祝贺广东财经大学成立四十周年！
祝贺广东新安职业技术学院成立二十五周年！

英语语言
疑难问题研究

颜钰 著

U0330367

中山大学出版社
SUN YAT-SEN UNIVERSITY PRESS
·广州·

图书在版编目（CIP）数据

英语语言疑难问题研究/颜钰著．—广州：中山大学出版社，2023.11

ISBN 978 - 7 - 306 - 07942 - 8

Ⅰ．①英…　Ⅱ．①颜…　Ⅲ．①英语—语法—学习方法—研究　Ⅳ．①H314

中国国家版本馆 CIP 数据核字（2023）第 215848 号

出 版 人：王天琪
策划编辑：熊锡源
责任编辑：赵　婷
封面设计：曾　斌
责任校对：陈晓阳
责任技编：靳晓虹
出版发行：中山大学出版社
电　　话：编辑部 020 - 84110283，84113349，84111997，84110779，
　　　　　　　　　84110776
　　　　　发行部 020 - 84111998，84111981，84111160
地　　址：广州市新港西路 135 号
邮　　编：510275　传　真：020 - 84036565
网　　址：http://www.zsup.com.cn　E-mail：zdcbs@mail.sysu.edu.cn
印 刷 者：佛山家联印刷有限公司
规　　格：787mm×1092mm　1/16　11.5 印张　285 千字
版次印次：2023 年 11 月第 1 版　2023 年 11 月第 1 次印刷
定　　价：45.00 元

前　　言

　　本书《英语语言疑难问题研究》，顾名思义，要探讨英语语言中的一些疑难问题。所谓疑难问题，是难以理解或翻译的英语句子。如 "If ever there was a treasure house that's going to wreck and ruin，it's this library." （David Aikman："Reading Between the Lines"）（要是说一座宝库将会遭到破坏和毁灭的话，那就是这个图书馆。）这句话看起来似乎简单，实际上却是个难句，因为句中的 if 从句并不表条件，而表强调。还有一些难句，表面上看来也容易，实际含义与字面意义大相径庭。如：The boy is good and bad. （这孩子很坏。）若望文生义译为"这孩子既好又坏"，就大错特错了。本书第一部分要探讨的就是这个问题：英语学习的陷阱——望文生义和歧义。笔者收集了望文生义 114 例，认真阅读，读者定能对望文生义有一个比较全面的了解，从而跳出望文生义的陷阱；读了对 55 组歧义句的剖析，定能增强语言识辨能力，提高语言水平。

　　本书第二部分是 18 篇精选论文，都是在外语刊物上发表过的，每篇论文就一个专题进行探讨，真正起到答疑解惑的作用。《特殊的 if 从句》一文介绍了 if 从句不表条件的种种情况，如表强调、表目的、表让步、表时间、表对比、表原因等等。《关于 be going to 用于条件句的主句中》一文介绍了 be going to 用于条件从句的主句的种种情况，从而批驳了一般语法书关于 be going to 不能用于条件句的主句中的不实说法。《英语动词不定式 to be 的几种特殊用法》介绍了动词不定式的几个特殊用法和应注意的问题。《试论 will 用于 if 从句》中所列举的种种情况，说明并非如一般语法书所说"will 不能用于 if 从句"。as 的用法极为复杂，本书用《引导状语从句的 as》和《引导定语从句的 as》两篇文章做了专门介绍。《英语介词 in 用法三则》明确指出，与表地点的名词连用时，in 用于较大的地方，at 用于较小的地方，但这并非一成不变的规则，用 in 或 at，要看上下文或依具体情况而定；表位置时，表示"在……上"意义时，并非总是要用 on，有时甚至不能用 on，而要用 in；对于"in a week（month，year…）"这样的词组，什么时候表示"在一周（月、年……）之内"，什么时候表示"在一周（月、年……）之后"，作者从理论上做了较为详尽的论述。如果说疑问句不表疑问，你可能不信，读一读《英语疑问句的一个用法——不表疑问》一文，你的疑惑就解除了。谈到人称代词，你可能会认为这不是很简单吗？其实不然，《人称代词用法札记》一文会使你耳目一新，收获多多。

　　本书第三部分是"英语 There 存在句研究"专题。there 存在句方面的文章不少，但专论却少见。提醒大家注意两个问题：一是 there 存在句的主语可以是表示确定意义的人或物；二是要区分各种不同的 there 存在句，包括没有 there 的 there 存在句。

　　笔者早已进入耄耋之年，一辈子在高校从事英语教学，能与读者交流，深感荣幸，真诚希望能够听取来自读者，特别是青年读者的批评和建议。

目　　录

上编：英语学习的陷阱

中编：英语语言疑难解惑 18 讲

下编：英语 There 存在句研究

上编：

英语学习的陷阱

英语学习陷阱之"望文生义"

　　望文生义，又叫缘文生义，是指"只从字面上去牵强附会，不求确切了解词句的内容"（to misinterpret words through taking them too literally）。我国一位著名翻译家曾将英语中的 the Milky Way 译成"牛奶路"，成了翻译界的一大笑料。无独有偶，一位英国翻译家在翻译我国古典名著《水浒传》时，将"放你妈的狗屁"译成"Your mother passes wind like a dog."，从而贻笑千古。还有将成语"美中不足"译成"Both America and China are insufficient."。翻译家尚且如此，更何况一般的语言学习者呢！因望文生义而造成的错误可以说比比皆是，现略举几例，可见一斑：

　　dry goods 纺织品，谷物　　（不是"干货"）
　　sweet water 淡水，饮用水　（不是"糖水""甜水"）
　　family talk 庸俗的交谈　　（不是"熟悉的谈话"）
　　bad sailor 晕船　　　　　（不是"坏水手"）
　　eat one's words 收回说过的话（不是"食言"）

　　汉语中的红茶，译成英语是 black tea（不是 red tea），而英语中的 black coffee 却是"纯咖啡"，white coffee 则是"加牛奶的咖啡"，white wine 是"白葡萄酒"（不是"白酒"）。又如：

［例1］　The boy is good and bad.

这孩子很坏。（不是"这孩子既好又坏。"）

［例2］　He is the last man to accept a bribery.

他绝不是受贿赂的人。（不是"他是最后一个受贿赂的人。"）

［例3］　Don't drink and drive.

不要酒后开车。（不是"不要喝酒和开车。"）

［例4］　He has written to me frequently since I was ill.

自从我病愈以来，他经常给我来信。（不是"自从我生病以来……"）

为什么会产生如此之多的"望文生义"错误呢？其原因是错综复杂的。既有只注意到句子的表层结构，而忽视了句子的深层结构的问题，又有只注意语言的规则，而忽视语言中起决定作用的有时并不是规则，而是"约定俗成"的问题；既有对母语为英语的国家——特别是英国和美国——对同一语言现象，有时可能有截然不同的理解缺乏认识的问题，又有对中西文化的差异缺乏了解的问题。此外，语言中大量存在歧义现象，对同一语言现象，如果只知其一，不知其二，也必然会产生错误的理解。这中间自然还包括英语初学者对英语语法，特别是惯用法不熟悉、不了解而造成的错误。

笔者愿将自己在学习的过程中收集、积累的望文生义的典型例句，奉献给读者。

1. It's natural to take offence if someone is rude.

误：如果有人粗蛮无礼，自卫是自然的。

正：如果有人粗蛮无礼，生气是自然的。

take offence 意为"生气"。

2．I had an appointment for three o'clock!

误：三点钟我还有约会！

正：我原预约好三点钟就诊的！

这里的 appointment 指的是与医生的预约。

3．They often talk horse.

误：他们常谈论马。

正：他们常吹牛。

talk horse = talk big。

4．That woman walks the streets.

误：那个女人常在那些街上走。

正：那个女人是妓女。

5．It was almost morning…

误：几乎半夜了吧……

正：差不多天亮了吧……

6．The Browns are the hospitality itself.

误：布朗一家本身是好客的。

正：布朗一家非常好客。

itself 作 extremely 或 very much 解。

7．A good thing itself may become harmful by its abuse.

误：一件很好的事，滥用了可能成为坏事。

正：即使是件好事，滥用了可能成为坏事。

8．It rains cats and dogs.

误：下猫和狗。

正：下倾盆大雨。

根据北欧神话，cat 被认为是对天气有巨大影响的动物，dog 被看作是强风的象征。dogs 伴随着 cats 而至当然就是"倾盆大雨"了。

9．small potato

据说一位大学教授外出讲学，开场白中他用了一句："I am a small potato."听众中有人不解，堂堂的教授怎么能说是个"小马铃薯"呢？很显然这是望文生义了。原来 a small potato 在美国口语中指的是 a person of no great importance or worth（"不重要的人"）的意思，相当于 nobody。间或可以用 big potato 来指"大人物"，但不多见。

10．I'll report that official.

误：我将向那位官员汇报。

正：我要告发那位官员。

report sb. 意为"告发某人"。

11．You make a fine mistake if you think so.

误：如果你这么想，你就会巧犯错误。

正：如果你这么想，你就大错特错了。

fine 在这里是 terrible 的意思。又如：Your shoes will be a fine state if you walk in the mud.（穿着鞋子在烂泥里走，鞋子准会弄得一塌糊涂的）

12．He is a bad drunk.

误：他是个很坏的酒鬼。

正：他是个不喜欢饮酒的人。

13．Don't call him names！

误：别叫他的名字！

正：别骂他！

call sb. names 意为"谩骂某人"。

14．The little boy is a love child.

误：那个小男孩是个可爱的孩子。

正：那个小男孩是个私生子。

a love child 意为"私生子"。

15．He is a writer，if a day.

误：他总有一天会成为一位作家的。

正：他确实是位作家。

if a day 意为"确实"，相当于 exactly。

16．The boss gave her the sack.

误：老板给了她一个麻袋。

正：老板解雇了她。

give sb. the sack 意为"解雇某人"。

17．"She was graduated from university at the age of 17．" "You don't say so！"

误："她17岁就大学毕业了。""你不要这样说吧！"

正："她17岁就大学毕业了。""那可未必吧！"（或"那不见得吧！"）

"You don't say so！"常用来表示说话者对某事感到不大相信或有所保留，相当于"That is incredible."。

18．We all stand up to the project.

误：我们都赞成这个工程。

正：我们都反对这个工程。

stand up to sth. 意为"反对某事"。

19．They are anything from ten to sixteen years younger than you.

误：无论是十岁的还是十六岁的，他们都比你年轻。

正：他们的年纪比你小十岁到十六岁不等。

anything 在这里用作副词，意为 in any way，to any degree，在句中起加强语气的作用。

20．"Make yourself at home，cut and come again."said Mr. Smith to his guests.

误：史密斯先生对客人们说："别客气，请把大馅饼切成几片吃。"

正：史密斯先生对客人们说："别客气，请尽量吃。"

cut and come again 是个习语，等于 eat heartily（尽量吃）。

21．"How goes the enemy?" "It's about ten，I guess."

误："敌人现在情况如何？""我想大概十点钟吧。"

正："现在什么时间？"（或"现在几点钟了？"）"我想大概十点钟吧。"

"How goes the enemy?" 是个习语，口语中常用，等于"What's the time?"。

22．Don't tell me you've missed the train！

误：不要告诉我，你已经误了火车。

正：恐怕你赶不上火车了吧！（或"你还不至于赶不上火车吧！"）

"Don't tell me…" 是习语，等于"I am worried by the fact that…"（恐怕，不至于……吧）。

23．There was nothing else I could do. So help me.

误：没有什么办法了，帮帮我吧！

正：我发誓我没有其他办法了。

so help me = I swear；may I be punished if I lie（我发誓；我保证）。

24．You are wearing your best clothes today. How come?

误：你穿上最漂亮的衣服，怎么来的？

正：你穿上最漂亮的衣服，为什么呢？

"How come?"美国口语等于"Why is it?""How does it happen?"，意为"怎么会……的？怎么搞的？"。

25．The headmaster made an example of the boy.

误：校长把这个男孩当作榜样。

正：校长惩罚这个男孩，目的在于警告其他的人。

make an example of sb. 意为 punish sb. so that others will be afraid to behave as he did。

26．He is a class table tennis player.

误：他是班里的乒乓球员。

正：他是优秀的乒乓球员。

class 意为 excellent（优秀的）。

27．She can speak French after a fashion.

误：她追求时髦，会说法语。

正：她法语说得不怎么好。

after a fashion 意为 not very well。

28．I'll teach you to meddle in my affairs.

误：我要教你管我的事。

正：你再管我的事我就要教训你了。

teach sb. to 意为 show the risk or penalty of（教训；告诫……不要做）。

29．The speaker carried the audience with him.

误：演讲者把听众带走了。

9

正：演讲者赢得了听众的赞同。

to carry 意为 to win the agreement of。

30. Don't make a fuss of them!

误：别对那些事大惊小怪！

正：别娇惯他们！

make a fuss of sb. 意为"娇惯某人"。

31. The old lady has gone to her rest.

误：那个老太太睡觉去了。

正：那个老太太去世了。

go to one's rest = die。

32. The exercises are all but finishied.

误：练习已全部做完。

正：练习都差不多做完了。

all but 意为 nearly，almost（几乎、差不多）。

33. I made up my mind to write a life of my poor father.

误：我决心要替我可怜的父亲作传。

正：我决定要替我死去的父亲作传。

34. My uncle remembered me on my birthday.

误：我叔父记得我的生日。

正：我叔父送了我一件生日礼物。

35. She is a homely woman.

误：她是一个家庭妇女。

正：她是一个朴素的女人。

36. He was a soldier of fortune.

误：他是一个幸运的军人。

正：他是一个冒险家。

37．He was used to being made fun of.

误：他常被人愚弄。

正：他习惯于被人愚弄。

38．They robbed his safe.

误：他们偷走了他的保险箱。

正：他们盗取了他保险箱内的东西。

我们说"The bandits robbed a bank."（土匪抢劫了银行），是抢去银行里的钱，绝不可能把银行搬走。

39．He stopped to think over his way of life.

误：他对于自己的生活方式已经停止不再想了。

正：他停下来思考人生。

stop doing sth. 意为"停止做某事"，stop to do sth. 意为"停下来去做某事"。

如：He stopped smoking.（他戒烟了）He stopped to smoke.（他停下工作，去吸一支烟）

40．His success is out of the question.

误：他成功是没有问题的。

正：他绝不可能成功。

out of question = beyond question，意为"无疑"，而 out of the question = not to be thought of，quite impossible，意为"绝不可能"或"无讨论的价值"。试比较：His success is out of question.（他一定成功）

41．He lost a cool thousand dollars.

误：他损失了一千元，还很冷静。

正：他整整损失了一千元。

cool 意为"整整的""实实在在的",如：We walked a cool twenty miles. （我们整整走了二十里路）

42．This is some war!

误：这是某种战争。

正：这是一场大战。

这里用 some 代替 great 在修辞学上是所谓的曲言法（meiosis），如：That was some storm! （好大的风暴！）

43．Catch me doing it!

误：我正在做着那个的时候，你抓住我吧。

正：谁要做那样的事！（反语）

44．It is a long lane that has no turning.

误：这是一条不转弯的长长的小道。

正：世界上没有一条不转弯的路。

45．I'm sorry I have other fish to fry.

误：很抱歉，我还有鱼要煎。

正：很抱歉，我还有别的事情要做。

46．I'm afraid you are a Jack of all trades and master of none.

你是一个干什么都会一点，但什么都不擅长的人。

Jack of all trades 是个成语，相当于我们汉语中的"万金油"。

据说含有 Jack 的习语在英语词典里有六七十个之多。如：

All work and no play makes Jack a dull boy.

只工作不玩耍，聪明孩子也变傻。

Jack of both sides. 骑墙派。

A good Jack makes a good Jill. 夫善则妻贤。

47．Where is john?

误：约翰在哪里？

正：厕所在哪里？

人名约翰必须大写 John，小写 john 不是人名，而是指 water closet（厕所）。英语中同一个词，大写和小写表示不同意思的情况还有一些。如：

China 中国—china 瓷器

Turkey 土耳其—turkey 火鸡

48．That's not quite my cup of tea.

误：那真的不是我的那杯茶。

正：那真的不是我所喜欢的东西。（That's not really the kind of thing I like.）

not be someone's cup of tea = not to be what someone likes, enjoys, is suited to, etc.（不是某人所喜爱的）

49．That man was so rude to me! I wouldn't go back to that job for all the tea in China.

误：那个家伙对我太无礼了！为了中国所有的茶叶，我也不愿回去为他干活了。

正：那个家伙对我太无礼了！不管他给多少报酬，我也不愿回去为他干活了。

50．Look out!

误：看外面！

正：注意！当心点！

据说，曾经有一位不太懂英语的外国人去英国旅行。一天，他坐上了当时新出的双层巴士在伦敦市内游览。他对伦敦的风光看得出了神，便不知不觉把头伸出车窗外，想看个真切。一位好心的英国人见状向他大喝一声："Look out！"意思是叫他当心，把头缩回来。谁知那位游客误解了，以为叫他往外看，于是把头伸得更出一点。当时汽车正急转弯，车身侧向一边，路角的灯柱与游客的脑袋相撞，造成游客严重受伤。

51．We cannot exaggerate its importance.

误：我们不能夸大它的重要性。

正：其重要性无论怎样夸大其词也不为过。

You cannot appraise this book too high.（此书无论给以怎样高的评价也不为过），也是同样的表示法。

52．I can't help thinking that he is still alive.

误：我不能帮助思想他还活着。

正：我不能不认为他还活着。

53．If you failed in your experiment，why，try for the second time.

误：如果你的实验失败了，为什么还要再来一次呢？

正：实验不成功的话，何妨再来一次。

54．He is a man of family.

误：他是一个有家庭的人。

正：他是一个世家子弟。

of family = nobly born，是一种含蓄的说法。

55．You don't say！

误：你不要说。

正：是吗？真的吗？

"You don't say."是美国人的一句口头禅，用来表示轻微的疑问或惊讶的语气。

56．**You can say that again！**

误：你可以再说一遍。

正：说得好！真妙！

"You can say that again. " 是一句赞美语。

57．**Give a dog an ill name and hang him.**

误：给狗一个恶名，把它吊死。

正：欲加之罪，何患无辞。

狗是人类忠实的朋友，英美国家的人特别喜欢养狗，有关狗的习语特别多，现略举数例：

Love me，love my dog. 爱屋及乌。

Every dog has his day. 狗有得意日，人有得意时。

Dog does not eat dog. 同类不相残。

Old dogs will learn no new trick. 老年人学不了新东西。

To let sleeping dog lie. 别自找麻烦。

Not even a dog's chance. 毫无机会。

a lucky dog. 幸运儿。

running dog. 走狗。

58．**Don't teach your grandmother to suck eggs.**

误：不要教你祖母吃鸡蛋了。

正：不要班门弄斧。（或不要对着耶稣讲道理。）

在英美国家，有关 egg 的习语很多，现略举数例：

Better an egg today than a hen tomomow.

今天一只蛋，胜过明天一只鸡。

Never cackle till your egg is laid.

事未完成莫先夸耀。

He that would have eggs must endure the cackling of hens.

如果你要享受的话，那便要先吃点苦头。

59. That young man has lost his heart.

误：那个青年人失去信心了。

正：那个青年人爱上了一个人。

lose one's heart to sb. = fall in love with sb., 意为"爱上了某人"。

60. The old man often takes his medicine.

误：那位老人常服药。

正：那位老人常忍受不愉快之事。

take one's medicine 意为"忍受不愉快之事"。

61. The day is ours.

误：日子是我们的。

正：胜利是我们的。

英语中，day 的用法很广，如 New Year's Day（元旦），National Day（国庆节），Christmas Day（圣诞节）。

此外，day（或 days）还可用来表示"胜利""得意的日子""辉煌的时期"等含义，如：

I've had my day, too. 我也有过一段黄金时代。

The day is ours! 胜利属于我们！

We've won the day! 我们赢了！

62. I will be drowned and no one shall save me!

我要淹死自己，任何人也不准救我。

一个法国人在伦敦游览，踏上泰晤士河上著名的伦敦桥时，不小心掉进河里。他在水中拼命挣扎，大呼"Help！"（救命！）。一群英国人本准备跳下水去营救，突然听到这个落水人大声呼喊："I will be drowned and no one shall save me！"

（我要淹死自己，任何人也不准救我！）大家以为他要自杀，便随他沉下去了。原来这个法国人把 shall 和 will 的位置掉转了，他本来是说"I shall be drowned and no one will save me!"（我快要淹死了，为什么没有人来救我呢!）。

63．That fellow did hard labour for three years.

误：那个家伙干过三年艰苦的劳动。

正：那个家伙劳改过三年。

do hard labour 意为"劳改"。

64．The woman in labour is his wife.

误：那个在劳动的妇女是他的妻子。

正：那个临产的妇女是他的妻子。

be in labour 意为妇女生孩子时的"阵痛"。

65．She is a medicine woman.

误：她是一个医务工作者。

正：她是个巫师。

66．What he has bought is invaluable.

误：他买的东西毫无价值。

正：他买的东西价值连城。

invaluable 意为 priceless（无法估价的）。

67．Make water.

误：制水。

正：小便。

在课堂上一个小学生有礼貌地问老师："Please, sir, may I go to W. C.?"老师有意考他，问道："Why are you going there?"该学生回答："Make water."上厕所比较文雅的说法是："May I be excused?"

68. I'm in trouble.

trouble 意为"烦恼"，当一个人身处困境之中时，常说"I'm in trouble."。不过，假如一位年轻的女性，而且是未结婚的，悄悄地对你说"I'm in trouble."时，就不是一般的烦恼了，而是说她"未结婚而怀孕了"。

69. a sporting house

误：体育室

正：妓院

sport 是运动的意思，它与其他词搭配时有很多有趣的用途，如：

Be a sport! = Be a man! 要像个男子汉！不要婆婆妈妈的！

He's really a sport. 他真是条好汉。

Don't make a sport of him. 不要愚弄他。

He is sporting with us. 他在愚弄我们。

70. I have a sweet tooth.

误：我有甜的牙齿。

正：我喜欢吃甜的东西。

71. She gave him the air.

误：她把空气给他。

正：她表示与他一刀两断。

英语中还有 to give sb. the axe 的习惯用法，意为"开除"或"消灭"，如：The manager gave him the axe. （经理已把他开除了）

72. It's an old story.

误：这是一个旧的故事。

正：这种事司空见惯。

与 story 连用的惯用语还有一些。如：

It's a long story. 说来话长。

to make a long story short. 简言之。

They are in one story. 他们众口一词。

They are telling stories. 他们谎话连篇。

I know her story. 我知道她的身世。

73．I am dead-beat today.

误：我今天被打成了重伤。

正：我今天筋疲力尽了。

"dead + *n*." 结构，如 dead letter 意为"无法投递的信"，dead language 意为"已废弃的语言"。

74．He is a book worm.

误：他是书呆子。

正：他是个爱好读书的人。

75．She is in the dock.

误：她在码头上。

正：她在被告席上。

be in the dock 意为"在被告席上"，be on the dock 才是"在码头上"。

76．No more（or：None）of your cheek!

误：不再有你的面颊。

正：别无礼!

77．Don't turn a cold shoulder to him.

误：不要把冷肩膀转向他。

正：不要冷淡他。

类似地，cry on one's shoulder 意为"向某人倾诉苦楚"而不是"在某人肩上哭"。

78. People did not shake off colonialist's yoke in order to put on hegemonist's.

误：人们没有摆脱殖民主义的束缚，是为了套上霸权主义的枷锁。

正：人们摆脱殖民主义的束缚，不是为了套上霸权主义的枷锁。

79. All are not friends that speak us fair.

误：恭维者都不是朋友。

正：恭维者并非全都是朋友。

all 与 not 连用表示部分否定。又如：

All are not thieves that dogs bark at.

误：凡遭犬吠者都不是小偷。

正：遭犬吠者并非都是小偷。

80. That's not half bad.

误：那不太坏。

正：那一点也不坏。（或：那好极了！）

81. Our proposal cannot possibly be taken into consideration and adopted.

误：我们的建议不太可能被考虑与采纳。

正：我们的建议根本不会被考虑与采纳。

82. The American tourist said he liked Hangzhou better than Shanghai, if you please.

误：这位美国游客说，同上海比起来，他更喜欢杭州，如果你乐意听的话。

正：这位美国游客说，同上海相比，他更喜欢杭州，这话你可不能不信。

if you please 常用来表示说话者对某事感到意外或惊讶，其含义相当于"Can you believe it?"。

83．You are looking very fresh.

你看起来真是朝气蓬勃！

这是一句地道的英国英语，但是一个名叫 Foster 的英国贵族在美国旅行时就因为说了这么一句话而引来了大麻烦。Foster 先生在美国旅行时，出席一个招待晚会。他遇见了一位活泼可爱的小姐，忍不住要献点殷勤，说点称赞的话，于是他用一句在英国很漂亮的话对她说："You are looking very fresh！"意为"你看起来真是朝气蓬勃！"。可是马屁拍在了马腿上，那位小姐听了大为生气，拂袖而去，不再理会这位贵族了。原来 fresh 在美国俚语中具有"鲁莽无理、厚颜无耻"的意思。例如女的说："Don't get fresh with me or I'll slap your face."（不要对我这样毛手毛脚，再来我就要打你的耳光）

84．We are here today and gone tomorrow.

误：我们今天在这里，明天就要到别处去了。

正：今日生存，明日死去。

85．I dare say he is honest.

误：我敢说他是诚实可靠的。

正：我想他是诚实可靠的。

86．He must needs go at once.

误：他必须立刻前往。

正：他坚持立刻要去。

must needs do = insist on doing，意为"主张一定要做……"。

87．I didn't know Mr．Wang from Mr．Li.

误：我不是从李先生那里认识王先生的。

正：我分不清谁是王先生，谁是李先生。

to know…from…意为"区别某人（物）和某人（物）"，相当于 to tell…from…。又如：

He could not tell wheat from rice when he first came to the countryside.

他第一次去农村时，分不清麦子和稻子。

You must tell right from wrong.

你们必须分清是非。

88．Hsiao Li is a boy of a girl.

误：小李是一个女孩子生的男孩。

正：小李是个像男孩一般的女孩。

a…of a…是个固定词组，意为"像……一般的……"。又如：

He is a fool of a man.

他是个呆子般的男人。

Have you seen his tyrant of a father?

你是否见过他那个暴君似的父亲？

89．Give me a pail of purifying water，please！

误：请给我一桶干净的水。

正：请给我一桶净化用的水。

purifying water 等于 water used for purifying sth.，意为"净化用的水"。

purified water 等于 water that has been purified，意为"净化过的水"。

又如：

boiling water 正在沸腾的水（即 100℃的滚水）

boiled water 烧开过的水（可能已经是凉水）

developing country 发展中国家

developed country 发达国家

90．She is being kind.

误：她是和蔼的。

正：她现在是和蔼的。

be kind 说明主语的特性和品质，being kind 表示目前的短暂涵义，因此，当有人说某某女人 being kind，而你对她的印象很不错，你完全可以说"She is always kind."。

91．I don't know whether they are not here.

误：我不知道他们是否在这里。

正：我想他们可能在这里。

这是个特殊句型，其内涵相当于"I think that they might be here."。句中 I don't know 并不是真的不知道，而是表示"没有十足把握"或"未经证实"的意味，其后的 whether they are not here 表示近乎肯定的猜测内容。

92．He lives in the country.

误：他住在这个国家。

正：他住在农村。

the country 是指"农村"或"乡下"，与 the town 相对应，相当于 the countryside。

93．Between you and me，it is nothing serious.

误：这件事对你和我来说并不怎么严重。

正：我私下对你说一句，这件事并不严重。

between you and me 是个固定说法，意为"你知我知""秘密言之"，相当于 I say it privately 或 in strict confidence。

94．The bus is stopped.

误：有人使这辆巴士停了下来。

正：巴士停了下来。

这个句子并非被动结构，而是系表结构，它不表示动作，而是说明主语的特点或处于某种状态。又如：

My daughter is just returned. 我女儿刚回来。

He is retired. 他现在已退休了。

95．They will get married in a month.

误：他们将在本月内结婚。

正：他们将在一个月后结婚。

in + 表示时间的名词构成的词组，如 in ten days（months，years），如果谓语动词是瞬间动词，in...作"……之后"解；如果是持续动词，in...作"……之内"解。

试比较：

They will graduate from Beijing University in two years.

他们将在两年后从北京大学毕业。

They will learn the English language in two years.

他们将在两年内学好英语。

96．No one man can fulfil the task.

误：没有一个人能够完成这项任务。

正：没有一个人能够独自完成这项任务。

one 和 a 都表示"一个"的意义，但涵义有所不同。one 强调数目观念"一个"，a 则不强调数目的意义，译成汉语时，常省略不译。试比较：

One child can not do it.

一个小孩子干不了这个活（，要两个或两个以上的小孩才可以）。

A child cannot do it.

小孩子干不了这个活（，要大人才干得了）。

97．Tyson is in jail.

误：泰森现在在监狱里。

正：泰森在坐牢。

in jail 是固定词组，意为"犯了法在坐牢"，而 in the jail 意为"在监狱里"，不是坐牢，可能是在监狱里工作，或者参观、访问等。

98．Now you and I are all in the same boat.

误：现在我们坐在同一条船上。

正：现在我们处境相同。

99．You shouldn't wake a sleeping dog in such a strange place.

误：你不要在这样一个陌生的地方把狗弄醒。

正：你不要在这样一个陌生的地方招惹是非。

100．He has a long head.

误：他有一个长脑袋。

正：他有远见。

101．Ask him．He is a walking dictionary.

误：问问他。他是一本走路的字典。

正：问问他。他是一本活字典。（或：他是个学识渊博的人）

又如：walking dictionary，意为"活字典，指学识渊博的人"。

又如：speak like a dictionary 讲话很有学问

102．That's your funeral.

误：那是你的葬礼。

正：此乃阁下之事。

be one's funeral 意为"某人自己需要操心的事"。

103．Stop pulling my leg, will you?

误：别拉我的腿，行吗？

正：别开我的玩笑，行吗？

104．She is a cold fish.

误：她是一条冷鱼。

正：她是一个古怪的人。

cold fish 意为"冷冰冰的人，不大与人来往的人"。

105．His old father kicked the basket while he was away from home.

误：他离家时，他父亲踢翻了水桶。

正：他离家时，他父亲去世了。

kick the basket 是英语俚语，意为"死、翘辫子"。

106．He is nothing but a gold brick.

误：他是一块金砖。

正：他是个二流子（游手好闲的人）。

107．Were your ears burning last night?

误：昨天晚上你耳朵发热吗？

正：昨天晚上你感觉到有人在议论你吗？

ears burning 耳朵发烧，意指有人背后议论。

108. You shouldn't do it. It will take the bread out of Tom's mouth.

误：你不要这么做，这会夺走汤姆的面包。

正：你不要这么做，这会敲掉汤姆的饭碗。

109. John can be relied on. He eats no fish and plays the game.

误：约翰为人可靠，他一向不吃鱼而且常玩游戏。

正：约翰为人可靠，既忠诚又正直。

误译是望文生义，是由于对原文所涉及的典故和习惯的用法无知而导致的理解错误。to eat no fish 出自英国伊丽莎白时代，耶稣教信徒为表示对当局忠诚而拒绝信守反政府的罗马天主教信徒在星期五只吃鱼的规定；to play the game 意为 to play fair.

110. For me personally, it was a blessing in disguise.

误：这对我而言，是化了装的幸福。

正：就我而言，这是因祸得福。

111. They were killed to a man.

误：他们被杀的只剩下一个人了。

正：他们全部被杀了。

（all）to a man 意为 all without exception（毫无例外，全部）。

112. Keep a thing seven years and you will find a use for it.

误：东西留七年，用处总会被发现。

正：东西保留一长，总会派上用场。

乍一读起来，误译并无差错，可它完全是望文生义。但人们不禁要问："东西一定要放七年才会派上用场吗?"这似乎不太符合常理。如果我们考察一下西方人使用 seven 的习惯,就会发现西方人使用的 seven 并非实指"七",而是虚指"较长的一般时间"。

113．I have my Power Book in the trunk of my car.

误：我车的行李箱里有一本动力书。

正：我车的行李箱中有一台笔记本电脑。

114．Rabbits never lie.

误：兔子从来不撒谎。

正：兔子试验一向很准。

把"Rabbits never lie."望文生义译成"兔子从来不撒谎"似乎并无什么差错。但如此译来岂不成了无稽之谈?此句中的 rabbits 显然是指用兔子所做的一种实验,可用反译法译成"兔子试验一向很准"。反译法在翻译中常常使用。

英语学习陷阱之"歧义"

　　我们在阅读或交际时，常碰到一些模棱两可的语句，使人不得其解而无所适从。有时一个句子、一个短语，甚至一个单词可以有多种解释。如："He doesn't read anything."一句，既可以表示"他什么东西都不读"，又可以表示"他并不是什么东西都读的（，只读某些特定的书籍）"。又如一个十分简单的句子"Light，please！"既可以表示"请开灯"，又可以表示"请关灯"，还可以表示"请拿火柴来"（如果是煤油灯的话）。这就是歧义。歧义与语言结构的本质联系具有普遍性，但并不意味着歧义不可消除。在多数情况下，歧义一经接触，随即消除。在口语中，通过语调，在书面中，通过上下文，均可排除歧义。有一句名言"No context，no meaning."（没有上下文就没有意义）就是这个意思。本章我们就来具体研讨一下歧义的问题。

一、否定的陷阱

　　英语否定结构形式繁多，其表达形式与汉语有许多不同之处，若按字面意义来翻译往往会弄错。对我们中国人来说，英语中的某些否定简直成了一种陷阱，稍不留意，就会掉入其中，不可自拔。

1．not…because

［例1］ He didn't wear an overcoat because it was cold.

此句显然不能按字面意义译为"他没有穿大衣，因为天气冷"，因为这不符合逻辑。正常人是绝不会因为天气冷反而不穿大衣的。此句的否定词 not 只能是否定 because 从句，意为"并不是因为天气冷他才穿大衣"（他穿大衣是出于别的原因）。

英语中 not…because 是一种歧义结构，否定词 not 表示两种不同的否定，一是否定谓语，一是否定 because 从句。本句属于后者，即我们通常所讲的"否定的转移"（transferred negation）。

［例2］ I didn't go because I was afraid.

这句话也可以有两个不同的意思。第一个意思是：我怕，所以没有去（I didn't go, and the reason was fear.）。第二个意思是：我不是因为怕才去的（我去是出于别的原因）（I went, but the reason was not fear.）。对于第一种否定，因为符合我们中国人的思维习惯，所以比较好理解，翻译时不会出错。而对于第二种否定，即否定的转移，却要多加留意，以免出错。下面各句均属于否定的转移：

［例3］ Thather said, "I do not say this because I believe that we should be in any way provocative towards the Soviet Union or anyone else."

撒切尔说："我这样说，并不是因为我认为我们应该对苏联或其他任何人采取任何挑衅的态度。"

［例4］ I do not want to support a candidate because of

blackmail and intimidation.

我不愿在讹诈和威胁之下去支持某一个候选人。

[例5] He was not ready to believe something just because Aristotle said so.

他不会因为亚里士多德说过某事如何如何，就轻易相信。

[例6] The mountain is not valued because it is high.

山不是以高为贵。

[例7] We do not eat because we want to eat.

我们不是为了吃饭而吃饭。

[例8] We should not scamp our work because we are pressed for time or because we have our hands full.

我们可不能因为时间太紧或工作太忙就对工作马马虎虎。（※我们对工作不能马马虎虎，因为我们时间很紧，工作很忙。）①

2．not …ing

[例1] They didn't go home thinking，"Boy，I did a great job today and I can't wait to get back tomorrow."

此句选自美国作家 Studs Tercel 的一篇描写普通工人生活的报道 "The Story of Welder"，讲述电焊工工作如何紧张繁忙、单调乏味，他们做工完全是为了生活，根本不关心工厂如何运营。句中的否定词形式上是否定谓语，实际上却是否定作状语的分词 thinking，属于否定的转移。因此，要译为：

他们回家时并不这样想："嘿，朋友，我今天的活干得相当出色，我巴不得马上回去再干，连明天都等不得。"

---

① 本书中※代表该句有语法上的错误或语义上的错误。

而不能译为：

他们没有回家，心想："嘿，朋友，我今天的活干得相当出色……"

下列一句也否定分词：

[例2]　The lazy boy did not sit listening to the teacher. He was watching something else.

这个懒小子坐在那里，并没有听老师讲，而是看别的东西。

3．not…to do…

[例1]　He said，"Now look，I didn't come here to get along with you guys. You're going to have to get along with me."

他说："喂，老弟们，我到这儿来不是来听你们的，该是你们来听我的。"

此句中的后面一句 you're going to 已清楚表明前句中的 not 不是否定 come，而是否定 to get along with 的。英语中谓语部分的否定词常转移到后面的不定式。又如：

[例2]　They don't come to see you killed.

他们到这儿来并不是要看你死亡的。

[例3]　It doesn't appear to be a true story.

这故事似乎并非事实。

[例4]　We are not here to watch the fun.

我们到这里来不是要看热闹。

[例5]　They do not conduct the dangerous experiment to serve their private interest，but to benefit man.

他们进行这种危险的实验，不是为了图私利，而是为了造福人类。

4．not...介词词组（或副词）

[**例1**]　Michelangelo did not learn to paint by spending his time doodling. Mozart was not an accomplished pianist at the age of eight as the result of spending his days in front of television set.

米开朗基罗并不是靠心不在焉地乱涂一气学会绘画的，莫扎特八岁成为一名造诣颇深的钢琴家也不是终日在电视机前消磨时光的结果。

很显然，此句中的 did not 和 was not 分别否定两个介词词组 by spending...和 as the result of...。下面是否定词转移到介词词组的例句：

[**例2**]　Rome was not built in a day. (= Rome was built not in a day.)

罗马非朝夕建成。

[**例3**]　He didn't go to work by bus.

他不是乘公共汽车上班的。

[**例4**]　He hasn't been speaking since three o'clock.

他不是从三点钟谈起的。　（※从三点钟起，他一直没说话。）

5．all...not

[**例1**]　All that glitters is not gold.

这是莎士比亚剧中的名言，意为"发光的东西未必都是金子"，不能按字面意义，译为"发光的东西都不是金子"。此句是部分否定，而不是全部否定（total negation）。如要表示"发光的东西都不是金子"的意思，要用"None that glitters is gold."。例如：

[**例2**]　You can't fool all the people all the time.

你未必每次都能成功地愚弄所有的人。

[**例3**]　Romulo said that all American proposals would not be acceptable.

罗慕洛说，美国的建议未必个个都是可以接受的。

[**例4**]　All the great truths are obvious truths. But all obvious truths are not great truths. （Huxley）

伟大的真理都是显而易见的道理。但是，不见得所有显而易见的道理都是伟大的真理。（赫胥黎）

[**例5**]　I do not know all of them.

他们我不全认识。

[**例6**]　He will not be here all the summer.

他将不是整个夏天都在这里。

every、everything、everywhere、always、altogether、entirely、wholly 等词在否定句中也表部分否定，而不表全部否定。

not always = sometimes

not everywhere = somewhere

not entirely = somewhat

not wholly = to some degree

[**例7**]　The good and beautiful do not always go together. （Shakespeare）

善和美不一定时常是相连的。（莎士比亚）

[**例8**]　Such a thing is not found everywhere.

这样的东西不是到处都可以找到的。

[**例9**]　The director claims he is a man of high principle, but he does not always act up to it.

这位局长自称有高度的原则性，可是有时候他却不按原则办事。

[例10] Everything is not good in that country, but equally everything is not bad.

在那个国家并非一切都好，同样也并非一切都坏。

[例11] Every man cannot be a poet.

并非人人都可成为诗人。（※人人都不能成为诗人。）

6．both…not

[例1] Both his parents are not at home.

他的父母亲不都在家里。（※他的父母亲都不在家。）

[例2] Both read the same Bible, and pray to the same God; and each invokes his aid against the other. The prayers of both could not be answered.

双方念的是同一本圣经，拜的是同一个上帝，但各方都要求他帮助去打倒对方。所以，双方的祈祷不可能都得到满足。

7．not…and

[例1] Don't drink and drive.

不要酒后开车。（※不要开车，不要喝酒。）

在否定句中，and 表部分否定。上句表示，说话人并非禁止对方"喝酒"，也不是禁止对方"开车"，而是禁止将二者结合在一起，即"喝了酒就不能开车"，"开车就不能喝酒"。在否定句中，or 才表全部否定。试比较下列两句：

[例2] He did not speak clearly and correctly.

他不曾讲得既清楚又正确。

[例3] He did not speak clearly or correctly.

他讲得既不清楚又不正确。

二、否定形式表示强调的肯定意思

肯定和否定是一对矛盾的两个方面，二者同是思维和言语中不可缺少的范畴，我们讲 "He is not a teacher." 是对 "He is a teacher." 的否定。否定句是借助否定词 no、not、never、none 等来表示的。在一般情况下，形式和意义是统一的，但是，有时也有形式和意义不一致的情况。即否定形式并不表否定，而表肯定；肯定形式不表肯定，而表否定。这是英语学习的一大陷阱，稍不留意，就会出差错。

8．cannot…too

[例1] You cannot praise him too much. （= It is impossible to over-praise him. = The more you praise him, the better. = You should praise him as highly as you can.）

cannot…too 这种结构形式上否定，实际上肯定，表示 "不可能过分""怎么也不为过""越……越……"。此句要译为：

你无论怎样称赞他也不过分。(※你不能过分称赞他。)

[例2] A teacher cannot be too patient with his students.

教师对学生不管如何耐心都不为过。

[例3] We cannot recommend this book too strongly.

这本书很好，无论我们如何推荐也不过分。

[例4] You cannot begin the practice too early.

练习开始得越早越好。

cannot…too 结构句中的 too 可换成 enough、sufficient(ly)、over 等，not 也可换成 hardly、scarcely、never、impossible 等否

定词。如：

［例5］ I can never thank you enough for your help.

对你的帮助我感激不尽。

［例6］ You cannot take sufficient care.

你要特别小心。

［例7］ We cannot over-emphasize the importance of physical exercise.

体育锻炼的重要性，我们无论怎样强调都不为过。

在这种结构中，如果去掉 too 或 enough 等词，就只表否定意义。试比较：

［例8a］ You can't praise this film too highly.

对这部电影无论评价怎么高都不为过。

［例8b］ You can't praise this film highly.

对这部电影不能评价过高。

9．cannot wait…

［例1］ I cannot wait to see him.

我渴望看见他。(※我不能等着见他。)

"cannot + wait + 动词不定式"这种形式上为否定的结构，实际上不表否定，而表强调的肯定，意为 be eager to（急于做……)。又如：

［例2］ I hear there are new books in the library. I can't wait to get hold of them.

听说图书馆到了一些新书，我巴不得马上就去借几本。

10．not + 比较级（或 so）

［例1］ I couldn't feel better. (= I felt best.)

我感觉好极了。

[**例2**]　　Nothing is more humiliating than to look poor among a gathering of rich ladies.　(= It is the most himiliating to look…)

在阔太太们中间露出一副穷酸相是再难堪不过的了。

[**例3**]　　None is so deaf as those that won't hear.

没有比故意不听的人更聋的了。(※没有比听不见的人更聋的了。)

11．not a little, no little, not half, not nearly, not slightly

这些词语均表示强烈的肯定。如：

[**例1**]　　We don't like it a little.

我们很喜欢它。(※我们一点也不喜欢它。)

[**例2**]　　It serves no little purpose to continue public discussing of this issue.

继续公开讨论这一问题是大有用处的。(※……是没有一点用处的。)

[**例3**]　　It is not half raining today.

今天的雨下得很大。(※今天的雨下得不大。)

注意 not a little 和 not a bit 的区别：

[**例4a**]　　He has not a little experience.　(not a little = much)

他有丰富的经验。(※他一点经验也没有。)

[**例4b**]　　He is not a bit like his brother.　(not a bit = not at all)

他一点也不像他的兄弟。

[**例5a**]　　He has no small chance of success.

他大有成功的可能。(※他没有什么成功的可能。)

试比较：

[**例5b**]　　He has no smallest chance of success.

他完全没有成功的可能。

前句是用否定形式表达肯定意义，no small = great；后句是用表微量意义的形容词（或副词）最高级表示强否定。又如：

[例6a]　He has no small reputation as an artist.

作为一个画家，他的声誉是很高的。

[例6b]　He has no smallest reputation as an artist.

作为一个画家，他没有什么声誉。

注意下列各句中的否定词的用法：

[例7]　He will finish it in no time.（in no time = at once 立刻）

他马上就会把这事做完。（※他将永远不能完成此事。）

[例8]　There is nothing like home.

任何地方都没有家里好。（※没有像家一样的东西。）

[例9]　His English leaves nothing to be desired.

他的英语棒极了。（※他的英语毫无希望。）

12．重复否定

[例1]　I don't lend my books to nobody.

我不把书借给任何人。

本来这句话的意思用一般否定句就可以了。即"I don't lend my books to anybody."（我不把书借给任何人）。但是"I don't lend my books to anybody."可能产生歧义，它既可以表示"我不把书借给任何人"（这时 anybody 念降调），又可以表示"我的书不是任何人都借的"（这时 anybody 念降升调）。为了排除歧义，可将 anybody 改为 nobody："I don't lend my books to nobody."。这种两个否定词在一起仍然表否定的方法叫重复否定（repeated negation）。重复否定在口语中，特别是黑人英语中至今使用广泛，甚至伦敦人也常说。又如：

[例2]　I don't know nothing about it.（＝I don't know anything about it.）

但在正式文体中常避免使用。

13．don't say（tell）

don't say 是美国人的口头禅，用来表示惊奇或轻微的疑问，意为"不会吧""哪能啊""真的吗""不见得吧"。不能照字面译为"你不要说"。如：

[例1]　"We're going to get married.""You don't say!"

"我们要结婚了。""真的吗?"

"Don't tell me…" 也有轻微疑问之意，如：

[例2]　Don't tell me you've fallen in love with her.

你总不会一下子就爱上她了吧。

类似用法，又如：

[例3]　"The food was awful!""You said it!"

"这食物很糟糕!""一点不假!"

当别人称赞或恭维你时，你一方面想表示谦虚，对他的恭维不大相信，另一方面，你又很高兴接受这种称赞或恭维，那么用"You don't say.""Don't tell me." 是最好不过的。如：

[例4]　"Your pronunciation is excellent!""You don't say!"

"你的发音好极了!""别开玩笑了。"

14．no more than

[例1]　He has no more than ＄10 in his pocket.

他口袋里只有10块钱。

这句不能译为"他口袋里的钱不超过10块"。要表达此意，应该说：He has not more than ＄10 in his pocket.

no more than = only；而 not more then = at most，意为"至多不过"。试比较：

[例2a] There are no more than five film tickets left now.

现在只剩下五张电影票了。

[例2b] There are not more than five film tickets left now.

现在剩下的电影票最多（不超过）五张。

上面讲的是 no more than，not more than 与数字连用的情况。它们也可用来比较两个事物的特点，这时 no more than 意为"两者都"，not more than 意为"不如""不及"，试比较：

[例3a] I am no more mad than you are. （＝I am cool-headed as you are.）

我和你一样并没有发狂（头脑清醒）。

[例3b] I am not madder than you are. （＝I'm not so mad as you are.）

我发狂发得没有你那样厉害。

注意与 no more than 相反的表示法 no less than。no more than 连接的前后两项都是否定，而 no less than 连接的前后都是肯定。no less than = as many（much）as。如：

[例4] A whale is no less a mammal than a horse is.

鲸是哺乳动物，就和马是哺乳动物一样。

no less...than 还可以做 as...as（和……一样）解。如：

[例5] She is no less beautiful than her sister. （＝She is as beautiful as her sister.）

她长得和她妹妹一样美。

15．yes 和 no

［例1］　　—Don't you like swimming?

　　　　　　—Yes，I do.

　　　　　　（—No，I don't.）

—你不喜欢游泳吗?

—不，我喜欢。

（—是，我不喜欢。）

回答一般否定疑问句时，英语与汉语由于习惯不同，有时差别很大。英语是说明实际情况，如答语是肯定的，即用 yes + 肯定结构；如果答语是否定的，则用 no + 否定结构。而汉语是就问句表态，然后再说事实。因而上述的 yes，要译成"不"，而 no 要译成"是"。陈述部分为否定式的附加疑问句的答语也是如此。如:

［例2］　　"He is not a teacher, is he?""Yes, he is."

"他不是教师，是吗?""不，他是。"

［例3］　　"You don't like Chinese food?""Oh, yes, I do like it very much!"

"你不喜欢中国菜?""哦，不，我喜欢，我很喜欢中国菜。"

［例4］　　"You've not changed enormously.""Yes, I have. I have changed enomously."

"约翰，你没有变多少。""不，我变了，我变了很多。"

对陈述部分是否定的附加疑问句和答语，英汉语也有这种差别。试比较:

［例5］　　—He is not a teacher, is he?

　　　　　　—Yes, he is.

（—No，he isn't.）

—他不是教师，是吗？

—不，他是。

—是，他不是。

[例6]　Hude：I am not in the least frightened of Carlotta.

　　　　Hugo：Oh，yes，you are. The very idea of her fills your soul with fear.

胡德：我一点也不怕卡罗塔。

休戈：不，你就是害怕。一想到她就会使你心里充满着恐惧。

16．no 和 not a

[例1]　He is no writer.

他不会写文章。

句中的 no 等于 quiet other than，意为"根本不是"，是一种特殊否定。这句相当于"He is anything but a writer.""He is far from being a writer.""He is not a writer at all.""He can't write."。要表示"他不是作家"的意思，要用"He is not a writer."。

由此可见，名词在系词后作表语时，其前用 no 比用 not a 更多强调含义。又如：

[例2a]　He is no fool.

他很聪明。

[例2b]　He is not a fool.

他不是傻瓜。

[例3a]　He is no musician.

他不懂音乐。

［例 3b］　He is not a musician.

他不是音乐家。

［例 4a］　It is no joke.

这是件正经事。

［例 4b］　It is not a joke.

这不是笑话。

但是当名词作 have 的宾语或作 there is（are）的主语时，其前用 no 或 not a 表示数量，not a 比 no 语气更强。试比较：

［例 5a］　He has no English dictionary.

他没有英语辞典。

［例 5b］　He has not an English dictionary.

他连一本英语辞典也没有。

17．not/no＋比较级

［例 1a］　This book is not better than that one.

［例 1b］　This book is no better than that one.

不细心的读者一定以为这两句表示的意义没有什么差别。其实，差别很大。前句属于普通的比较结构，意为"两本书都好"（"Both of the books are good."），只是在"好"的程度上，这本并不超过那本。因此，要译为"这本书没有那本好"。而后一句 no beter than 是比较级的特殊用法，所表示的是该形容词（或副词）的相反意义。no better than ＝ as bad as，因此要译为"这本书同那本书一样坏。又如：

no richer than ＝ as poor as

no bigger than ＝ as small as

no heavier than ＝ as light as

no later than ＝ as early as

no wiser than = as stupid as

no darker than = as bright as

再请比较：

［例2a］　Joe is not richer than his friend.　（ = Both of them are rich.)

乔不比他的朋友更富。

［例2b］　Joe is no richer than his friend.　（ = Both Joe and his friend are poor.　= Joe is as poor as his friend.)

乔和他的朋友都是穷光蛋。

18．否定转移

［例1］　He didn't come to see me.

这句话既可以是"他没有来看我"，也可以是"他来不是看我"。究竟是表示哪一种意思，往往取决于上下文，在口语中取决于语调。表示第一种意义时念降调：He 'didn't 'come to ˎsee me.　（ = He failed to come to see me.) 表示第二种意义时是否定的转移，含降升调：He 'didn't 'come to ˇsee me.　（ = He came not to see me, but to see sb. else.)。

下面两组句子中的第一句念降升调也都表示这种否定的转移：

［例2a］　I 'didn't 'come because of the ˇrain　（ = I came not because of the rain.)

并非因为下雨我才来。

［例2b］　I 'didn't 'come because of the ˎrain　（ = I failed to come because of the rain.)

因为下雨我没有来。

［例3a］　I 'have not 'studied Russian for ˇtwo years.　（ = I

have studied Russian for less than two years.)

我学俄语不到两年。

[例 3b]　　I 'have not 'studied Russian for 'two years. (= It is two years since I studied Russian.)

我不学俄语已经两年了。

19．not happy 和 unhappy

[例 1a]　　He is not happy.

[例 1b]　　He is unhappy.

这两句都表示否定意义。第一句是借助否定副词 not 否定谓语，第二句是用带否定前缀的词作表语。尽管否定的方式不同，但意义并无差别，都是"他不高兴"的意思。但是，如果加上表程度的副词，如 very 后，它们的含义就大不相同了。试比较：

[例 2a]　　He is not very happy.

他不是很高兴。

[例 2b]　　He is very unhappy.

他很不高兴。

这是因为，第一句是真正的否定句，否定句使用程度很高的副词时，不但不能加强否定的意义，反而使程度有所减弱。第二句从语义上看是否定，在语法上是个肯定句，因而可以用 very 等程度很高的副词加强语气。

20．a bit 和 not a bit

[例 1a]　　He spends ￡ 200 a year.

他一年要花两百英镑。

[例 1b]　　He lives on ￡ 200 a year.

他一年只靠两百英镑过活。

[**例2a**]　I am a little tired.

我有点疲倦。

[**例2b**]　I am a bit tired.

我有点疲倦。

上面每组句子中的两个句子，均为肯定句。虽然措辞不同，但其意义却基本相同。但是，如果变成否定句，它们的意义则完全不相同了。试比较：

[**例3a**]　He doesn't spend £ 200 a year.　（＝less than）

他一年花不到两百英镑。

[**例3b**]　He doesn't live on £ 200 a year.　（＝more than）

他一年不只靠两百英镑过活。

[**例4a**]　I am not a little tired.　（＝I am very tired.）

我很疲倦。

[**例4b**]　I am not a bit tired.　（＝I am not tired at all.）

我一点也不疲倦。

21．besides 和 except

[**例1a**]　There is nothing on the table except a pencil.

[**例1b**]　There is nothing on the table besides a pencil.

besides 和 except 本是意义不相同的两个介词。besides 意为"除……之处（，尚有……）"，表示在整体中加入一部分，而 except 意为"除……之外（，不再有……）"表示在整体中除去一部分。试比较：

[**例2a**]　We all went besides him.

除他以外，我们大家也都去了。（他去了）

[**例2b**]　We all went except him.

除他以外，我们都去了。（他没有去）

但是，在否定句中，except 和 besides 表示的意义却相同。因此，"There is nothing on the table besides a pencil." 和 "There is nothing on the table except a pencil." 意义一样，都是：桌上只有一支笔。

22．a good many 和 a good few

请比较下列两组句子。

[例 1a]　　He excuses my not going there.

[例 1b]　　He excuses my going there.

[例 2a]　　I want a cloth that will wear.

[例 2b]　　I want a cloth that will not wear.

第一组中 excuse 有两种含义。第一句的 excuse 作 pardon 解，等于 "He pardons me not going there."（他原谅我不去）。第二句中的 excuse 作 dispense 解，等于 "He dispenses me from going there."（他免除我去）。因此，两句尽管一个为肯定，一个为否定，形式相反，而意义却相同。

第二组中的 wear 也有两种含义。第一句中的 wear 作"经穿"（endure continued use）解，"我要一种经穿的布"。第二句中的 wear 作"磨损"（become less useful）解，"我要一种不会穿破的布"。因而，实际上两句意义相同。

英语中有些意义相反的词，加上一些限制语后，意义变得相同，如 many（很多）和 few（很少）意义相反，但 a good many 和 a good few 却意义相同，都作"许多""相当多"解。如：

[例 3a]　　There are a good many students there.

[例 3b]　　There are a good few students there.

那儿有很多学生。

23．表示否定的肯定句

［例1］　Catch me doing it!

我可不会再干那种事了!

这是一个肯定句，为什么表示强烈的否定意义？原来这是一句反语（reverse remark）。反语就是说反话，即用正面的话来表达反面的意思。这句相当于：You won't catch me doing it. 言下之意即"I won't do it again."。

反语往往引人深思，表现出深刻的思想感情，特别是用来讽刺、挖苦时更为深刻有力。反语常以感叹句形式出现，如：

［例2］　A fat lot you know!（ = You know nothing.）

你懂得真多!（你什么都不懂!）

［例3］　You may do that for all I care.　（ = I don't care if you do that!）

你愿做就做吧，我才不在乎呢!

有些用 as...as 表示的明喻（simile）也可用反语，即将两个相反的东西作比较，衬托出否定的意思。如：

［例4］　You might as well expect a river to flow backward as hope to move me.

你不能动摇我的心，正如不能使河水倒流一样。

［例5］　He is as sensitive to music as a deaf-mute.

他就像一个聋哑人一样对音乐不敏感。

前面我们探讨了否定句产生歧义的情况。肯定和否定是一对矛盾的两个方面，二者同是思维和言语中不可缺少的范畴，否定的意义除了用带有否定词的否定句表达外，还可以用肯定形式表达。如"我不懂这首诗"，除可以用"I don't understand the poem."表达外，至少还可以有以下一些表达方法：

（1） I fail to understand the poem.

（2） I am at a loss to understand the poem.

（3） I am in the dark about the poem.

（4） I am in total ignorance of the poem.

（5） The poem is beyond me（beyond my understanding）.

（6） The poem puzzles me.

（7） The poem beats me.

（8） The poem gets me.

（9） The poem is（all）Greek to me.

（10） The poem is a sealed book to me.

（11） It is out of my power to understand the poem.

（12） The poem is too difficult for me to understand.

（13） If only I understood the poem.

（14） I wish I understood the poem.

（15） Who says I understand the poem?

三、并列结构的陷阱

24．good and…

[例1] The boy was bad. Yes! He was good and bad.

那孩子坏呀。是的！他真是很坏。（※……他既好又坏。）

and 通常是并列连词，它所连接的两个词、词组及句子在意义上通常也是并列关系。但是，当 and 连接的两个形容词的第一个是 good、nice、fine、lovely、rare、bright、big 等时，它们不再是并列关系，而是从属关系，第一个形容词相当于一个同义的副词，起"强意词"（intensifier）的作用，加强第二个形容词的语义，相当于 very，thoroughly，quite 等，通常译为"很""非常"等。因此，此句决不能按字面意义译为"……他既好又坏"。但却有人望文生义将"It's nice and warm today，isn't it?"译成"今天的天气睛朗而且温暖，你说呢?"，这自然是错误的。又如：

[例 2]　　The book is fine and expensive.

这本书很贵。（※这本书好又贵。）

[例 3]　　He got good and angry.

他很生气。

[例 4]　　I like the article. It was good and short.

我喜欢这篇文章，它十分简短。

[例 5]　　The boss was always big and busy.

老板总是很忙。

good and…作定语时，and 有时可以省略，如：

[例 6]　　I prefer good black coffee.

我要喝很浓的咖啡。

人类在语言思维上有时是相通的，在汉语中也可以见到这种用法。如"这孩子好坏"译成英语正好是"The boy is good and bad."。

25.　复数名词并列重复

[例 1]　　There are books and books.

有各种各样的书，有好书也有坏书。（※有很多书。）

复数名词重复一次有时不是为了强调，而是表示同一类人或物的不同性质。此例是由"There are good books and not good books，and even bad books."一句压缩而来的。不说出 not good 和 bad 是为了达到委婉的效果。据钱歌川先生称，这种表现法似乎出自 Bacon 说的 "There are dinners and dinners." 一语，现应用到其他一切事情上。又如：

[例 2]　You can find doctors and doctors in Hong Kong.

在香港，既有好医生，也有坏医生。（※在香港，你能看到很多很多医生。）

[例 3]　There are translations and translations.

翻译有好坏之分。

但是，如果复数名词重复两次以上，则表示"大量的""许多的"。如：

[例 4]　There were rats and rats and rats all over the house.

从前这幢房子里到处都是老鼠。（※从前这幢房子里有各种各样的老鼠。）

[例 5]　We saw students and students and students.

我们到处看见很多很多的学生。

26．表示单数意义的并列结构

[例 1]　The writer died in poverty and distress.

这位作家在极端贫困中死去。（※这位作家死于贫困和悲伤。）

and 是个并列连词（coordinator），通常用来连接并列的单词、词组或句子，意为"和、与、同、及、又"等。但有时它所连接的并非并列关系而是从属关系，相当于从属连词，此句中的 distress 修饰 poverty，等于 distressed poverty。又如：

[例 2]　I felt it was time for conversation and confidence（= for confidential conversation）.

我以为该是推心置腹地谈一谈的时候了。（※我以为该是谈话和有信心的时候了。)

[例3] They work with might and main. (= with main might)

他们尽全力工作。

and 连接两个名词，后一个修饰前一个的这种结构很多，翻译时不能望文生义。如：

death and honour (= honourable death)，意为"光荣牺牲"（※牺牲和光荣）。

cups and gold (= golden cups)，意为"金杯"（※杯子和金子）。

bread and butter (= buttered bread)，意为"涂有奶油的面包"（※面包和奶油）。

a watch and chain，意为"有链条的表"（※表和链条）。

a lock and key，意为"有钥匙的锁"（※锁和钥匙）。

a needle and thread，意为"穿了线的针"（※针和线）。

a cup and sauce，意为"放在茶碟上的茶杯"（※茶杯和茶碟）。

coffce and milk，意为"加牛奶的咖啡"（※咖啡加牛奶）。

brandy and soda，意为"加苏打的白兰地酒"（※白兰地酒和苏打）。

a knife and fook，意为"一副刀叉"（※刀和叉）

27．as well as 引出的并列结构

[例1] He has experience as well as knowledge.

他既有知识，又有经验。（※他有知识和经验。※他既有经验，又有知识。）

as well as 用作并列连词时，其意义相当于 not only...but

also，均为"不但……而且"。但二者侧重点有所不同。as well as 侧重在前面的词，而 not only…but also 侧重在后面的词。上句可改为：He has not only knowledge but also experience. 又如：

[例2]　She is a talented musician as well as being a photographer.

她不但是摄影师还是个天才的音乐家。(※她是天才的音乐家和摄影师。)

[例3]　He grows flowers as well as vegetables.

他不但种菜，而且养花。(※他不但养花，而且种菜。)

但是，as well as 有时也可用来代替 and，特别是列举三个或三个以上的人或物的情况下更为常见。这时，前后各部分没有轻重之分，通常译成"和""以及"等。如：

[例4]　The president has said that leaders from Britain，West Germany，France，Italy as well as Japan will be present at the meeting.

总统说英国、西德、法国、意大利和日本的领导人将出席会议。(※不但日本，而且英国……)

如果 as well as 所连接的是主格和宾格形式相同的人称代词或名词，则可能产生歧义。如：

[例5]　I love her as well as Comrade Li（or you）.

这句话即可理解为："不但李同志（或你）喜欢她，我也喜欢她。"［此时 Comrade Li（or you）为主格］也可理解为："我不但喜欢李同志（或你），也喜欢她。"［此时 Comrade Li（you）为宾格］

28．as well as 与否定结构选用

[例1]　I have received no letters from John as well as from

Peter.

我接到了彼得的信,但不曾接到约翰的信。(※我没有接到约翰的信,也没有接到彼得的信。)

在否定句中,有时 as well as 在句中的位置不一样,意义上差别很大。此句中的 as well as from Peter 不在否定的范围之内。但如果将 as well as 的位置挪动一下,将它置于否定词的范围之内,即 "From John as well as from Peter, I have received no letters.",全句意义就发生了变化,成了"我不曾接到彼得的信,也不曾接到约翰的信"。在否定句中,有时 as well as 的位置不一样,意义上差别很大。试比较下列各组句子:

[例2a] I shall not go as well as you.

你将去,但我不去。

[例2b] I, as wall as you, shall not go.

你将不去,我也将不去。

[例3a] He doesn't study hard as well as his brother.

他的弟弟学习努力,而他不努力。

[例3b] He, as well as his brother, doesn't study hard.

他和他的弟弟一样,学习不努力。

四、比较结构和其他结构的陷阱

29. know better than to do

[例1] This subject— the death of the city of New York— continues to be discussed by those of us who should know better.

这个话题——纽约城的衰亡——继续被一些人谈论着,而这些人本来应该明智些不去谈论这个话题的。(※……还在继续被我们这些对纽约比较熟悉的人们谈论着。)

know better 常表示否定，意为 be wise or well-trained enough not to，be not so foolish as to do［明白事理而不至于（做某事）］，因此，上句中的…who should know better 应为：…who should know better than to discuss it，即…who should be wise enough not to discuss it。又如：

［例2］　She should know better than to spend all her money on books.

她应该懂得不能把所有的钱都花在买书上。

［例3］　You ought to know better than to trust her.

你应当明白她这人不能相信。

［例4］　I know better than to move another leg.

我知道还是站着不动为妙。

［例5］　He knew better than to interfere in our affairs.

他明白事理，不至于干涉我们的事。

［例6］　I thought you know better than to go to such places as that.

我想你不会去那样一些地方。

30．none the worse

［例1］　He is none the worse for falling into the river.

他跌进河里但什么事也没有。

"none + the + 比较级" 意为 "一点也不" "毫不"。句中的 "for + 名词结构" 表达一个已发生或即将发生的事实，而不是一个被否定的事实。又如：

［例2］　I'm afraid I'm none the wiser for your explanation.

恐怕你的解释没使我有所开窍。

[例3]　He is none the worse for a single failure.

他并不因仅仅一次失败就垮了下去。

[例4]　He is none the wiser for all his experience.

他并不因为有经验而聪明一点。

[例5]　He is none the happier for all his wealth.

他并不因富有而快乐些。

31．as I live

[例1]　He is dead，as I live.

他的确是死了。（※他死了，我还活着。）

此句中的 as I live 并不表示比较或方式，而表示强调。用确切无疑的事实"我活着"（I live）来强调前面主句 he is dead（他死了）也是确切无疑的，as I live 相当于 indeed。类似的说法还有 as I am here、as the sun shines、as you stand here、as my nose is in my face，等等。

32．since "自从"

[例1]　I haven't written to her since she lived in London.

自从她离开伦敦以来，我还没给她写过信。（※自从她住在伦敦以来……）

[例2]　Two years has passed since I smoked.

我戒烟已经两年了。（※我抽烟已经两年了。）

[例3]　He has written to me frequently since I was ill.

我病愈之后他常给我写信。（※自从我生病以来……）

since 作连词引导时间状语从句，表示从过去某一时刻到现在或从过去某一时刻到过去另一时刻为止的一段时间。从句常用一般过去时，所表示的时间是从这个动作结束时算起。如果是短暂动词（momentary verb）如 leave、see、come，因为动作的发生和结束都是在瞬间完成的，动词的词汇意义和语法意义具有一致性，since 从句所表示的时间从谓语动词所表示的动作完成时算起，不会造成理解上的困难。如：

[例4]　We've been friends since we left school.

我们从学校毕业后一直是朋友。

[例5]　Where have you been since I last saw you?

自从我上次见到你以后，你到哪里去了？

但是，如果是持续动词（durative verb）或状态动词的过去时，如上述几句中的 lived、smoked、was ill，表示的时间也应从这些动词所表示的动作完成或状态结束时算起，即"不居住""不抽烟""不生病"时算起。如果要表示动作或状态延续至今，那就要用这些动词的现在完成时。试比较：

[例6]　I have met him often since I have lived here.

自从我在这里住下来之后，我常看见他。

[例7]　I have not written to her since I have been home.

自从我回家以来，一直没给她写信。

33．表示赌咒的 I'll eat my hat

[例1]　I'll eat my hat if I do.

我绝不做。（※如果我做的话，我就吃掉我的帽子。）

此句中的 I'll eat my hat 是赌咒用语，hat 也可以换成 boots、hands、head。if 从句与包含赌咒词语的主句连用，强调地表示 if 从句的反面意思。又如：

[例2]　If I understand you, Mr. Lorry, I'll be hanged.

劳雷先生，我丝毫不了解你。（※绞死我，我也不了解你，劳雷先生！）

[例3]　I wish I may die if I like it.

我真不喜欢它。

［例4］　I am damned if I agree with him.

我绝不会同意他的意见。

［例5］　Well，then…I'm jiggered if I don't see you home.

啊，好吧，我非送你回家不可。

有时这种赌咒词语可以省去，只剩下一个 if 从句，表示的意义不变。如：

［例6］　If this is human life!

这真不是人过的生活!

34. if an inch 表示强调

［例1］　This mountain is 1,685 metres high，if an inch.

这座山的确有 1,685 米高。（※如果这座山有一英寸高的话，它就有 1,685 米高。）

此句中的 if 从句并不表条件，不能按一般条件从句来理解。这是一种断言性条件从句（asseverativa condition），是表强调的一种手段，是从最小的单位条件说起，作为说话人立论的根据。也就是说，如果你承认这座山有一英寸高（要否定这一点，显然是荒谬的），这座山就有 1,685 米高。同例如：

［例2］　She is forty if she is a day（or an hour）.

她确确实实四十岁了。

［例3］　The audience were ten thousand，if a man.

听众无论如何也有一万人。

［例4］　The alteration in the house cost full 5000 pounds if they cost a penny.

改造这座房屋至少花了整整五千英镑。

［例5］　He is a writer，if a day.

他确实是位作家。（※他总有一天会成为一位作家。）

35．nothing if not 表示强调

［例 1］　It is nothing if（it is）not a hoax.

这是个十足的骗局。（※如果不是骗局，它什么都不是。）

此句中的 nothing if not 也起强调作用。此句是 "It is a hoax." 的强调句型。又如：

［例 2］　He is nothing if（he is）not a basketball player.

他确实是位篮球运动员。

［例 3］　The current situation is nothing if not fine.

目前形势好极了。

36．as sure as eggs is eggs

例：It will happen as sure as eggs is eggs.

那是必定会发生的。

此句中 as sure as eggs is eggs 是口语体，表示强调，意为"的的确确，千真万确"。注意此中的 eggs is eggs 不可改为 eggs are eggs，因为这里是把 eggs 看作一个整体。把 eggs 改为 a gun、death、nails、fate、one's lives 也可以。

37．it is a wise man that…

［例 1］　It is a wise man（a good workman）that never makes mistakes（blunders）.

智者千虑必有一失。（※聪明人从来不做错事。）

在 "It is a＋形容词＋名词＋that 从句" 句式中，that 从句并不是修饰其前面名词的定语从句，而是说明句首作主语的先行词 it（anticipatory it），因而实际上是主语从句，具有否定意义。这种句式多见于谚语或格言，翻译时一定要从反面着笔。此句等于 "The man that never makes mistakes is wise." 或

"However wise a man is, he makes mistakes."。它的字面意义是：从不犯错误的才是智者。其实义则是：世上没有不犯错误的人。转译成：智者千虑必有一失。同例如：

[例2]　It is a good horse that never stumbles. (= However good a horse is, it stumbles.)

人有失误，马有失蹄。(多好的马也会失足。)

[例3]　It is an ill wind that blows nobody good. (= It is an ill wind that never blows anybody good. = However ill a wind is, it blows sb. good.)

人死和尚乐。(世界上没有对人人都不利的事。)

[例4]　It is an ill bird that fouls its nest. (= However ill a bird is, it never fouls its own nest.)

家丑不可外扬。(多坏的鸟也不会弄脏自己的巢。)

38. 非限制性定语从句与限制性定语从句

[例1]　We can read of things that happened 5,000 years ago in the Near East, where people first learned to write.

我们能够通过阅读了解五千年前近东所发生的事情，因为那里的人们首先学会了书写。(※早在五千年前的近东，人们首先学会了写字。关于这一点，我们可以从书本上读到。)

此句中两个定语从句，that happened 5,000 years ago in the Near East 是限制性定语从句，修饰先行词 things，其意为"我们能够从书本上读知五千年前在近东所发生的许多事情"。where people first learned to write 是非限制性定语从句，对先行词进行补充说明，表原因。误译将非限制性定语从句理解为修饰 the Near East 的限制性定语从句，而把限制性定语从句译成非限制性定语从句。

39．as 作关系代词与作连词的区别

［例 1］　　Whales are not fish，as some people think.

鲸鱼不是鱼，但有些人认为是鱼。（※正像有些人认为的那样，鲸鱼不是鱼。）

此句中的 as 为连词，意义上相当于 but，引导的是方式状语从句。从句本身是省略了宾语的复合句，省去的是整个主句，但不包括 not。这句话如果不省略，则为：Whales are not fish，as some people think whales are fish.

40．反身代词的歧义用法

例：You must stick the stamp on yourself.

你必须自己把邮票贴上去。（※你必须把邮票贴在自己身上。）

反身代词（reflexive pronoun）有两种不同的用法：强调用法和非强调用法（emphatic and non-emphatic use）。强调用法的反身代词在句中作同位语，要重读；非强调用法通常放在动词或介词的后面，作宾语，一般不重读。不了解这两种用法，则可能造成理解上的错误。

有一个故事讲的是一位法国人到英国旅游。他英语不怎么好。一天，他去邮局寄信。买好邮票后，他把信连同邮票一起交给售票员。售票员对他说："You must stick the stamp on yourself."这位法国人听了以后大为不解，问道："Why must I stick the stamp on myself?"售票员知道他理解错了，向他解释说："I mean you must stick the stamp on the letter and must do it yourself."这自然是个笑话，却说明了分清反身代词强调和非强调用法是非常重要的。售票员说"You must stick the stamp on yourself."意为"你必须自己把邮票贴上去"。句中 yourself

是强调用法，作主语 you 的同位语，要重读。而那位法国人却把 yourself 误为介词 on 的宾语，不重读。这句就成了"你必须把邮票贴到你自己身上"，难怪他要感到吃惊了。

41．限制性与非限制性定语从句

［例 1a］　She has a brother who is an artist.

她有一个兄弟是艺术家。（限制性定语从句，她可能有多个兄弟，其中一个是位艺术家）

［例 1b］　She has a brother, who is an artist.

她有一个兄弟，他是艺术家。（非限制性定语从句，表示"她只有一个兄弟"）

例 1a 是限制性定语从句，与主句之间不用逗号，口语中无停顿；例 1b 是非限制性定语从句，与主句之间有逗号，口语中有停顿。有无逗号对区分限制性和非限制性定语从句关系重大，有时引起意义上很大差别。Eckersley 讲了一个牧师不喜欢穿平常的牧师服的故事。这个牧师说："I will wear no clothes which will distinguish me from my fellow-men."（我将不穿与众不同的衣服）但是，他的话在报上刊载时误加了一个逗号，原来的限制性定语从句变成了非限制性定语从句，句子成了："I will wear no clothes, which will distinguish me from my fellow-men."（我将不穿衣服，这样我就会与众不同了）这位牧师因此受到人们的奚落。这个故事十分生动地阐明了限制性定语从句与非限制性定语从句的区别。又如：

［例 2a］　There were very few passengers that escaped without serious injury.

没有受重伤逃出来的旅客很少。

［例 2b］　There were very few passengers, who escaped

without serious injury.

旅客很少，他们都逃出来了，没有受重伤。

例 2 的两句也只是因为一个小小的逗号引起意义上的重大差别。随着语言的发展，也出现了一些非限制性定语从句不用逗号的情况。有人对 *New Concept English* 第三册作过统计，不带逗号的非限制性定语从句就有 70 句左右。因此，不能单纯看有无逗号，主要应从意义上区分限制性定语从句和非限制性专语从句。

42．show sb. sth. 和 show sb. to sth.

［例 1a］　He showed me the door.

他赶我出门。

［例 1b］　He showed me to the door.

他送我到门口。

show sb. the door 是一个习语，意为"逐出，要某人离开"（require sb. to leave and see that he does so）。此中的 the door 如改为其他名词，则意义大为不同。试比较：

［例 2］　He showed me the pictures.

他把他的图画给我看。

［例 3］　Show him the room.

告诉他是哪一个房间。

而例 1b 句中的 show me to the door 中的 show 意为"引导、陪伴"（guide，escort），me 是直接宾语，to the door 表示"送行"的目的地，并非习语。又如：

［例 4］　He showed me to the station.

他送我到车站。

［例 5］　He showed me into the living room.

他把我带进起居室。

[例6] The guide showed us over the old castle.

向导带我们走遍那古堡。

43．be absent in

[例1] He is absent in Beijing.

他在北京。(※他不在北京。)

be absent in 表示"在某地"，相当于 be present in。要表示"不在、缺席"（not present, not in existence）后面要接介词 from。"他不在北京"要译为"He is absent from Beijing."。又如：

[例2] Several students were absent from the lecture.

有几个学生没有来听课。

be absent in 实际上是 be absent（from...）in...的省略结构。如说"他不在广州，而在北京"可译为"He is absent from Guangzhou in Beijing."。

名词 absence 的用法亦同。如：

[例3] The war broke out during my absence（from this place）in the country.

这战事发生在我（不在那个地方而）在乡里的时候。

[例4] During their absence in Shanghai, they paid a visit to the Chinese Economic and Trade Exhibition.

在上海逗留期间，他们参观了中国经济贸易展览会。

但是，说到不会动的东西时，absent（or absence）in 却作"不在……里""在……里没有"解。如：

[例5] This word is absent in that dictionary.

在那本词典里没有这个词。

44．"英国教师"还是"英语教师"

[例1]　He is an English teacher.

这也是歧义句，既可以表示"他是一个英国教师"，又可以表示"他是一个英语教师"。这时，重音起决定作用。重音在 teacher 上，English ′teacher 表示"英国教师"（不一定教英语），重音在 English 上，′English teacher 即"英语教师"（不一定是英国人）。

45．forget to do 和 forget doing

[例1]　I forgot posting the letter.

我忘记我已经把信寄走了。(※我忘记寄信了。)

forget 作"遗忘"（fail to remember）解时，后面可接名词、代词、动名词、动词不定式或从句作宾语。接动名词作宾语时，表示把某件发生过的事情忘记了；如接不定式作宾语，则表示忘记去做某事。试比较下面两句：

[例2a]　They forgot telling me.

他们忘了他们已经告诉我了。

[例2b]　They forgot to tell me.

他们忘记告诉我了。

值得注意的是，要表示"把什么东西忘记在什么地方"的意思，也就是说，有具体的地点时，不能用 forget，如可以说：

[例3a]　I've forgotten my book.

但不能说：

[例3b]　I've forgotten my book in the library.

表示"把……遗忘在某地"，要用 leave，上句应改为：

[例3c]　I've left my book in the library.

注意 forget 在某些习语中的用法：

［例4］　Don't get dizzy with success and forget yourselves.

不要让胜利冲昏头脑，忘乎所以。

［例5］　"I'm sorry I hurt your feeling. " "Forget it. "

"很抱歉伤了你的感情。""甭提了，没什么。"

［例6］　Thanks for reminding me. I'd forgotten all about him coming this afternoon.

谢谢你提醒我，他今天下午要来的事我完全忘了。

46．a few 和 few

［例1］　I have a few novels at home, fifty in all.

我家里有一些小说，总共有五十本。

［例2］　There are few novels in the library, only fifty in all.

图书馆里没有什么小说，总共才五十本。

［例3］　I can lend you a little money. Will ten dollars be enough?

我可以借些钱给你。十美元够吗？

［例4］　I am afraid I can give you little money this time. Will ten dollars be all right?

我恐怕这次不能给你什么钱了。十美元行吗？

表示"一点儿"，可以用 few、a few（与可数名词连用），也可以用 little、a little（与不可数名词连用）。什么时候用 a few、a little，什么时候用 few、little，不在于它们绝对的数或量的多少，而在于说话人的语意是肯定还是否定。一个人家里有五十本小说，自然是多啦，所以用 a few，而图书馆才有五十本小说，自然是少了，所以用 few。例3、例4的区别亦同。

又如一篇作文中有五个错误，如果你认为写得好，只有五个错误，你就可以说："There are few mistakes in it." 如果你认为写得不好，五个错误太多了，你就可以说："There are a few mistakes in it."

又如热水瓶中有一定量的水，从不同角度，可以有不同的说法。如果说"There is little water in it." 那你是持否定态度，说瓶里没有什么水；如果说"There is a little water in it."，那你是肯定态度，说里面还有一些水。

a little 和 a few 前面加上否定词 not，不是没"有一点"，而是"不只是一点儿"，意思是"不少"或"相当多"。所以 not a little 和 quite a little、not a few 和 quite a few 意思相近。如：

[例5]　Not a few people have visited the city.

不少人参观过这个城市。

[例6]　Not a little money was paid back to her.

付了她不少钱。

47．There will be a meeting next Thursday.

你可能会认为，这句话不是很简单吗？不就是"下星期四有一个会议"吗？其实不然，这里有歧义。如果在星期五、星期六、星期日说这个话，自然是"下星期四有个会议"。但是如果在星期一、星期二说这个话，就只能是"本周星期四有个会议"了。

同样，这句话如果在星期三、星期四说的，便只能指下周星期四。这是因为说话人指本周（即包含说话时间在内的这一周）的话，则应说 tomorrow（明天）或 today（今天）。因为"今天""明天"这两个词与历法专有名词（Thursday）相比，具有优先选择权。

48. much thanks 和 many thanks

[例1] Much thanks!

多谢!

当别人为我们做了好事、帮了忙时，我们常说 "Thank you!" "Thank you very much!" "Many thanks." 或 "Much thanks." 表示感谢。thanks 复数名词，照理只与 many 连用，怎么可以与 much 连用呢？但是，much thanks 却是地地道道的英语，英美人至今常用。初学者必然要问：这是为什么？我们不妨查一下比较大型的英文辞典，看一看 much 的含义。

在 *Universal English Dictionary* 中，much 条第二个解释是："（archaic）great in number, many"。在 *Webster's New Twentieth Century Dictionary* 中，much 条第一个解释是："many in number（obs）"，并附有一例："Edon came out against him with much people." 由此可见，在古英语中 much 有一种用法等于 many，现在这种用法已经陈旧，谁也不讲 much people、much books 了，而要讲 many people、many books。但是，much thanks 却保存了下来，当然用法上也不如 many thanks 普遍。

much 与复数名词连用不仅限于 much thanks，还可见于下列几种情况：

第一，一些表示数量的词组，如果只考虑"量"的多少，而不考虑具体的个数时，可用 much 来修饰。如：

[例2] She has five children, which I think is too much.

她有五个小孩，我认为太多了。

这句中把 five children 看作一个整体，而没有考虑到各个可数的人，因而用 much，不用 many。这从句子的谓语动词用单数 is 也可得到证明。

第二，有些抽象名词，虽然用复数形式，但意义上不可数，仍表示抽象概念，因而可与 much 连用。如：

［例3］ He has much brains.（much 不可改为 many。）

他很有头脑。

［例4］ How much wages does he get a month?（much 不可改为 many。）

他一个月多少工资？

第三，much 可加在一些物质名词复数前面，表示"数量之大""范围之广"。如：

［例5］ Don't give the dog so much potatoes.

不要给狗吃太多土豆。

［例6］ There is much grounds in front of our house.

我们家门前有大块空地。

第四，当复数名词与单数名词构成一个整体，可以用 much 来修饰，如：

［例7］ There is too much cinema, cigarettes and chocalates.

电影院、香烟、巧克力之类的东西太多了。

第五，买东西问价格时，总是用"How much…?"，尽管回答时可能是复数名词词组。如：

［例 8］ "How much does this coat cost?" "Twenty dollars."

"这件衣服多少钱?""二十元。"

49．at table 和 at a table：不定冠词引起语义变化

［例1］ We sat at a table.

我们坐在桌旁。

［例2］　We were at table when he came in.

他进来时，我们正在吃饭。

例1中的 table 是单数可数名词，前面有冠词 a。例2中 at table 中的 table 已经不再表示具体的桌子，而表示抽象的概念，其意思是"进餐"，因而变成不可数名词，前面没有冠词 a。英语中有不少这样的情况，常见的有：

第一，可数名词 school、college、market、prison、court、hospital、camp、bed、table、sea、class、church 等与介词 at、after、in、to、from 等连用时，常失去可数名词的具体意义，不表示这些名词所代表的建筑物或事物，而表示与这些建筑或事物有关的情形或活动，或表明它们使用的目的，转变为抽象名词，具有不可数名词的特点。它们前面不能有冠词。如：

［例3］　He goes to school every day.

他每天上学。

［例4］　When he was a boy his greatest wish was to go to sea.

他儿时最大的愿望就是去当水手。

第二，表示交通工具的一些名词，如 bicycle、car、bus、train、boat、plane 等与 by 连用，表示乘车、乘船、坐飞机等抽象概念。如：

［例5］　He goes to work by bicycle.

他骑自行车上班。

［例6］　He came by boat.

他坐船来的。

50．职位前是否加冠词

［例1］　His father is professor of Peking University.

他父亲是北大教授。（※他父亲是北大的一位教授。）

一些表示职位、身份、职业的可数名词，在句中作表语、补足语及同位语，表示该名词具有的抽象意义，用作不可数名词。句中的 professor 相当于 professorship。此句不能译为"他父亲是北大的一位教授"。要表示"一位"的意思，应为"His father is a professor of Peking University."。又如：

［例2］　　She is all woman.

她女性味十足。

［例3］　　I am more engineer than soldier.

与其说我是士兵，倒不如说我是个工程师。

51．非限制性定语从句和限制性定语从句：标点符号

［例1a］　　Her son who is a surgeon has gone to Yemen.

［例1b］　　Her son, who is a surgeon, has gone to Yemen.

以上两句文字完全相同，稍有不同的是，例1b 句中 who is a surgeon 前后多了一个逗号，也就是这个逗号使得它们表达的意义有所不同。例1a 要译为"她那当外科大夫的儿子到也门去了"（暗示她不止一个儿子）；例1b 要译成"她的儿子是个外科大夫，他到也门去了"（暗示她只有一个儿子）。可见标点符号也可能引起歧义。又如：

［例2a］　　Mary Robinson says Mrs. Abington is the greatest actress in London.

玛丽·鲁宾逊说阿宾顿夫人是伦敦最伟大的女演员。

［例2b］　　Mary Robinson, says Mrs. Abington, is the greatest actress in London.

"玛丽·鲁宾逊，"阿宾顿太太说，"是伦敦最伟大的女演员。"

可见有无一个逗号，能使伦敦最伟大的女演员易位。

标点符号的使用在汉语中也是十分重要的。因标点符号的差异造成意义上差别的，不乏其例。如甲对乙下了一个遂客令：

下雨天留客天留我不留

甲写这个逐客令的本意为：

下雨天留客，天留我不留。

但因甲没有用标点符号，乙却念成了：

下雨天，留客天。留我不？留。

这样，"逐客令"就变成"留客令"，与甲的原意完全相反了。

52．day 和 days

［例1］　My day is gone.

误：我的日子完蛋了。

正：我得意的日子已经过去了。

在一部美国西部电影中，一位新警长请一位功劳卓著的老警长重新出山平匪，老警长说了"My day is gone."这么一句。be gone 有"死去""完蛋"的意思，很显然这里不是这个意思。老警长说这么一句是表示"我老了，以前的辉煌、得意都过去了"，以此来拒绝新警长的请求。

与 day 搭配的习惯用语很多，现略举数例：

［例2］　His days are numbered.

他的寿命指日可数了。

［例3］　The poor old man ended his miserable day by jumping into the sea.

这可怜的老人投海自尽，了却残生。

［例4］　We've won the day.

我们赢了！

[例5]　　When it was day, the fishermen went out.

破晓时，渔夫们就出发了。

[例6]　　How goes the day?

战况如何？

53．be being +形容词

[例1]　　She is being kind.

误：她待人和蔼可亲。

正：她装出和蔼可亲的样子。

is being kind 不表示主语的特性和品质，只表示"目前"或现在"短暂"的状况。即"她平时待人并不和蔼，现在故意装出一副和蔼可亲的样子"。要表示"她一向待人和蔼可亲"，要说"She is kind."。比较下面每组里的两句：

[例2a]　　She is angry with you.

她跟你发怒了。

[例2b]　　She is being angry with you.

她装作跟你发怒的样子（，实际上她一点也不生气）。

[例3a]　　I am fair to both sides.

我对双方都公平。

[例3b]　　I am being fair to both sides.

我正在留意做到对双方公平。

54．some time 和 sometime

[例1]　　It took him some time to finish the letter.

他花了好些时间写完这封信。

[例2]　　I'll write to him sometime this evening.

今晚我要给他写封信。

例 1 中，some time 意为"一段时间"（for some period of time）；例 2 中的 sometime 意为"在将来或过去的某一个时候"（at some uncertain time in the future or in the past）。又如：

[**例 3**]　I haven't been feeling well for some time.

我感到不舒服已经有一段时间了。

[**例 4**]　I will see you again sometime.

改日再来看你。

[**例 5**]　He was sometime professor of physics at the university, and will publish a new work before long.

他曾是这所大学的物理学教授，不久就要出版一本新书。

表示"有时"（at some times, now and then）要用 sometimes。如：

[**例 6**]　Sometimes he comes by train and sometimes by bus.

他有时乘火车来，有时候乘汽车来。

中编：

英语语言疑难解惑 18 讲

英语"开始"情貌意义的表达手段[*]

英语中，有<u>些</u>动词，如：begin、start、commence，其本身的词汇意义就表示"开始"。如：

[例1]　I <u>began</u> to study English last year.

[例2]　She sat down at the piano and <u>started</u> to play.

[例3]　We <u>commence</u> building on March 18th.

这里，"开始"的情貌意义是通过动词的词汇意义表现出来的。

可是，这一类动词在英语中为数并不多，在更多的情况下，"开始"的情貌意义不是通过动词本身的词汇意义，而是通过其他方式表示出来的。有些动词或动词词组，本身并无"开始"的意义，但在一定的语言环境中，却可以表示"开始"的情貌意义。下面我们试图分类作一介绍。

1. 某些表示状态改变或位置转移的动词（transitional event verb），如 get、become、grow、turn、change、arrive、reach、leave、die、fall、land 等，用于进行时含有"开始"意义。如：

[例1]　It is <u>getting</u> dark.

*　本文原发表于《外国语文教学》（四川外国语学院学院）1986 年第 3 期。

〔例2〕　　The old man was <u>dying</u>.

〔例3〕　　The train was <u>arriving</u>.

〔例4〕　　Winter is here. The leaves of the trees are <u>turning</u> yellow.

有一些限界动词（conclusive verbs）① 有时也可以表示"开始"的意义。如：

〔例5a〕　I <u>was painting</u> the table this morning. （＝I began to paint the table…）

〔例6a〕　I <u>was translating</u> an article a few days ago. （＝I began to translate an article…）

如果动词改用一般时，则表示行为达到了界限。试比较：

〔例5b）　I <u>painted</u> the table this morning.

（"桌子"已漆好，行为已完成。）

〔例6b）　I <u>translated</u> an article a few days ago.

（文章已经在几天前译好，行为已完成。）

有些表示状态变化的动词，如 get、become、grow 等，有时不用进行时，但仍表示"开始"意义。如：

〔例8〕　　He often <u>gets</u>（becomes）quarrelsome when he's been drinking.

〔例9〕　　They <u>got</u> to words and then to blows.

〔例10〕　I <u>got</u> to know him in the autumn of 1963.

〔例11〕　On leaving school he <u>became</u> a bank clerk.

---

①　限界动词表示动作有一个终极的限界，到了一定的限界，动作便无法继续下去了，它包括瞬间动词和一部分持续动词；非限界动词表示动作是在持续过程中，它包括状态动词和没有目的或界限的持续动词。

［例12］　He grew to believe that it was true.

2．有些被动语态句表示动作或状态的开始。如：

［例1a］　The gate is shut at ten o'clock.

［例2a］　The buildings are painted every year in May.

这里"开始"的意义是借助时间状语 at ten o'clock, in May 表示出来的，没有这种时间状语，就无"开始"的含义。试比较：

［例1b］　The gate is shut.

［例2b］　The buildings are painted.

3．某些动词＋-ing 可以表示"开始"意义。如：

［例1］　He burst out laughing.

［例2］　We got talking and did not notice the time.

［例3］　A flip of the switch sent water gushing out.

4．有不少短语动词可表示"开始"意义，它们大多由一些非限界动词（non-conclusive verbs）加上副词构成，常见的有 sit down、lie down、stand up、ride away、blow up、burn up、clear up、light up、doze off、set about 等，以及由某些瞬间动词加副词或介词构成，如 fall to、fall into、burst out、burst into、break into 等。如：

［例1］　The doctor had a hard time persuading him to lie down.

［例2］　On our way to the peak, a fierce storm suddenly blew up.

［例3］　The child cried out.

［例4］　We set about our task at once with great enthusiasm.

［例 5］　He fell to speculating on the probable reasons for her refusal to marry him.

5．一些表示感觉、认识或关系的非限界动词，在一定的上下文中常表示动作或状态的开始。如：

［例 1］　We have English classes at 8 every day.　（＝We began to have…）

［例 2］　I am 55 next week.

［例 3］　Lunch is at twelve（＝Lunch begins at twelve.）

［例 4］　When did you first know each other?（＝When did you get acquainted with each other?）

6．祈使句，不论是限界动词还是非限界动词，都表示说话人要求对方立即开始某一动作或状态，含有"开始"意义。如：

［例 1］　Be quiet, comrades!

［例 2］　Come and have a cup of tea.

［例 3］　Those in favour of the plan, please raise your hands.

7．由形容词或名词加后级 -en 变来的动词，如 quicken、widen、lengthen、blacken、fatten、sicken、whiten、highten、strengthen 表示"开始"含义，等于"become ＋形容词比较级"，如 quicken ＝ become quicker，widen ＝ become wider。如：

［例 1］　The patient's pulse quickened.（＝…became quicker.）

［例 2］　His interests widened.（＝… became wider.）

［例 3］　The days are lengthening.（＝…are becoming longer.）

这些动词也可以用作及物动词，这时含有使役意义，也表示动作的开始。如：

［例4］ The sun ripened the apples. （ = ...caused the apples to ripen. ）

8. 持续动词（durative verbs）的现在完成时带有表示一段时间的状语时，往往表示动作的开始。如：

［例1］ I have studied English for three years. （ = I began to study English three years ago. ）

［例2］ He has lived in Changsha for 20 years. （ = He began to live in Changsha 20 years ago. ）

上述两句中，因为用了以 for 引导的表一段时间的状语，所以 have studied、has lived 表示没有终止的动作，只有开始和发展阶段。但是，如果没有这种时间状语，则表经验，而不表动作的开始。试比较：

［例3］ I have studied English.

［例4］ He has lived in Changsha.

9. 在一定的上下文或情景中，since 特别是 ever since 引导的从句中的谓语动词，有时可以表示某种动作或状态的开始（from the beginning of some state）。如：

［例1］ I never dealt better since I was a man. （ = since I became a man）

［例2］ Her husband has been in love with her ever since he knew her. （ = since he began to know her）

［例3］ We have enjoyed the beautiful scenery around us ever since we stayed here. （ = since we came to stay here）

［例4］ We never had any intercourse with the family though since we lived here we have enjoyed the range of their pleasure grounds. （ = since we came to live here）

[例5] He has written to me frequently since I <u>have been</u> ill. （ = since I began to fall ill）

[例6] I have played a great deal ever since I <u>can remember</u>. （ = since the beginning of the time I can remember）

上述各 since 从句中的谓语动词 was、knew、stayed、lived、have been、can remember 显然都是表示动作或状态的开始。一般说来，表时间的 since 从句中的动词，如果是非限界动词或状态动词的完成时态（常见的是 have been，have known 等），或者是含有像 can 之类的情态动词，或者是瞬间动词的过去时，表示动作或状态的开始。如果是持续动词或状态动词的过去时，有时可以表示动作的开始（如前例所示），但在更多的情况下，表示从该动作结束后产生的状态的开始。如：

[例7] He hasn't written to me since he <u>lived</u> here. （ = since he left here）

[例8] Two years has passed since I <u>smoked</u>. （ = since I gave up smoking）

10. 有些表示意志、爱好或偏爱的及物动词，后接动词不定式的被动语态作宾语补足语，含有"开始"意义。如：

[例1] I want these letters <u>to be posted</u> as soon as possible.

[例2] Would you like the window <u>to be closed</u>?

第一句，表示说话者希望这些信被拿出付邮。他要看到有人把信带走，准备去邮寄才会放心。第二句表示说话者询问对方是否该把窗户关上。因此，说话者的着眼点都在动作的开始，依拉德斯把它叫作"开始体"。如果省去 to be，即只用过去分词作宾语补足语，则强调的不是动作的开始，而是动作的结果，依拉德斯把它叫作"终止体"。因此，一些强调动作结果，而不强调动作开始的使役动词，如 get、make、have 等后面从不用动词不定式的被动语态作宾语补足语。如：

　　[例3]　　I'm afraid I shan't be able to get it <u>done</u> in time.（不说"…to get it to be done in time."）

　　以上是英语"开始"情貌意义的主要表示法。尽管很不全面，但从中我们也不难看出，"开始"情貌意义可以通过各种方式表示出来。如通过动词本身的词汇意义，通过增加副词或介词，通过动词的体性或使用祈使语气等。

特殊的 if 从句

以连接词 if 引导的从句，通常表示条件，用以限制或说明主句中的动作或情况。如：

[例1]　If John comes tomorrow, he will work in the garden.

约翰明天来的话，他会到花园里干活的。

[例2]　If he were here, everything would be all right.

要是他在这儿，一切都会没问题。

例 1 中的 if John comes tomorrow 是主句 he will works in the garden 存在的条件，这种条件是可能实现的，因而叫做真实条件句（real condition）。例 2 中的 if he were here 也是主句 everything would be all right 存在的条件，不过这种条件只是一种设想，实现的可能性很小或根本不可能实现，因而叫作非真实条件句（unreal condition）。此外，还有一些 if 从句，形式上看起来像是条件从句，但实际上并不真正表示条件。我们姑且把它叫作特殊条件句（special condition）或准条件句（pseudo-condition）。如：

[例3]　If you want to know, I haven't seen him.

[例4]　She and I are friends, if you follow me.

上面两句中的主句所说的"我没有看见他""我和她是朋

友"都是客观事实，并不以 if 引起的从句为条件。

这种形式上像条件从句，而又不是真正表条件的 if 从句，是属于真实条件句的范畴。但是和一般真实条件句不同，它和主句之间的关系并非因果关系，而是其他关系。这种特殊条件句通常可以用于以下几个方面：

1. 以 if 引起的从句，在句中作插入语，用以提醒听话人注意，或对整个句子进行解释。如：

［例1］ If I may say so, that dress doesn't suit you.

如果我可以这么说的话，这件衣服你穿不合适。

［例2］ If you'll believe me he went through with flying colors on examination day!

信不信由你吧，考试那天他旗开得胜。

［例3］ And how much did you pay for your new car, if I may ask?

如果我可以这样问的话，你买这辆新汽车花了多少钱？

［例4］ I'd like some information if you don't mind, Mr. Birling.

伯林先生，如果你不介意的活，请告诉我一些消息。

［例5］ I did not attend the funeral in character, if I may venture to say so.

我并未如所预料般参加葬礼，如果我可以冒昧地这样说的话。

这种 if 从句有一个共同点，那就是虽然也可以译成汉语的"如果""要是"，但它并不包含条件或假设的意义。在结构上它可以放在句首，也可以放在句尾，通常用逗号与主句隔开。放在句首时，表明说话人就说话内容向听话人表态，让听话人在思想上有所准备，因而显得委婉而有礼貌。如例 1：

［例1］　If I may say so, that dress doesn't suit you.

例 1 中，说话人真正要说的是 "That dress doesn't suit you."，但他不直截了当地说，怕听话人难以接受。所以，采用了曲折方式，加上客套式的 if 从句 if I may say so，这样语气较前缓和得多，便于听话人接受。这种 if 从句作为附加语放在句尾时，对前句的内容加以补充说明。有人把这种附加语叫作句子状语（sentence adverbial），也有人叫分离语（style disjunction）。常见的这类 if 从句有：if I may be frank、if I can speak frankly、if I can put it frankly、if you follow me、if I may say so、if you don't care、if you don't mind、if you allow me to say so、if you remember、if you please、if you like 等。

2. 以 if 引起的从句表强调。如：

［例1］　If the girl's death is due to anybody, then it's due to him.

如果有人要为这个女孩的死负责任的话，这个人就是他。

［例2］　If ever there was a treasure house that's going to wreck and ruin, it's this library.

要是说一座宝库将会遭到破坏和毁灭，那就是这个图书馆。

［例3］　…if ever they had known what it was to bear a good name, that time had gone by.

即便他们有过好名声，那个时候也已经过去了。

［例4］　But if he was ever happy, it was in these first 10 years in Vienna.

如果说他曾有过幸福的时刻，那便是在维也纳的最初十年。

[例5]　　If ever anyone on this earth was simple and unaffected, Moltke was.

如果世界上有纯朴、真挚的人的话，莫特克便是。

[例6]　　He despises honour, if anyone does.

世界上果真有人轻视名誉的话，他便是一个。

上述各句中的 if 从句都是用来加强语气、突出主句中所陈述的内容的，它们分别为下列各句的强势语。

[例1b]　　The girl's death is due to him.

[例2b]　　This library is going to wreck and ruin.

[例3b]　　The time they had known what it was to bear a good name had gone by.

[例4b]　　He was happy in these first 10 years in Vienna.

[例5b]　　Moltke was simple and unaffected.

[例6b]　　He despises honour.

这类 if 从句形式上也是条件从句，通常也译成"如果""要是"，但实质上只是表强调的一种手段。表强调的 if 从句一般放在主句前面，句中常有 anybody（anyone）、anything、ever 等词，主句中的主语常是代替从句内容的 it 或 that。但是这种 if 从句也有放在主句后面的，如最后一句。当然这句改为"If anyone despises honour, it is he."也是可以的。

此外，if you like 也常用来表强调。如：

[例7]　　That's a tall story, if you like.

这是一个难以令人相信的故事。

[例14]　　It's a duty if you like, rather than a pleasure.

这与其说是一种乐趣，不如说是一种责任。

还有一种断言性条件从句（asseverative condition）也表示强调。如：

［**例15**］　She is forty if she is a day.

她至少四十岁了。

这里是从最小的单位条件说起，作为说话人立论的根据。也就是说，如果你承认她活了一天（要否定这一点，显然是荒谬的），她就至少有四十岁了。又如：

［**例16**］　If I've heard him say that once, I've heard him say it a hundred times.

我听他讲过不止一百遍了。

［**例17**］　The alterations in the house cost full 5,000 pounds if they cost a penny.

改建这座房屋至少花了整整五千英镑。

［**例18**］　He must be sixty if he is an hour.

他至少六十岁了。

这种断言性 if 从句常用来表示年龄、距离、重量、钱数等。它可以放在主句之前，也可以放在主句之后。

3．以 if 引导的从句表目的。如：

［**例1**］　If everyone is to hear you, you must speak up.

要使大家都听得清楚，你就必须大声讲。

［**例2**］　If she wants to lose weight she must go on a diet and do more exercise.

要是她想减轻体重的话，就得节食，还要多参加锻炼。

第一句中的 you must speak up 不是以 everyone is to hear you 为条件，而是以它为目的，这句相当于：You must speak up so that everyone can hear you. 第二句中的 she must go on a diet and do more exercise 也不是以 she wants to lose weight 为条件，而是以它为目的，这句相当于：She must go on a diet and do more exercise in order that she can lose weight.

if 从句表目的时，从句中常有表"意愿"的动词或动词短语，如：want、wish、be + to 不定式等，主句中的谓语通常包含有 must、should、ought to、need 等表示"必须"意义的情态动词。

4. 以 if 引起的从句不表条件，而表让步。如：

[例1]　If he is poor, at least he's honest. （= Though he is poor, at least he's honest.）

他虽穷，却至少是诚实的。

[例2]　If I'm mistaken, you're mistaken too. （= Though I'm mistaken, you're mistaken too.）

就算我错了，可你也错了。

[例3]　I shall finish it, if it takes two years. （= I shall finish it, even if it takes me two years.）

即使要花两年的时间，我也要把这件事干完。

上述各句中的 if 从句都不是主句存在的条件，它与主句在意义上是相反的。if 相当于 even if、though（although），作"即使""虽然"解。if 从句是让步状语从句，表示让步的 if 是从表条件的 if 演变而来的，因而，有时 if 从句究竟是表让步还是表条件，要根据主句的意义而定。试比较下面两句：

[例4a]　If he is inexperienced, he won't be able to accomplish it. （条件）

要是没有经验，他就不可能完成这项任务。

[例4b]　If he is inexperienced, he is at any rate eager to

learn.（让步）

虽然他没有经验，但是他很好学。

if 引导的让步状语从句，常可采取省略形式。如：

[例5]　　He seldom，if ever，goes out.

他即使外出，也很少。

[例6]　　The hotel is certainly comfortable if rather dear.

这家旅馆确实很舒适，虽然价钱贵了一点。

[例7]　　There is little，if any，difference between the two sentences.

这两句即使有差别也是细微的。

5．以 if 引导的从句表时间。如：

[例1]　　If winter comes，can spring be far behind?（＝When winter comes，can spring be far behind?）

冬天来到了，春天还会远吗？

[例2]　　If I do not understand what he says，I always ask him.（＝When I do not understand what he says，I always ask him.）

我不懂他所说的话时，我总是问他。

[例3]　　If you mix yellow and blue，you get green.（＝When you mix yellow and blue，you get green.）

将黄色与蓝色混合，便会得到绿色。

if 从句表时间时，相当于 when 或 whenever。从句中的时态可以与主句中的时态相同，用陈述语气而不用虚拟语气。

6．以 if 引起的从句表对比。如：

[例1]　　If I was a bad carpenter，I was a worse tailor.（＝I really was bad as a carpenter，but worse as a tailor.）

我不是一个好木匠，更不是个好裁缝。

［例2］　If you're the queen, then I'm Julius Caesar. （ ＝ You're no more the queen than I am Julius Caesar. ）

你不是皇后，正如我不是恺撒大帝一样。

上面两句都表示对比。第一句陈述一个事实，而第二句则表示一种假设，但是用的是陈述语气，而不是虚拟语气。

7．以 if 引导的从句用来委婉地陈述一种事实，而主句是这种事情发生的原因。如：

［例1］　If she did wild or wicked things it was because she could not help them.

要是她做出了鲁莽的或者顽皮的事儿，那是因为她情不自禁。

［例2］　If you don't like your job, why don't you change it? （ ＝ Since you don't like your job, why don't you change it? ）

既然你不喜欢你的工作，为什么不换一个？

8．有一种 if 从句，它和主句之间也不构成条件和结果的关系，它仅仅指出与主句有关的条件，说明说话者之所以要叙述主句的原因。如：

［例1］　If you're going out, it's raining.

这里，"你要出去"和"天在下雨"并不互为条件和结果。"你要出去"并非"天在下雨"的条件；"天在下雨"也不是"你要出去"的结果。但是，"天在下雨"这句话，只有在"你要出去"的情况下讲出来才有意义，否则，就没有必要了。这实际上是一个省略句。是"If you're going out, it is relevant to say it's raining."（如果你要出去，那我就告诉你，天在下雨呢）的省略形式。又如：

[例2]　If you want to know, I haven't seen him. (= If you want to know, it is relevant to say I haven't seen him.)

如果你想要知道的话，那就告诉你，我并未见过他。

[例3]　If you ask me, she is Swiss. (= If you ask me, I can tell you, she is Swiss.)

你要问我的话，我就告诉你，她是瑞士人。

这种 if 从句中的谓语动词通常用一般现在时，但主句中谓语动词的时态则不受限制，可以用各种时态。又如：

[例4]　If you want to know, I see (have seen/shall see/saw/had seen) him.

以上八种用 if 引导的从句的共同点是，它们形式上是条件从句，实质上都不表示条件或假设。它们与主句之间的关系不是一般 if 从句与主句之间的那种因果关系。

此外，还有一种特殊的 if 从句，它们与条件或假设毫无关系，纯粹用来表示说话人的某种感情，因而译成汉语时，一般也不用"如果""要是"等表示条件的字眼。这种 if 从句又可分为以下几种情况。

1. if 引导的从句独立使用，作感叹句，表示惊奇、沮丧、恼怒等感情。如果句中谓语动词是否定式的话，则表示强烈的肯定意义；反之，如果是肯定式，则表示强烈的否定意义。如：

[例1]　Well, if this isn't my old friend Harry Hawk! （相当于：This is my old friend Harry Hawk! ）（表示惊奇）

天哪，这不是我的老朋友哈里·霍克吗！

[例2]　And if he didn't try to knock me down! （相当于 What do you think he did? He tried to knock me down. ）

你猜他想干什么？他想把我打翻在地。（表示恼怒）

［例3］　Well, if I haven't left my coat on the bus! （相当于：I have left my coat on the bus.）（表示沮丧）

真倒霉，我把衣服忘在汽车上了。

［例4］　Well, I'm sure, if this is English manners! （相当于：This is not English manners at all.）

啊，这哪里是英国人的礼节！

［例5］　If this is Christian work! （相当于：This is not Christian work at all.）

这哪里是基督徒干的活！

if 的这种用法，通常只用从句，而省略主句。有时也可以加上被省略的主句：I'm（I'll be）damned（或 dashed、darned、blessed、blowed、doomed、hanged、jiggered、shot、switched 等）。如：

［例6］　I'll be hanged if I'm going to be responsible for every blamed.......

就是要我的命我也不能担当每一桩该死的……

2. if 从句独立使用，而省略了 I'm blessed 之类的主句，可以表示说话人的愿望，相当于汉语中的"但愿""要是……就好了"。如：

［例1］　If only she had known about it! （but she did not know!）

她那时要是知道这事就好了！

［例2］　If only I could remember his name! （＝I do wish I could remember his name!）

但愿我能记住他的名字！

[例3] If only they would stop making so much noise.

但愿他们不这样大吵大闹的。

3．if you please 常作插入语，用来表示说话人的感情，通常表示有礼貌的请求，也可以表示惊讶或愤怒等。常可译成"请""对不起""竟然""真想不到""出人意外""岂有此理"等。如：

[例1] I will have another cup of tea, if you please. （表示请求）

对不起，请再来一杯茶。

[例2] And now, if you please, she left us at the dead of night.

真想不到，她竟在深更半夜离家出走。（表示惊讶）

[例3] He's broken my bicycle, and now, if you please, he wants me to get it mended so that he can use it again.

他把我的自行车搞坏了，还要我修好再给他用，真岂有此理！

试论 will 用于 if 从句*

一般说来，在 if 引起的条件从句中，要用一般现在时代替一般将来时，而不能用 will，因此，下面例 1a 是正确的，例 1b 则是错误的；

[例1a]　I shall go for a walk if the rain stops.

[例1b]　※I shall go for a walk if the rain will stop.

"如果雨停的话，我就去散步。"这里，"去散步"和"停雨"都是尚未发生的将来事件，但用的时态却不同。前者用将来时 shall go，而后者用一般现在时 stops，且不能改为表将来的 will stop，因为"停雨"是"散步"的前提条件，而在条件从句中是不能用将来时态的，因此，用 will stop 就错了。但是，任何事物都是相对的而不是绝对的，will 也不是绝对不可以用于 if 从句中的。请看以下二例。

[例2]　If you will sign this agreement, I will let you have the money.

[例3]　If you will make that noise, please shut the windows so the neighbours can get to sleep.

上两句中，if 所引起的从句也都是条件从句，但谓语动词

---

* 本文原发表于《福建外语》1986 年第 3 期。

中却用了 will。可见，问题不在于 will 能否用于 if 从句中，而在于在什么情况下用，表示什么含义。本文试图就这个问题发表一点粗浅的看法。在下列情况下，will 可以用于 if 引起的条件从句。

一、当 will 用作情态动词时

情态助动词 will 可以表示下列意义：

1. 表示"同意"。如：

［例］ If you will help me, we can finish by six. （＝If you consent ［are willing, will be so kind as］ to help me...）

假如你同意帮助我，我们在六点钟以前可以完成。

2. 表示"拒绝"，常用否定式 won't. 如：

［例］ If you won't help us, all our plans will be ruined. （＝If you refuse to help us...）

如果你拒绝帮助我们，我们所有的计划都将落空。

3. 表示"坚持"，这时 will 要重读。如：

［例］ If you will eat so much pastry, you can't complain if you get fat. （＝If you insist on ［or：keep on］ eating so much pastry...）

假如你一定要吃那么多糕点，你长胖了就不要抱怨。

4. 表示"许诺"。如：

［例］ If you will keep the secret, I will confide it to you. （＝If you promise to keep the secret...）

如果你答应保守这个秘密，我就告诉你。

5．表示"选择"。如：

[**例**] If you will take that one, I will take this one. (= If you choose to take that one…)

假如你挑那个，我就挑这个。

从时间上看，上述各句中的 will 都不是表将来，而是表现在，是说话者或句中主体现在的意愿——同意、拒绝、坚持、许诺或选择。如果不表示上述含义，则不能用 will。如不能说：※If you will fail, your parents will be displeased. （应改为：If you fail, your parents will be displeased. ）

因为，谁也不会愿意失败，因此，本句的从句中不可能有"意愿"的含义，而只能是主句赖以存在的条件。因此，要用一般现在时表将来，不能用 will。有时，用不用 will 都可以，但意义有所不同。试比较下列两句：

[**例 2a**] If he comes here tomorrow, I'll give him this book.

如果他明天到这里来的话，我就把这本书给他。

[**例 2b**] If he will come here tomorrow, I'll give him this book.

如果他明天愿意到这里来的话，我就把这本书给他。

二、if 从句不表示条件

当 if 引起的从句形式上是条件从句，实际上并不表条件，而表其他含义时，if 从句中可以用 will。

1．if 从句表示有礼貌的请求。如：

[**例**] If you will wait a moment I'll go and tell the manager that you are here. (= Please wait a moment and I'll go to tell the manager that you are here.)

请等一下，我去告诉经理你来了。

这种 if 从句不表示条件，而表示客气的请求，相当于祈使句。

2．if 从句用作插入语，表示婉转客气。如：

［例1］ If you will believe me, he went through with flying colors on examination day!

信不信由你吧，考试那天他旗开得胜。

［例2］ He is a careless man, if you will. (= ...if you wish him to be so called.)

如果你愿意那样说的话，他是个粗心的人。

英语中这种插入语很多，可以用 will，也可以不用 will。如：if you please, if you don't mind.

if 除引导条件从句外，还可以引导其他从句（比如宾语从句）。这时，可以用各种时态，自然也可以用 will。如：

［例3］ I'd like to know if (= whether) you will be using the car tomorrow. （宾语从句）

我想打听一下，明天你是否用这辆车。

三、其他情形

1．当 if 从句中假设的条件实际上是主句中动作完成后的结果时，可以用 will。如：

［例］ If it will make you happier, I'll stop smoking.

如果我戒烟会使你快乐，那我就戒烟。

2．有时 if 从句并不是主句动作的结果，仅仅表示从句动作发生在主句动作以后，也用 will。如：

[例]　If the play will be cancelled, let's not go.

这句话的含义是：如果我们去了以后，戏不演的话，那么我们就不去了。"戏被取消"是在"去"以后发生的，是将来时间，因此，可以用 will。

关于 be going to 用于条件句的主句中[*]

当代著名的语法学家 Randoph Quirk 等四人在其合著的《当代英语语法》（*A Grammar of Contemporary English*）一书中说，be going to 通常不能用在条件句的主句中（*Be going to* is not generally used in the main clause of conditional sentences.）。如只能说 "If you leave now, you'll never regret it."，而不能说 "If you leave now, you are never going to regret it."。Eckersley 父子合著的《综合英语语法》（*A Comprehensive English Grammar*）中也认为，be going to 不常用在条件句的主句中（*Going to* is not often used when the futurity is contingent on a condition.），因为这时 "说话者的意图已无关紧要"（the intention of the person is no longer important），并举例说：If you ever go to France you will like（not: are going to like）the food there. 也有语法学家对这个问题的提法略有不同，如《当代英语语法》的作者之一 Leech 在另一著作《意义和英语动词》（*Meaning and the English Verb*）中认为，"在大多数表示将来时间的条件句的主句中 be going to 不适用，但是，如果 if + 分句是现在的条件，而不是将来的条件，那么，be going to 就适用了。例

---

* 本文原发表在《福建外语》1989 年第 3 - 4 期。

如：We are going to find ourselves in difficulty if we carry on like this.”。英国当代另一语法学家 Hornby 认为，条件句的主句中，如果有"主观意图"的话，可以用 be going to，否则不行。他认为"If Tom passes the examination, his father is going to buy him a bicycle."一句是正确的；而"If Tom asks his father to buy him a bicycle, his father is going to do so."一句不正确（应改为"…will probably do so."），因为前者包含他父亲的意图，后者没有。这些语法家们的看法从表面上看来似乎并不一致，其实并无大的不同，只是各人强调的角度不同而已。Quirk 和 Eckersley 说"be going to is not often（or：generally）used"，这里，在否定句中加上了 often（or：generally）使得否定程度减弱，其含义并非"不能用"，而是"不常用"或"通常不用"。言下之意，在一般情况下不用，但是，在某些特殊情况下是可以用的，只不过他们没有把这种特殊情况指出来。而 Leech 和 Hornby 在肯定通常不用的同时，指出了能够用的特殊情况，这就更有利于我们对这个问题有一个全面的了解。在实际语言中，我们也发现 be going to 用在条件句的主句中的情况并非罕见。现略举几例。

[例1] If I have enough money, I'm going to take a trip.

[例2] I was going to take you into this cottage if you please.

[例3] We aren't going to see very much if she keeps her hat on.

[例4] Are you going to go to Chicago if John goes?

[例5] If you've eaten those tables, you're going to be very sick.

[例 6] If Winter bottom's calculations are correct, this Planet is going to burn itself 200,000,000 years from now.

[例 7] But if you ask me, it's going to be a long job, and we'll need heavy cranes, and…

下面我们就来谈谈 be going to 在什么情况下可以用在条件句的主句中。

1．当 if 从句指现在的条件时，主句中可以用 be going to

在表示将来时间的条件句中，主句是在这种将来条件下的必然结果，因此，主句中通常要用 will，不用 be going to，如：

[例 1] He'll tell you if you ask him.

因为"他将告诉你"是以"你（将）去问他"为条件的，换句话说，只有"你问他，他才会告诉你"。但是，如果表示现在条件，在主句中可以用 be going to。如：

[例 2] We're going to find ourselves in difficulty if we carry on like this.

如果我们继续这样下去，我们将陷入困境。

这里 if we carry on like this 是现在条件，这种现在条件是通过动词 carry on 的词性和状语 like this 表现出来的。如果不表示现在的条件，就不能用 be going to，而要用 will。如：

[例 3] If you accept that job, you'll never regret it.

这里的 accept 只可能表将来，因此，不能说：※If you accept that job, you're never going to regret it.

2．表示"可能性"时，主句可以用 be going to

条件句要求在 if 条件下，主句的动作一定会发生，而 be going to 在表示将来时，只说明某事很可能会发生，但不一定会发生，因此，be going to 通常不用在条件句的主句中。但是，在现代英语里，特别是在口语中，主句可以仅仅表示某种可能性，这时，可以用 be going to。如：

[例 1]　 I'm going to get wet if the bus doesn't come soon. (＝ I'm likely to get wet if the bus doesn't come soon.)

[例 2]　 If he's been telling lies again, he's going to get into trouble. (…likely to get into trouble.)

[例 3]　 If he's not careful, he's going to have an accident. (＝ …he's likely to have an accident)

上面几句都表示说话人认为已有迹象表明在某一条件下很可能会发生某事。第一句表示"如果车不快来的话，我可能就会淋湿"，第二句表示"要是他再扯谎的话，那他可能会陷入困境"，第三句表示"如果他不细心，他可能要出事"。

3．当表示说话者的某种感情色彩时，主句中可以用 be going to

条件句的主句通常表示在某种条件下所产生的结果，而与说话者的感情无关，因此，通常不用 be going to。但是，如果需要表现说话者的某种感情时，可以用 be going to。如：

[例 1]　 If Tom passes the examination, his father is going to buy him a bicycle.

假如汤姆考试及格，他的父亲将要给他买一辆自行车。

[例 2]　 If he comes, I'm going to leave.

要是他来，我就走。

[例 3]　 If he comes, there's going to be trouble.

他要是来了，就糟了。

[例 4]　 I'm going to hit you if you do that again.

你要是再这么干，我可要揍你了。

［例 5］　　He is going to come if the rain stops.

如果雨停，他就会来。

以上各句中的 be going to 都表示说话者的感情。第一句表示汤姆父亲的意图，尽管这种意图的实现有赖于汤姆考试及格；第二句表示说话者对"他来"一事感到不满，对此进行威胁（threat）；第三句表示在说话者看来，"他来"必然会导致一场"不可避免的灾难"（an inevitable disaster）；第四句表示说话者强烈的决心，是对听话人所做出的一种警告；第五句表示句中主体的决心，说话者知道已经没有其他事情能阻碍他了。

4. 当 if 从句形式上是条件从句，实际上并不表条件时，be going to 可以在主句中使用。如：

［例 1］　　But if you ask me, it's going to be a long job, and we'll need heavy cranes, and…

这句里的 if you ask me 形式上是条件从句，但它并不是主句赖以存在的条件，因为"这将是一项长期的工作"是客观存在的，与"你是否问我"毫无关系。这里，if you ask me 相当于 in my opinion，起插入语的作用，用来缓和语气，表示委婉客气。全句相当于：In my opinion, it's going to be a long job, and we'll need heavy cranes, and…既然 if 从句不表条件，主句也不表在这种条件下必然产生的结果，从句对主句就没有语法影响，因此，主句完全可以用 be going to 这一结构。对这种句型我们也可以理解为在主句之前省略了 I will tell you，即"But if you ask me, I will tell you it's going to be a long job, and we'll need heavy cranes, and…"。英语中用作插入语的 if 从句很多，常见的有：if I may be frank、if I can speak frankly、if I can put it frankly、if you follow me、if I may say so、if you don't care（mind）、if you allow me to say so、if I remember rightly、if you must know、if you please、if you like，等。

［例2］　I'm going to get to the top if it kills me.

这里 if 所引导的是让步状语从句，if = even if，因此，主句中完全可以用表示意图的 be going to。

［例3］　If I am to command here, I am going to do what I like, not what you like.

这句中的 if 从句形式上是条件从句，实际上表目的，因此，主句中可用 be going to，这句相当于：I am going to do what I like, not what you like in order that I can command here.

if 从句表目的时，从句中常用 want、wish、be + to 不定式等表示意愿的动词，主句中常有 must、should、have to 等表示"必须"含义的情态动词。

以上是 be going to 用于条件句的主句中的几种情况。还有一点必须指出，随着语言的发展，be going to 这一结构本身的意义也发生了一些变化。例如，它现在常常可以用来代替单纯将来时（plain future），如：He is going to be 32 tomorrow. 这句话按照传统的观点，是不能用 be going to 的，而要用 will，因为一个人的年龄是客观存在的，是不以人的意志为转移的。但是，这种用法现在在口语中却常见。这里 be going to 等于 will。因此，在当代英语中，尤其在美国英语中，be going to 用在条件句的主句中的情况也远非我们前面所讲的几种情况，这有赖于我们在阅读中细心观察。

英语动词不定式符号 to 的省略[*]

在一次考试中，不少考生将"All we can do is wait here."这样一个正确的句子当作病句，改为"All we can do is to wait here."，而将病句"The farmhands were made work fourteen hours a day."误认为是正确的。产生这种错误的原因在于，他们不懂得英语动词不定式符号 to 在什么情况下可以省略，什么情况下不能省略。在英语中，动词不定式叫 infinitive，不带 to 的动词不定式叫 infinitive without *to* 或 bare infinitive。不定式短语在句中可以作各种成分：

[例1] To know all about English is one thing, to know English is quite another. （主语）。

[例2] Our plan is to finish the work in two days. （表语）

[例3] His daughter wants to be a doctor. （宾语）

[例4] I have an announcement to make. （定语）

[例5] We'll go there to work and struggle to overcome these difficulties. （状语）

[例6] John asked him to write to you. （宾语补足语）。

不带 to 的动词不定式用得远没有这么广，主要限于用作

---

* 本文原发表于《湖南师范学院学报（外语版）》1981 年第 1 期。

动词复合谓语的一部分、宾语及宾语补足语和表语。本文就不带 to 的动词不定式的用法作一些整理和说明。拟从两方面来讨论这个问题：第一，动词不定式符号 to 一定要省略的；第二，动词不定式符号 to 可以省略，也可以不省略的。

一、动词不定式符号 to 一定要省略的场合

1. 在助动词和情态动词 can（could）、do（did）、may（might）、shall（should）、will（would）、must、need、dare 等后面，作动词性复合谓语的一部分的动词不定式要省略 to。如：

[例 1]　A weak nation can defeat a strong, a small nation can defeat a big.

[例 2]　They don't show their noses here.

[例 3]　Our goal must be attained.

但是，与情态动词 ought、used 连用的动词不定式要带 to。如：

[例 4]　Communists ought to work for the good of all, so that everyone can live well.

不过，在美国，当 ought 用于否定句或疑问句时，与之连用的动词不定式有时可以省略 to，如：

[例 5]　You oughtn't smoke so much.

[例 6]　Ought you smoke so much?

其次，与助动词 be 连用的动词不定式表示事先安排好了的或将要发生的事情，与助动词 have（或 have got）连用的动词不定式，表示因客观环境促使不得不做的事情，要带

to。如：

　[例 7]　　We are <u>to meet</u> at seven this evening.

　[例 8]　　You have <u>to be</u> in my office by nine o'clock.

　[例 9]　　I have got <u>to do</u>（have to do）it now.

此外，当 do、need 和 dare 不作助动词或情态动词，而作实义动词时，与它们连用的动词不定式要带 to。如：

　[例 10]　　I did it <u>to please</u> you.

　[例 11]　　We need <u>to unite</u> with them.

　[例 12]　　She dares <u>to go</u>.

　2. 在某些表示生理上的感觉的动词，如 see、watch、hear、listen to、look at、notice、feel、observe（观察）、perceive（察看）、behold（注视，看）、mark（注意）、sense（意识到，觉察）等的宾语后面，作宾语补足语的动词不定式要省略 to。如：

　[例 1]　　Gao Yubao saw the landlord <u>steal</u> into the court-yard.

　[例 2]　　We observed tears <u>come</u> into her eyes.

　[例 3]　　We marked them <u>do</u> it.

　[例 4]　　He sensed her <u>hesitate</u>.

此外，hear say（或 tell）是习惯用法。say 或 tell 前都没有 to。如：

　[例 5]　　I <u>hear say</u> that there will be an election soon.

　[例 6]　　Have you ever <u>heard tell</u> of such things?

但 see、feel、perceive 等动词后面作宾语补足语的如果是动词 to be，一般不省略 to。如：

　[例 7]　　When the figure got nearer, I perceived it <u>to be</u> a woman.

[例 8]　As it came near I saw it <u>to be</u> Magwitch，swimming.

[例 9]　I felt this <u>to be</u> very true.

[例 10]　The author has something to say which he perceives <u>to be</u> true and useful，or helpful beautiful.

[例 11]　Now I saw him <u>to be</u> the man who walked up the hill every morning.

3．在使役动词 have、make、let 等后面的动词不定式不带 to。如：

[例 1]　Let us <u>be</u> the best friends in the world！

[例 2]　The landlord made her <u>suffer</u> a lot.

[例 3]　She likes to have the house <u>look</u> clean and tidy.

此外，make believe 是习惯用法，意为"假装"，believe 前没有 to。如：

[例 4]　Sometimes when children play they make <u>believe</u> they are grown-ups.

如果 believe 后面接有不定式，不定式符号 to 也可省略（动词 to be 一般不省略 to）。如：

[例 5]　The child made believe <u>do</u> his homework.

[例 6]　He made believe to be ill.

make do 也是习惯用法，意为"设法应付，凑合着用"（= manage），do 前面省略了不定式符号 to。如：

[例 7]　I don't know how she makes <u>do</u> on so small an income.

[例 8]　If you haven't the right tool for the job we shall have to make <u>do</u> without it.

　　let 与动词 go、fall、slip 连用时，如果 let 的宾语是人称代词，则放在 let 之后、不带 to 的不定式之前；如果是名词，则要放在不定式的后面。如：

　　[例9]　　Let it <u>go</u>（<u>fall</u>，<u>slip</u>）.

　　[例10]　　Keep hold of the rope and don't let <u>go</u> the horses.

　　[例11]　　He let <u>fall</u> a hint about his intentions.

　　[例12]　　Don't let <u>slip</u> any opportunity of practising your English.

　　let go 和 let go of 意思相同，只是用 let go of 时，宾语不管是名词或者是人称代词，均放在后面。如：

　　[例13]　　Let <u>go of</u> it.

　　leave go（of）"松手放开"与 let go（of）同义，go 前面也省略了不定式符号。如：

　　[例14]　　Don't <u>leave go</u> until I tell you.

　　[例15]　　Make that dog <u>leave go of</u> my coat.

　　但当 make 作"制造"，have 作"有"，let 作"出租"解时，后面的动词不定式作状语或定语，一定要带 to。如：

　　[例16]　　The workers make many sewing machines <u>to meet</u> the needs of the market. （状语）

　　[例17]　　I'll have a lot of work <u>to do</u> tomorrow. （定语）

　　在谚语"Money makes the mare to go."中 go 前面的不定式符号 to 可以保留。

　　上述2、3两项都是主动语态。如果改为被动语态，动词不定式符号 to 一般就需要保留。如：

　　[例18]　　He was seen <u>to cross</u> the street. （试比较：I saw

him cross the street.)

[例 19] I was made to repeat the story. （试比较：They made me repeat the story. ）

本文开头所说的病句 "The farmhands were made work fourteen hours a day. " 的错误就在于动词 work 前面少了一个不定式符号 to，改为 "The farmhands were made to work fourteen hours a day. " 就对了。

但是，let fall、let go、let slip 用在被动语态时，fall、go、slip 前都没有 to，这是习惯用法。如：

[例 20] A few hints were let fall by the girl.

[例 21] The prisoners were soon let go.

[例 22] The opportunity was let slip.

let 除在上述三语中可用于被动语态外，let 和形容词、副词或介词构成的词组，如 let loose、let out、let off、let in、let into 等也常可用于被动语态。如：

[例 23] They were very lucky to be let off like that.

let 和动词连用时，也间或见用于被动语态。如

[例 24] I was let know.

[例 25] They were let look over the house.

注意 know、look 前面的 to 也常省略。但 let know、let look 通常不用于被动语态，用被动语态时常用 allow、inform 等词代替 let 结构。如：

[例 26a] They cannot let the matter rest here.

[例 26b] The matter cannot be allowed to rest here.

[例 27a] We'll let him do it.

[例 27b] He will be allowed to do it.

［例 28a］　He <u>let</u> me <u>know</u> about it.

［例 28b］　I <u>was informed</u> of it.

4．在一些习惯用法，如：**had better**、**had best**、**had（would）rather**、**had（would）sooner**、**had as soon**、**rather than**、**need hardly**、**would fain** 等后面，不定式符号 to 要省略。如：

［例 1］　She would rather <u>die</u> with her head held high than betray Marxism，Lenin-ism and Mao Zedong Thought.

［例 2］　He would sooner <u>put</u> his head under the gas than tell her the truth.

［例 3］　I had as soon <u>walk</u> as go by bus.

［例 4］　I would soon <u>go</u>.

5．与介词 **but**、**except** 连用的动词不定式，如前面有实义动词 **do**（不论是限定形式还是非限定形式）时，不定式符号 **to** 要省略。如：

［例 1］　The little boy <u>does</u> nothing but <u>play</u> all day.

［例 2］　What could I <u>do</u> then except <u>watch</u> them carry you away?

［例 3］　Not knowing the language，the foreigner could <u>do</u> nothing but <u>smile</u>.

［例 4］　You <u>do</u> nothing but（except）<u>play</u>.

否则，不定式符号 to 不能省略。如：

［例 5］　It had no effect except <u>to make</u> him angry.

如果不定式是作定语，则 to 可省可不省。如：

［例 6］　I am sure we in England had nothing <u>to do but（to）fight</u> the battle out.

［例 7］ There was nothing for James <u>to do but（to）wait and see</u>.

介词 save、besides 后面有时也可接不带 to 的动词不定式。如：

［例 8］ What had she done for her father <u>save leave</u> him at the first opportunity?

［例 9］ What do you like to do <u>besides play</u> basketball?

［例 10］ That afternoon I had nothing to do <u>besides answer</u> letters.

在介词短语 instead of 的前面如果已经出现不带 to 的动词不定式，它后面的动词不定式也要省略 to。如：

［例 11］ You must go instead of <u>stay</u> here.

［例 12］ A word of encouragement might have made me respect instead of <u>hate</u> him.

6. 在 why、wherefore 开始的疑问句中，当不定式具有谓语的意义时不需用 to。如：

［例 1］ Why <u>ask</u> me?

［例 2］ Why not <u>go</u> there?

［例 3］ Why <u>pay</u> rent when one could buy a house for less.

［例 4］ Men of England，wherefore <u>plough</u> for lords who lay ye low?

how 后面间或也有用不带 to 的不定式。如：

［例 5］ How <u>leave</u> her there?

"Why ask me?" 这类句型，有人认为是省略了 do you，即 "Why do you ask me?"。也有人认为是省略了 should you，即 "Why should you ask me?"。但是，疑问词 what、which、when、 where、how 等后面加动词不定式，在句中作主语、宾语、表语等成分时，动词不定式符号 to 不可省略。如：

[例6]　When to start remains undecided.

[例7]　I don't know where to go.

[例8]　The question is what to do.

7．当两个或两个以上作用相同的动词不定式并列使用时，往往只第一个动词不定式前有 **to**，而后面的动词不定式前不用 **to**。如：

[例1]　They told me to go home and not be an old silly.

[例2]　What we want is to stay in our labs，experiment，and think.

但是，如果强调对比，则不省。如：

[例3]　To be or not to be that is the question.

[例4]　To know it and to do it are two different things.

二、动词不定式符号 to 可省可不省的场合

在下列情况下，动词不定式符号 to 可省，也可不省。

1．在动词 help、find、bid、know 等的后面作宾语或宾语补足语。如：

[例1]　Shall I help you (to) carry that box upstairs?

[例2]　Help me (to) put the room to rights.

[例3]　Constant practice will help you to acquire correct pronunciation.

[例4]　When I was only ten，I had to help support the family.

动词 help 后面什么时候用带 to 的不定式，什么时候用不带 to 的不定式呢？基本原则是当这种帮助意味着 help 的主语实际上参与做该事情时，可以用不带 to 的不定式。比如"Help me lift this box."这个句子，含有被请求帮助的人实际上与请求者一起抬了箱子的意思。同样"I help him mend his car."含有"我和他一起修理汽车"的意思。例 3 中 to acquire 之所以不省略 to，是因为 constant practice 不会去掌握正确的发音，正确的发音全部要 help 的宾语 you 去掌握。同样，"This book will help you to use English."一句中 to use English 也不省略 to，因为 this book 不会使用英语。有学者建议，我们在弄不清该不该用 to 的时候，最好一律加 to，因为加 to 总是正确的。

　　[例 5]　　We have found the farm (to) do well.

　　[例 6]　　Do you find it (to) pay?

上面两句中的 to 可有可无。但如果不定式是 to be 的话，不可省去 to，如：

　　[例 7]　　We find him to be dishonest.

　　[例 8]　　I found him to be a good assistant.

例 7 和例 8 中的 to 不能省去，不过把 to be 一起省掉却是可以的。如：

　　[例 7b]　　We find him dishonest.

　　[例 8b]　　I found him a good assistant.

但是例 8b 除了表示"我发现他是一个好助手"的意思外，还可以表示"我已经替他找到了一个好助手"的意思，因为 find 可以带双宾语。所以，当 to be 后面是名词时，最好不省掉 to be，以免引起误解。

动词 bid（作"命令""吩咐"解）的宾语之后的动词不

定式符号 to 可省可不省，不过省去的情况多。如：

[例 9]　　They bade us (to) take good care of the old man.

[例 10]　　He bade me (to) go in.

动词 know 表示"经验""观察""看过""听过"等意义时，它的宾语后面的不定式，有时有 to，有时没有 to。know 用于这种意义时，只有过去时或完成时态。一般说来，用于肯定意义时，to 可有可无，用于否定意义时，一般没有 to。如：

[例 11]　　I have known him (to) say this before.

[例 12]　　I have known him walk with Tiny Tim on his shoulder very fast indeed.

[例 13]　　I never knew him say this before. (or：I have never known him say this before.)

此外，动词 mean、say 后面作宾语的动词不定式，也可省略 to。如：

[例 14]　　You mean have my hair cut?

上述结构用于被动语态时，都需带 to 的不定式。如：

[例 15]　　He was helped to carry that box upstairs.

[例 16]　　The farm has been found to do well.

[例 17]　　We were bid to take good care of the old man.

[例 18]　　She has never been known to lose her temper.

2. 作表语的动词不定式，有时也可以省去"to"。这主要是用于当主语部分使用或暗含有动词 to do（暗含有动词 to do 通常指表示欲望的动词，如 want、need、say、require、ask 等），而动词不定式用以进一步阐发 to do 的含义。如：

[例 1]　　All I wanted to do was hide.

[例 2]　　All I wished was go home and rest. (= All I

wished to do was <u>go</u> home and <u>rest</u>.）

［例3］　All I want to do is <u>resign</u> and <u>get</u> out of this, but it's still too much to expect me to betray myself like that.

［例4］　I'll ask you a favor while I'm here. That's <u>take</u> me seriously.

注意，此时联系动词通常只是动词 be 而且是一般现在时或一般过去时。

本文开头提到的句子"All we can do is wait here."就是作表语的不定式 to wait 省略了 to。如果动词不定式不是进一步阐发动词 to do 的含义，而是其他动词的含义时，则动词不定式符号 to 不能省去。如：

［例5］　What he had not expected was <u>to be drawn</u> in, mentally, as much as he had.

但是，当主语是形容词最高级时，作表语用的动词不定式虽不是阐发动词 to do 的含义，也可省略 to。如：

［例6］　The most important thing is（to）serve the people heart and soul.

3．在动词 come、go、run、try、stop、look 等后面作目的状语的动词不定式常可以省略 to，但这种用法只有当 come、go 等动词用于祈使句或不定式时才可以。如：

［例1］　Come <u>have</u> supper with us.（＝Come <u>to have</u> supper with us.　＝Come and have supper with us.）

［例2］　Let's go <u>talk</u> to the other fellows.

［例3］　You can run <u>get</u> me a spoon.

［例4］　It makes people stop <u>look and listen</u>.

4．better（more、worse、less....）than...后面的动词不定式符号 to 可有可无。如：

[例1]　I cannot do <u>better than（to）quote</u> Shakespeare.

[例2]　He went to Michael Mont，the junior partner of the film，but Mr. Mont could do no <u>more than give</u> him two pounds out of his own pocket.

[例3]　I know <u>better than to do</u> such a thing.

[例4]　You should know <u>better than talk</u> nonsense.

[例5]　Rollie knew <u>better than to ask</u> who the boss was.

综上所述，不带 to 的动词不定式主要是与助动词、情态动词连用作动词性复合谓语的一部分；与表示生理现象的动词、使役动词连用作宾语补足语；与少数介词及介词短语连用作介词的宾语；当主语部分使用或暗含有 to do 时，不带 to 的动词不定式可作表语；此外，它还可以用在一些习惯用法中。不带 to 的动词不定式一般只用于主动语态，不用于被动语态；在由主动语态变为被动语态时，不带 to 的动词不定式（与助动词、情态动词连用的及某些习惯用法除外）一般要改为带 to 的动词不式。

英语动词不定式 to be 的几种特殊用法[*]

不定式 to be 在用法上和其他动词不定式有共同的地方，也有不同的地方。本文要探讨的是它们不同的地方，即动词不定式 to be 的几个特殊用法。

1. 在感官动词（verbs of perception），如 see、hear、feel、observe、perceive 等后面，作宾语补足语的动词不定式通常不带 to，如例 1 ~ 3；但是，如果不定式为 to be，则 to 不可省略，如例 4 ~ 7。

　　［例1］　　I see him **come**.

　　［例2］　　I heard her **sing**.

　　［例3］　　Watch that boy **jump**!

　　［例4］　　I see it **to be** so.

　　［例5］　　I heard him **to be** very foolish.

　　［例6］　　Our guest at last perceived him **to be** known.

　　［例7］　　We all felt the plan **to be** unwise.

例（4）~（7）中的 to be 分别作动词 see、hear、perceive、feel 的宾语补足语，to 不可省略。这里的 see、hear 等动词不表示感官的感觉（physical perception），而表示心理上

＊　本文原发表于《外语与外语教学》1986 年第 1 期。

的感觉（mental perception）。表示心理上的感觉的动词还可以以一个 that 从句作宾语，如：

［例 8］ I saw **that** he disliked the cat.

［例 9］ I hear **the wilder forces have fallen out with the Smiths**.

［例 10］ I felt **that you would like to know**.

因此，上述带 to be 作补足语的结构可以用 that 从句来代替，而意义不变。如：

［例 11］ I saw it to be impossible. →I saw that it was impossible.

但是，不能用分词 being 来取代 to be，不能说：※ I saw it being impossible.

与此相反，除 to be 以外，其他动词不定式作 see、hear 等动词的宾语补足语时，可用分词来代替不定式，其意义上并无多大差别。试比较：

［例 12a］ I saw him come into the classroom.

［例 12b］ I saw him coming into the classroom. ①

但是，用 that 从句来代替这种结构，往往引起意义上的变化。试比较：

［例 13a］ I heard him **sing** in the next room. 我听见他在隔壁唱歌。

［例 13b］ I heard **that he sang in the next room**. (hear ＝learn/be informed) 我听见他在隔壁唱歌。

---

① 这两种结构之间有细微的区别，用不定式表示一个已经完成的动作，用分词表示动作还在进行。

不过表示感官感觉的动词 see，有时也以 that 从句作宾语。如：

［例 14］　He saw **that the children were eating their lunch**.

［例 15］　I saw **that the box was empty**.

此外，用于这种结构的 to be 同其他动词不定式一样，只是一般式，而不是完成式。如不能说：※I see（hear）him have come. ※I saw it to have been impossible. 因为这里的动词不定式所表示的动作是和谓语动词同时的，不可能是先于谓语动词所表示的动作。

还有些动词（如 find）和动词词组（如 make believe、make do）后面的不定式作宾语补足语时，to 可有可无。但如果不定式是 to be 时，通常要用 to。如：

［例 16］　I find him **to be** dishonest. ［试比较：We have found the farm **(to) do** well. ］

［例 17］　He made believe **to be** ill.

（试比较：The child made believe **do** his homework. ）

不少语法学家，如 Poutsma、Jespersen、Curme 对这一现象都有论述。Poutsma 把这种接不定式 to be 作宾语补足语的 see、hear 等动词称为 mental perception（心理感觉），Jespersen 称之为 inference（推论）。葛传椝先生在他的《英语惯用法词典》see 条中举有一例："Now I saw him to be the man who walked up the hill every morning."，并且指出这里的 saw 作"知悉、了解"解。可见葛先生的看法与 Poutsma 是一致的。钱歌川先生也引用过这种用法的例句："I saw it to be a mistake."（我看到这是一个错误）但是，国内出版的大多数语法书和辞书都很少提及这一用法。我们认为，see、hear 这类动词的这一用法，并非罕见，语法书和辞书理应有所反映。

2. 作表语的不定式 to be，不定式符号 to 不可省略。

Quirk 等在《当代英语语法》一书中指出："动词不定式作为补足语（即表语——笔者注），用以进一步阐明动词 do 的含义时，其 to 可有可无。"如：

　　[例1]　　All I did was **(to) turn** off the gas.

　　[例2]　　What I did was **(to) learn** the language.

但是，如果动词不定式是 to be 的话，即使在这种情况，to 也不能省略。如：

　　[例3]　　What I did was **to be** careful.

3. 动词不定式符号 to 可以单独出现在句末，省略后面的动词。如：

　　[例1]　　—Would you like to go to the party?

　　　　　　　—I would like **to**.　（= I would like **to go**.）

在有些动词，如 want、ask、allow 后面，to 也可以一起省略。如：

　　[例2]　　You can borrow my pen, if you want.

　　[例3]　　—May I go out this evening?

　　　　　　　—Yes, I'll allow you.

但是，如果不定式是 to be 或被动态的话，则不能只留下 to，而将 be 省略。如：

　　[例4]　　—Are you on holiday today? —No, but I'd like **to be**.（不能说：※No, but I'd like to.）

　　[例5]　　—They are going to give a dinner party. I want you **to be invited**.

—And I want you to be, too. （不能说：※ And I want you to.）

4．动词不定式 to be 的省略。

第一，作宾语补足语 to be 的省略。英语中有不少表示意见、判断、信念、料想、声明、心理感觉或情感状态的动词，用 to be 作其宾语补足语时，to be 常可以省略。如：

[例1]　We consider him（to be）a genius.

[例2]　Do you believe such inquiries（to be）useful?

[例3]　I found her（to be）an entertaining partner.

[例4]　Perhaps this book will prove（to be）of some use to you in your studies.

这类动词很多，常见的如 acknowledge、consider、believe、discover、imagine、judge、think、guess、show、suspect。但有以下几点值得注意：

其一，虽然大部分这类动词的宾语补足语前面的 to be 可以省略，但有些动词，如 know、dislike、urge 等后的 to be 不可省略。下列几句都不对：

[例5a]　※I know him a writer.

[例6a]　※I disliked him a smoker.

[例7a]　※I urged him a good father.

上面几例都应该在 him 后面加上 to be：

[例5b]　I know him to be a writer.

[例6b]　I disliked him to be a smoker.

[例7b]　I urged him to be a good father.

其二，to be 的省略仅局限于它的一般式，而它的完成式 to have been，因为是用以表示过去时间，不能省略。如：

［**例8**］　We believe it to have been a mistake.

句中的 to have been 不可省略。

其三，有时省略 to be 会发生歧义。如：

［**例9a**］　We have found him to be a good assistant.

我们已经发现他是一个好助手。

［**例9b**］　We have found him a good assistant.

例9b 除含有上面的意思外，还可能有"我们已经替他找到一个好助手"的意思，相当于"We have found a good assistant for him."，这是因为 find 可以带双宾语。因此，在可能产生歧义的情况下，to be 以不省略为好。

其四，to be 能否省略，有时与 to be 的补足语的词性有关。例如：

［**例10**］　Most people supposed him（to be）innocent.

［**例11**］　All the neighbours supposed her to be a widow.

例10 和例11 中的谓语动词都是 suppose，但第一句中的 to be 的补语是形容词，Hornby 认为 to be 可以省略，第二句中 to be 的补语是名词，他认为 to be 不可省略。又如：

［**例12**］　I supposed him **to be** a work man, but he was in fact a thief. He was commonly supposed（to be）foolish.

其五，当宾语或 to be 的补语前置时，to be 习惯上不省略。如：

［**例13**］　The prisoner, whom I consider **to be** innocent...

［**例14**］　The visitor, whom I guessed **to be** about sixty...

［**例15**］　You're not so clever as I believed you **to be**.

第二，表示意愿的动词，如 want、wish、desire、like、expect 等后面跟不定式 to be，再加分词（或形容词），to be 常可以省略。如：

[**例16**]　I want these letters（to be）posted as soon as possible.

[**例17**]　Would you like the window（to be）closed?

根据荷兰语法学家依拉德斯的看法，这里有无 to be 是体的区别。"He wants some letters to be posted. "表示他希望这些信被拿出付邮，着眼点在这个动作的开始，因此是开始体；而"He wants some letters posted. "着眼点是动作的结果，是终止体。因此，一些只强调动作结果而不强调开始的动词，如 get、make、have 等，后面从来不用 to be 加分词的形式。如：

[**例18**]　I must get my hair cut.（不说：※I must get my hair to be cut.）

Quirk 等把动词分为"现状动词"（current verbs）和"结果动词"（resulting verbs）。"现状动词"（表意愿的动词属此类），如 believe、call、consider、declare、find、imagine、keep、leave、like、prefer、think、nant 等，可以用 to be 词组或 as 词组作其宾语补足语，而"结果动词"如 get、have、paint、render、set 等则不行。如可以说：

[**例19**]　They considered it to be（as）beautiful.

但不能说：

[**例20a**]　※They painted it（as）white.

只能说：

[**例20b**]　They painted it white.

第三，一些表示命名意义的动词（naming verbs），如 announce、appoint、elect、name、pronounce 等，常用于"动词＋名词（或代词）＋名词"的结构，如：

［例21］　They appointed him chairman.

在这种结构中，作补足语的名词前常可使用 to be。如：

［例22］　The President named him（to be）Secretary of State.

［例23］　They pronounced him（to be）a good boy.

［例24］　They elected Smith（to be）chairman.

不过，to be 省略的居多。这种结构中的 to be 也可以换成 as 或 for。如：

［例25］　The President named him as Secretary of State.

［例26］　They selected him for president.

第四，在连系动词 appear、seem、prove、turn out 等后面，to be 短语作主语补足语时，to be 常可省略，而意思不变。如：

［例27］　The patient seemed（to be）asleep.

［例28］　This appears（to be）the only exception to the rule.

［例29］　The day turned out（to be）a fine day.

在 there seems to be 后面接名词的句式中，to be 也可省略。如：

［例30］　There seems（to be）every hope that business will get better.

但是，to be 的完成式 to have been 不可省略。如：

［例56］He seems **to have been** ill.

下列句中的 to be 也不可省略：

［例31］　The patient seemed **to be** asleep/abroad/there.

因为 abroad 和 there 都是副词，而副词只能作 be 的表语性的附加语，而不能作其他内涵动词（intensive verb）的表语性附加语。如可以说：

［例 32］　All our men are abroad.

不能说：

［例 33］　※The patient seemed abroad.

这种结构可以转换成"It seems（appears…）that（as if）…"的结构。如：

［例 34］　I seem（to be）unable to solve his problem.

［例 35］　It seems that（as if）I am unable to solve this problem.

happen 后面的 to be 不能省略。如：

［例 36］　He happens **to be** a friend of mine.

第五，在一些及物动词之后，可以用"there + to be + 名词（或代词）"的结构作宾语。如：

［例 37］　I don't want there to be any misunderstanding.

我不希望有任何误解。

［例 38］　I expected there to be no argument above this.

我预期在这事上没有争辩。

［例 39］　We don't want there to be any disturbance.

我们不希望有任何干扰。

能够这样用的，只能是"there + to be"，不能是其他动词。这种结构可以转换成带复合宾语的结构、宾语从句或以 have 作宾语的结构。试比较：

［例 40a］　I don't **want there to be** any misunderstanding.

［例 40b］　I don't **want any of you to misunderstand** me.

［例 40c］　I don't **want that** there will be any misunderstanding.

［例 40d］　I don't **want to have** any misunderstanding.

在有些动词，如 wait、ask、look 之后还可以用"for +
there + to be + 名词（或代词）"作宾语。如：

［例 41］ John was waiting for there to be complete silence.

"for + there + to be"也可以作主语。如：

［例 42］ **For there to be** so few people in the streets was
unusual.

街上人这么少真是有点奇怪。

［例 43］ It's impossible **for there to be a war** between
your country and mine.

你我两国之间发生战争是不可能的。

浅谈及物动词不带宾语[*]

及物动词通常都需要带宾语，不及物动词则不带宾语。但是，在实际运用语言中，可以发现有些及物动词可以不带宾语。如：

[例1]　　He has left for Shanghai.

[例2]　　I wrote to my mother yesterday.

而某些不及物动词却可以带宾语。如：

[例3]　　He lived a happy life.

[例4]　　She smiled a sweet smile.

本文打算谈一谈及物动词不带宾语的几种情况。

1.　当我们考虑的只是动作的本身，而不是接受该动作的某个人或物时。如：

[例1]　　He likes to give.

他喜欢赠送东西。

[例2]　　I neither lend nor borrow.

我既不借东西给别人，也不向别人借。

[例3]　　It is my turn to milk.

轮到我挤奶了。

---

* 本文原发表在《中小学外语教学》1984 年第 11 期。

在上例中，我们所关注的只是 to give、to lend and borrow、to milk 这些动作的本身。至于给什么、借出借进什么、挤什么奶，并非我们关注的。因此，其宾语往往可以省略。

2．在一定的语言环境中，宾语所指已很清楚的情况下，宾语常可以省略。如：

［例1］　I wrote ［a letter］ to him a fortnight ago，but he hasn't answered ［my letter］ yet.

［例2］　Thanks，I don't smoke ［a cigarette］.

［例3］　A horse rears ［its legs/itself］.

上例中的宾语是不言而喻的。wrote to him 自然指的是写信，smoke 当然是指吸烟，a horse rears 其宾语自然是 its legs 或 itself。因此，省略宾语并不影响理解句子的确切含义。但这些句子译成汉语时却往往要加上被省略了的宾语。又如：

［例4］　His knees seemed to give ［＝give way］.

［例5］　He had hung up ［＝hung up the telephone］.

［例6］　Shut up ［＝Shut up your mouth］.

［例7］　Verreker shrugs ［＝shrugs his shoulders］.

有时孤立的一个句子，很难确定它省略的宾语究竟是什么。如 "He plays well." 既可以说是"他球打得好"，也可以说是"他乐器演奏得好"，还可以说是"他牌打得好"。但只要在具体语言环境中，所省略的是什么，就一目了然了。

3．有些及物动词后跟有带宾语的介词，因而，动词的宾语常可省略。如：

［例1］　She has left for London.

［例2］　Send for the doctor，please.

［例3］　I didn't want to add to mother's misery.

我不愿增加母亲的痛苦。

上面几句中被省略了的宾语有些虽然很容易补上，但最好不补。如我们可说"He has left Beijing for London."，但却很少有人说"Send somebody for the doctor."。在 add misery to mother's misery 中，add 的宾语和介词的宾语相同，因而动词的宾语往往省略。如果宾语不同，则不可省。试比较：

［例4］ That was adding fuel to the fire.

这真是火上加油。

此外，及物动词和副词构成的动词词组有时也省略宾语。如：

［例5］ John made a trip to the South and considered setting up［business］there.

约翰去南方跑了一趟，打算在那儿开业。

英语中这样的短语动词为数不少。

4. 在对别人的叙述或提问表态时，我们常用"I know." "Yes，I see." "I remember." "I had forgotten." 之类的句式。这些都是省略了宾语的句子。如：

［例1］ —Is this a nonsmoker?

—I don't know［whether this is a nonsmoker or not］.

［例2］ —There's going to be a meeting tonight.

—I know［that 或 there's going to be a meeting tonight］.

［例3］ —She's having a baby.

—How do you know［that 或 she's having a baby］?

—She told me［she was having a baby］.

上面几句中的意思因为上下文已交待清楚，不会引起歧义，所以省略宾语，不省略反倒显得有些累赘。

5. 在现代英语中，有些以反身代词作宾语的动词，如 dress、wash、shave、hide、prove 等，常可省略反身代词，但仍具有反身的意义。如:

［例1］　He often washes［himself］in cold water.

［例2］　She rose and began to dress［herself］very quickly.

［例3］　You must prepare［yourself］for all emergencies.

一般说来，用作 wash、dress 和 shave 等动词宾语的反身代词在现代英语中省略的居多。有些动词，如 prove、prepare、recover、withdraw 有无反身代词意义略有不同。有反身代词的，强调"经过努力渐渐达到"，而没有反身代词的则只表明事实的本身。如"He proved himself（to be）a good teacher."含有"他已经渐渐被人认为是……"之意，而"He proved（to be）a good teacher."则含有"他到后来已经被人认为是……"的意思。有些动词后的反身代词不可省略，省略后，其句子不能成立。如:

［例4］　Please help yourself to some fish.　（不能说：※ Please help to some fish. ）

有时作宾语的反身代词省略与否可根据英国英语和美国英语用法上的习惯。

［例5］　The Ohio empties itself into the Mississippi.

［例6］　He qualified himself for office.

例5和例6是英国英语，美国英语则省略 itself 和 himself。

［例7a］　I do not trouble myself to learn.

[例7b]　I do not trouble to learn.

例7a 是美式英语（用 myself 作宾语），例7b 是英式英语（省略 myself）。

6. 作宾语的相互代词的省略。有些动词，如 meet、cross、intersect、touch、kiss、marry、embrace 等，由于它们本身的词汇意义表示出相互关系，后面跟的相互代词（each other、one another）通常可以省略。如：

[例1]　Their hands touched（each other）.

[例2]　How have you been since last we saw（each other）in France?

[例3]　They kissed（each other）and parted.

省略反身代词后，上述这些动词可看作不及物动词。

此外，有些及物动词，当它们用于现在完成时态时，宾语不可省略。如：

[例4a]　I generally read in the afternoon.

[例4b]　※I have read.

[例4c]　I have read the book.

上面例4a、例4c 都是正确的句子，例4b 则不符英语表达习惯。

试谈不及物动词用作及物动词[*]

英语动词有及物和不及物之分。通常及物动词要带宾语，而不及物动词不带宾语。但是，通常是不及物的动词，有时也可以用作及物动词，即可以带宾语，如：

[例1] He lived a simple life.

他生活简朴。

live 通常是不及物动词，但在上句中却用作及物动词，带了一个同源宾语 a simple life。本文拟谈不及物动词用作及物动词的问题。

请先看下列各组例句。

第一组

[例2] She died a heroic death.

她英勇献身。

[例3] He breathed a deep breath.

他深深地吸了一口气。

[例4] The wind blew a gale.

刮了一阵大风。

[例5] He had left word that he was going a long walk.

他留话说他要散步到很远的地方。

[例6]　Bernadine saw that she had come a long journey.

伯纳迪恩看出她刚长途旅行回来。

第二组

[例7]　He stood the bottle near the window sill.

他把瓶子放在窗台附近。

[例8]　He lifted the child and sat her at a little table.

他把孩子抱起来，让她在一张小桌边坐下。

[例9]　He walked the children across the road.

他领着孩子们过了马路。

[例10]　I'll run you to the station.

我将用车送你去车站。

第三组

[例11]　I cried myself well-nigh blind.

我的眼睛几乎哭瞎了。

[例12]　He stared the man out of countenance.

他把那人盯得局促不安。

第四组

[例13]　Won't you stay supper?

请留下来吃晚饭好吗？

[例14]　They talked literature all the evening.

他们一整晚都在谈论文学。

[例15]　He has travelled the whole world.

他已周游全球。

第五组

[例16]　One of you must leg it up to the hotel.

你们中得有一个人跑到旅馆去。

［例 17］　　We'll foot it.

我们将步行去。

［例 18］　　Shall we tram it or bus it home?

我们坐电车回家，还是坐公共汽车?

［例 19］　　We therefore decided that we would sleep out on fine nights; and hotel it and inn it and pub it…when it was wet.

因此，我们决定如果晚上天气好，我们就睡在外面，下雨就住旅馆、客栈……

［例 20］　　Don't lord it over others.

不要对别人称王称霸。

［例 21］　　She was really going it today—she did more work than she did during the whole of last week.

她今天拼命干，一天做的工作比上周整一周还多。

上面五组例句，代表了不及物动词带宾语用作及物动词的五个方面。下面我们分别来讨论一下它们是如何用作及物动词的。

1．不及物动词接同源宾语

A 组中的例 2 和例 3 中的动词 die、breathe 都是不及物动词，后面带了一个与它们的词汇意义完全相同的名词作宾语，而成为及物动词。这种宾语叫做同源宾语（cognate object）。同源宾语前往往带有形容词修饰语，在语义上相当于副词作状语。它们可以分别改为：

［例 2b］　　She died heroically.

［例 3b］　　He breathed deeply.

例 4 中的 a gale 的意义不完全与动词 blow 相同，是一种引

138

申的同源宾语，它不能改为与之相应的副词，但可以用表示程度的副词替换。这句可改为：

[例4b]　　The wind blew hard.

同源宾语多是习惯用法。例 5 和例 6 中的 a long walk、a long journey 也可看作 go 和 come 的同源宾语。

2．不及物动词接施事宾语作宾语

第二组各句中的不及物动词后面都加上了一个施事宾语，因而变成及物动词。例 7 和例 8 中的 stand 和 sit 加上施事宾语后变成了使役动词，stand = cause to stand，sit = cause to sit。例 9 和例 10 中 walk 和 run 很少有使役意义，而含有"伴随"的意义，即表示主语和宾语同时进行这个动作，施事宾语相当于作状语的 with 词组。例 9 相当于"He walked across the road with the children."，例 10 相当于"I'll run the car with you in it to the station."。

3．不及物动词接复合宾语

第三组例 11 和例 12 中的动词 cry、stare 本也是不及物动词，但其后接了一个主谓结构 myself well-nigh blind、the man out of countenance 作宾语。与第二组不同的是，它不表示"伴随"，也很少有"使役"意义，而表示"结果"。这两句可分别改为：

[例11b]　　I cried until（or：so much that）I was almost blind.

[例12b]　　He stared at the man until（or：so much that）he（the man）became nervous.

4．由短语动词省略后的不及物动词，后面接宾语

第四组例 13 ～ 15 中的动词 stay、talk、travel 实际上是由

stay for、talk about、travel over 短语省略介词而来的。因为省略了介词，原来的介词宾语就成了动词的宾语，因而这些动词也就变成及物动词。英语中这样的动词词组还有一些，如：range［through］the woods（在森林里来回走），wait［at/on］table（侍候进餐）。

5. 由名词转化而来的不及物动词接 it 作宾语

第五组例 16～21 中的 leg、foot、tram、bus、hotel、inn、pub 是由名词转化而来的动词，通常不及物，但是，它们后面可以加上一个无确切含义的 it（the unspecified *it*），这样它们就用作及物动词了。这里 to leg it = to run；to foot it = to walk on foot；to tram（bus）it = to go by tram（bus）；to hotel（inn，pub）it = to sleep in a hotel（inn，pub）。此外，在一些习惯用语中，通常是不及物的动词后面也可以加上一个 it（如例 20 和例 21 两句）。这样的习惯用语还有一些，如 rough it（生活简单，过艰苦的生活）；walk it（走去）；pig it（像猪一样生活，过困苦生活）；hop it（走开）。

上面我们讨论了某些不及物动词在特定情况下通过增添宾语用作及物动词的情况。还必须指出的是，多数辞书对这些动词及物用法的一面也程度不同地有所涉及，本文只不过是企图作一番比较系统的归纳而已。

语态转换问题几则*

1. 英语主动句转换成被动句时，其时态通常须保持一致。如：

[例1a]　　Everybody likes this book.

[例1b]　　This book is liked by everybody.

[例2a]　　We will take good care of them.

[例2b]　　They will be taken good care of.

但是，如果主动句中谓语动词是完成进行时态或将来进行时态，转换成被动句时，常用完成时态或一般时态代替。如：

[例3a]　　We've been discussing the problem for two days.

[例3b]　　The problem has been discussed for two days.

[例4a]　　We shall be discussing it tomorrow.

[例4b]　　It will be discussed tomorrow.

2. 英语中有些动词如 **cut**、**build**、**pack**、**close**、**sell** 等，其现在完成时往往用来说明动作的结果。如：

[例1a]　　I've packed the cases.

我把箱子装好了。

[例1b]　　The cases have been packed.

---

* 本文原发表于《中小学英语》1986 年第 6 期，此处稍有改动。

141

箱子已装好了。

而这些动词的一般现在时的被动态也表示结果。如"The cases are packed."（箱子已装好了）。所以，这些动词的一般现在时被动式（例 2a、3a）转换成主动句时，要用现在完成时而不用一般现在时（例 2b、3b）。

［**例 2a**］　The cases are packed.

［**例 2b**］　We have packed the cases.

［**例 3a**］　The vegetables are all cut up.

［**例 3b**］　I've cut up all the vegetables.

3．英语主动句和被动句相互转换时，通常不产生意义上的变化，但有时也有例外。如：

［**例 1a**］　I can't teach the boy.　(= I am unable to teach the boy.)

［**例 1b**］　The boy can't be taught.　(= The boy is unable to learn.)

［**例 2a**］　People suppose that they will arrive on the five o'clock train.

人们猜想他们会坐五点的火车到。

［**例 2b**］　They are supposed to arrive on the five o'clock train.

他们应该是坐五点的火车到。

例 1a 和 1b 意义的不同是由于情态动词运用而引起的。例 2a 和 2b 的意义的不同则是由于 suppose 和 be supposed 的意思不同而引起的。

4．有时同一个被动句转换为主动句时，可能有两种不同的方法。如：

[例 1a] Coal has been replaced by oil.

[例 1b] Oil has replaced coal.

[例 1c] People in many countries have replaced coal by oil.

例 1a 中的 by oil 有不同的含义，它既可以表示"施动者"，也可以表示手段，对应的主动句也有所不同。在同一被动句中，使用不同的介词，意义略有不同。如：

[例 2a] He was killed by an arrow.

[例 2b] He was killed with an arrow.

这两句都说明同一事件"他中箭身亡"。其差别在于：by an arrow 表示的是施动者，其相应的主动句为"An arrow killed him."；而 with an arrow 表示的是工具或手段，意味着还暗含有一个施动者，其相应的主动句为"Someone killed him with an arrow."，如果实际上不存在暗含的施动者，就不能用 with 短语，如不可说"We were driven indoors with rain."，而应改为"We were driven indoors by the rain."。正因为 by 和 with 表示的意义不同，所以，它们可以出现在同一个句子中，如：He was shot by the policeman with a revolver.

5．有些动词，如 allot、allow、assign、award、give、grant、hand、offer、pay、pass、tell 等，后面可接一个间接宾语和一个直接宾语；变为被动语态时，可将其中一个宾语转化为主语，另一个保留。如：

[例 1a] I gave him a book.

[例 1b] He was given a book.

［**例1c**］　A book was given（to）him.

不过，把间接宾语提前作被动语态主语的居多。如果把直接宾语作主语，在间接宾语前通常要加介词 to（在美国英语中 to 也可省略）；在另外一些动词，如 buy、choose、cook、make、order 等后面的间接宾语前要用 for，且不可省略，如：

［**例2a**］　I bought her a dictionary.

［**例2b**］　She was bought a dictionary.

［**例2c**］　A dictionary was bought for her.

在有些情况下，带双宾语的句子在变为被动语态时只有一种可能性，如：

［**例3a**］　He wrote her a long letter.

［**例3b**］　A long letter was written to her.

［**例4a**］　He found George a seat.

［**例4b**］　A seat was found for George.

在例3和例4中，转换为被动态时只能将直接宾语提前作被动句的主语。

6. 有些及物动词带一个名词（或代词）作宾语，后面还可接一个名词作补足语，如：

［**例1**］　They elected him president.

［**例2**］　He appointed Tom manager.

这种句子转化为被动句时，只能将宾语作为被动式的主语，而不能将补足语转换为主语，如上面两句的被动式是：

［**例1b**］　He was elected president.（不能说：※President was elected him.）

［**例2b**］　Tom was appointed manager.（不能说：※Manager was appointed Tom.）

在主动句中，有些宾语补足语的前面可以有动词 to be，但通常省略。转换成被动句时，要加上省去的 to be，如：

[例 3a]　He found George（to be）a bright pupil.

[例 3b]　George was found to be a bright pupil.

[例 4a]　Most people supposed him（to be）innocent.

[例 4b]　He was supposed to be innocent.

7. 在主动句中，有些动词如 see、hear、watch、make 等后面作宾语补足语用的不定式要省去不定式符号 to，但在被动句子中，to 却不能省。如：

[例 1a]　I saw the train come into the station.

[例 1b]　The train was seen to come into the station.

但动词 let 是个例外，如：

[例 2a]　They have let the grass grow.

[例 2b]　The grass has been let grow.

英语主动句表被动意义用法初探[*]

一、引言

在英语中，被动意义通常是用被动句表示的。如"The king was dethroned."。但是，有时候被动意义也可以用主动句来表示。如：

[例1]　　The article reads like a translation.

[例2]　　The window won't open.

[例3]　　What is worth doing at all is worth doing well.

[例4]　　This house is to let.

本文将对英语主动句表被动意义的问题作一初步探讨。

二、英语谓语动词主动形式表示被动意义

英语中有一些动词，其主动形式可以表示被动意义。如：

[例1]　　This kind of medicine sells dear.

[例2]　　The method proved highly effective.

＊　本文原发表于《湖南科技大学学报》1985 年第 2 - 3 期。

[例3]　　The stone moved.

[例4]　　The dinner is cooking.

上面四句形式上是主动句，但都表示被动意义。例 1 中的 medicine 实际上是"被卖"得贵，例 2 中的 method 是"被证明"非常有效，例 3 中的 stone 是"被搬走"了，例 4 中的 dinner 是"在被煮"。这种主动形式表示被动意义的句子分别属于几种不同的句型。例如上面例 1 和例 2 中 sells 和 proved 分别带了状语 dear 和补足语 highly effective，属于 S + V + 状语型；例 3 只有主语和谓语，没有状语，属于 S + V 型；例 4 谓语动词是进行时，属于 S + be + V-ing 型。下面我们就按这三种句型谈谈谓语动词的主动形式表被动意义的问题。

1．S + V + 状语型。如：

[例1]　　These novels sell very well.

[例2]　　This scientific paper reads like a novel.

[例3]　　A porcelain sink cleans easily.

[例4]　　The meat cuts tender.

[例5]　　Your pen writes quite smoothly.

[例6]　　The door locks easily.

这一类型的主动句表示被动意义往往要有方式或程度状语（或补足语），以表示同动作有关的情况和程度等，句子的意思才相对完整。没有这种状语，句子不成立。如不能说：

[例1b]　　※These novels sell.

[例2b]　　※This scientific paper reads.

[例3b]　　※A porcelain sink cleans.

[例4b]　　※The meat cuts.

[例5b]　　※Your pen writes.

［例 6b］　　※The door locks.

有时虽有状语，但不表方式或程度也不行。如不能说：

［例 7］　　This house sold yesterday.　（应改为：This house was sold yesterday.）

但是，谓语动词的否定式，特别是与情态动词连用时，可以不用状语。如：

［例 8］　　The figures will not add.

［例 9］　　The suit-case would not lock.

这种句型也可以改为被动句，但意义略有不同。试比较：

［例 10a］　　His novels don't sell.

［例 10b］　　His novels are not sold.

例 10a 说明小说本身质量不好，影响其销售，因此卖不出去；例 10b 仅仅说明一个事实，与小说本身无关，可能小说写得还好，但由于印刷质量差或别的什么原因，销售不出去。这类动词大多是表示感觉的动词以及表示"读写""洗刷""吃""煮"等既可是及物又可是不及物的动词。常见的有 feel、smell、sound、touch、look、test、tear、take、peel、wash、wear、read、write、translate、sell、eat、cook、cut、digest、act、add、compare、last、lock、pull、keep、spill 等。

2．S＋V 型。如：

［例 1］　　The meeting ended at 10.

［例 2］　　The train stopped.

［例 3］　　The fashion changes.

［例 4］　　The prospect brightens.

这一类型以主动形式表被动意义的句子，可以不要状语就表示完整的意义。这些动词大多表示"移位""运转""开始"或"结束"等意义，或表示某种容易的、自然的，甚至是自发的动作的动词，或由形容词变来的动词。常见的有 move、stir、roll、turn、change、begin、start、commence、end、stop、break、burst、boil、pass、drop、beat、spread、toss、shiver、slip、improve、burn、cool、warm、empty、brighten、blacken、ripen 等。

这些动词大多又能兼作及物动词，因此，这一类句子一般都可以改为被动句。如：

[例 5a]　The stone rolls.

[例 5b]　The stone is rolled.

这两句意义基本相同，但语义的重点不一样。第一句着重石头滚动这一事实，第二句则着重于石头突然被什么东西触发了滚动的动作。

3．S + be + V-ing 型。如：

[例 1]　The book is printing (reprinting, binding).

[例 2]　The meat is cooking.

[例 3]　The house is building.

[例 4]　The plan is working out successfully.

[例 5]　Her face was streaming with tears.

这种用进行时（主要是现在进行时和过去进行时，很少用于其他时态）形式表示被动意义的主动句是早期英语遗留下来的一种用法，使用范围比较小，限于少数动词，如 do、owe、cook、bind、print、build、prepare、show，且多见于描写性的文字中，表示某种动作或过程正在进行。它们也可以改为被动句。如：

[例 2a]　The meat is cooking.

［**例 2b**］　　The meat is being cooked.

［**例 3a**］　　The house is building.

［**例 3b**］　　The house is being built.

上述几种句型中谓语动词主动形式表被动意义时具有两个特点。其一，这些动词必须是不及物动词或兼作及物和不及物的动词；其二，作主语的通常都必须是作为动作对象的事物，而不能是人。如果是人，则意义发生变化。试比较下面两句：

［**例 6a**］　　What's cooking?

在煮什么?

句中 cook 是不及物动词，is cooking 主动形式表被动意义。

［**例 6b**］　　Who's cooking?

谁在煮东西?

句中 cook 是及物动词，省略了宾语。

三、英语非谓语动词的主动形式表被动意义

英语动词不仅是谓语形式有时可以用主动形式表被动意义，非谓语形式（即动名词、动词不定式、分词）有时也可以用主动形式表示被动意义。下面我们就来具体谈谈非谓语动词主动表被动的情况。

1. 动名词的主动形式表被动意义。

动名词是动词的非谓语形式之一，它也有主动和被动两种语态。当动名词逻辑上的主语所表示的是这动作的对象时，这个动名词一般要用被动语态。如：

［**例 1**］　　This question is far from being settled.

这个问题还远没有解决。

这里 being settled 不能改为 settling，因为 this question 是 settle 这个动作的对象，而不是它的发出者。但是，有时却可以用动名词的主动形式表示被动意义。如：

[例2] My watch needs repairing.

我的表需要修理。

这里 my watch 也是承受 repair 这个动作的，但用的是主动形式 repairing，而且不能改为被动形式 being repaired。下面我们就来讨论一下动名词的主动形式表示被动意义的问题。

第一，在 need、require、want、deserve、repay、choose 等动词之后作宾语的动名词要用主动形式，但表示被动意义。如：

[例3] My room needs whitewashing.

我的屋子要粉刷。

[例4] The house wants cleaning.

这房屋要打扫。

[例5] This problem requires studying with great care.

这个问题需要仔细研究。

[例6] This point deserves mentioning.

这一点值得提一下。

[例7] This book published twenty years ago will repay studying in these times.

这本书虽是二十年前出版的，但现在还值得学习。

以上各句中的动名词尽管表示被动意义，但不能改为被动语态，不过改用不定式的被动态却是可以的。如上面例3可以改写为：

[例3a] My room needs to be whitewashed.

但不能说：

[例3b]　　※My room needs being whitewashed.

此外，动词 take（作"需要"解时）后可以加 some 再加动名词作宾语表示被动意义。如：

[例8]　　This document takes some understanding.　（＝It takes some time to understand this document.）

[例9]　　A goods train takes some stopping.　（＝It takes some time to stop a goods train.）

在动词 take、stand（＝bear）（多用否定式）后作宾语的动名词可用主动表被动，意义不变。如：

[例10]　　These houses won't bear dancing in.

[例11]　　He can't stand criticizing.

当然也可以用被动形式：

[例12]　　These houses won't bear being danced in.

[例13]　　He can't stand being criticized.

第二，在形容词 worth 之后，作宾语的动名词也是主动形式表被动意义。如：

[例14]　　The book is worth reading.

[例15]　　The film is worth seeing.

这里的动名词 reading 和 seeing 不能改为被动态，也不能改用不定式的被动态。下面两句都不正确：

[例14b]　　※The book is worth being read.

[例15b]　※The book is worth to be read.

第三，在介词或短语介词 beyond、past、in need of 等之后，用动名词的主动形式表示被动意义也可以用被动形式。如：

［例 16 ］　The Turks are beyond bearing （＝being borne）.

［例 17 ］　Her ignorance is past believing （＝being believed）.

［例 18 ］　Your method is in need of improving （＝being improved）.

介词 of 和 for 之后的动名词位于句子或短语的末尾时，有时也可以用主动形式表被动意义。如：

［例 19 ］　These medals are of irregular awarding （＝of being irregularly awarded）.

［例 20 ］　There were in the book things that were not ripe for telling （＝for being told）.

［例 21 ］　The food is not fit for eating （＝for being eacten）.

主动形式表被动意义的动名词必须是及物动词或起及物动词作用的成语动词，因为动名词与句子中的主语构成逻辑上的动宾关系。句中作主语的通常是物，而不是人。

第四，有时，当动名词位于句首作主语，表示抽象化了的动作，可以用主动形式表被动意义。如：

［例 22 ］　Hanging and wiving goes by destiny. （＝To be hanged and to be wived goes by destiny.）

是被绞死还是娶妻，这是命中注定的。

2. 动词不定式的主动形式表被动意义。

动词不定式在下列结构中主动表被动。

第一，当不定式 to let、to rent （to hire）、to blame、to seek、to compare、to do 等作表语时。如：

［例 1 ］　The house is to let （＝to be let）.

本屋出租。

[例2]　I'm not to blame (= to be blamed).

不是我的过失。

[例3]　These cars are to rent (= to be rented).

这些汽车出租。

[例4]　The cause is not far to seek (= to be sought).

不难找到原因。

[例5]　Much remains to do (= to be done).

还有很多事情要做。

[例6]　I don't know any cities that are to compare (= are to be compared) to these oriental cities in brilliancy.

我想不出还有任何城市能象这些东方城市一样，如此辉煌动人。

to let、to rent、to blame 用主动和被动都可以，但用主动似乎更普遍。表对比时要用被动态。如：

[例7]　This house is to be let, not to be sold.

这房屋出租，不卖。

to compare、to seek、to do 等虽然可以用主动表被动，但用被动居多。to do 表被动时，只限于当 much、what、a great deal、a lot、something 等作主语时。

第二，不定式作定语时，下列三种情况可用主动形式表被动意义。

首先，在 There be 结构中，用来修饰主语的不定式可以用主动式，也可以用被动式，且意义相似。如：

[例8]　There's a lot of work to do (to be done).

[例9]　There are many questions to settle (to be settled).

[例10]　There remains much to say (to be said).

［例11］　There was no time to lose（to be lost）.

在口语中多用主动态，特别是有些习惯用法，主动态不能改为被动态。如：

［例12］　There was plenty to eat.

［例13］　There was the devil to pay with the girl's relations.

但在"There was no sound to be heard."一句中常用被动态 to be heard。有时，用主动态或用被动态含义不同。试比较：

［例14a］　There is nothing to do now.（＝There's nothing to occupy us.　＝We have nothing to do.）

现在没事干。

［例14b］　There is nothing to be done now.（＝There's nothing that can be done.　＝We can do nothing now.）

现在没有什么办法。

［例15a］　There was nothing to see.（＝There's nothing worth seeing.）

没什么可看的。

［例15b］　There was nothing to be seen.（＝There's nothing that could be seen.　＝There was nothing visible.）

看不见有什么东西。

其次，当不定式和它所修饰的名词构成动宾关系，而和句中的主语或另一名词构成主谓关系时，常用主动形式表被动意义，而不用被动式。如：

［例16］　We have many difficulties to overcome.

我们有很多困难要克服。

［例17］　I want a book to read.

我要一本书来读。

这两句中的 to overcome 和 to read 分别与 many difficulties 和 a book 构成动宾关系,而与主语 we 和 I 构成主谓关系,因此,用主动形式表被动意义。

[例 18]　He'll show you the right path to take.

他将告诉你要走哪一条路。

[例 19]　Will you lend me a book to read?

请你借我一本书看,行吗?

这两句中的 to take、to read 也分别与 the right path 和 a book 构成动宾关系,但不是与主语 he 和 you,而是与谓语动词的宾语 you 和 me 构成主谓关系,因此,也用主动形式表被动意义。

如果不构成主谓关系,在表示被动含义时,仍应用被动式。如:

[例 20]　Have you anything to be taken to the city?

你有什么东西需要带到城里去吗?

句中 you 和 to take 不构成逻辑上的主谓关系,因此,to take 要用被动式。

最后,当不定式所修饰的名词前有形容词修饰语,表示"需要""适合"(a necessity, a suitability or a fitness)等意义,或虽无形容词修饰语,但含有上述意义时,作宾语的不定式,其主动形式表被动意义。如:

[例 21]　It's the only thing to do.

[例 22]　You admit it was not the thing to do.

如果不表示上述含义,用不定式的被动态。如:

[例 23]　He was not a man to be lightly played with.

当不定式作状语，修饰作表语的形容词，而又和句中的主语构成逻辑上的动宾关系时，其不定式的主动式表被动意义。如：

[例24]　　The horse is not easy to control.

[例25]　　The book is difficult to read.

[例26]　　He is easy to convince.

[例27]　　The coffee is ready to drink.

上述各句中主动形式的不定式都含有被动意义，与 to be controlled、to be read、to be convinced、to be drunk 相当，但不能改为被动语态。因为我们可以用 for 作媒介给不定式前面加上一个逻辑主语。

[例24b]　　The horse is not easy (for her) to control.

[例25b]　　The book is difficult (for me) to read.

[例26b]　　He is easy (for you) to convince.

[例27b]　　The coffee is ready (for us) to drink.

too...to 结构，也属于这种用法。如：

[例28]　　The tea is too hot to drink.

[例29]　　It is a too obvious thing to do.

能用于这一句型的形容词很多，常见的有 easy、hard、difficult、impossible、good、heavy、lovely、ready、pleasant、comfortable、convenient、exciting、fit、frosty、flimsy 等。

3．现在分词的主动形式表被动意义。

英语分词有两种，一种是现在分词，一种是过去分词。过去分词通常表被动意义，现在分词一般表主动意义。如：

[例1]　　The news is exciting.

这消息激动人心。

157

如果要表示被动意义，通常要用现在分词的被动态。如：

[例 2]　　We must keep a secret of the things being discussed.

我们这儿讨论的事必须保密。

但是，现在分词的主动形式有时也可以表示被动意义。如：

[例 3]　　There can hardly be much doing.

没有多少办法。

这里，现在分词 doing 作定语修饰主语 much，much 是它的逻辑宾语，照理要用被动式，但这里用的是主动形式表被动意义，相当于 "There can hardly be much that can be done."。现在分词的主动形式在以下情况表被动意义：

第一，当现在分词作定语，修饰 There be 句型中的主语时。如：

[例 4]　　There is nothing doing.　（＝There is nothing that can be done.）

[例 5]　　There is a glorious dish of eggs and bacon making ready（＝that has been made ready）.

[例 6]　　I guessed there was some mischief contriving（＝being contrived）.

第二，有些动词的现在分词作表语时，主动形式表被动意义。如：

[例 7]　　*The Pickwick Papers* were then publishing in parts（＝...were then being published）.

[例 8]　　A page is missing.

[例 9]　　Preparations were making to receive Mr. Creakle

and the boys.

第三，作某些感觉动词（verbs of perceiving）（间或也有其他意义的动词）的宾语补足语时。如：

［例10］　I hear some fiddles tuning（ = being tuned）.

［例11］　I have read of such things in books of ancients, and I have watched them making（ = being made）.

［例12］　I saw the things shaping（ = being shaped）.

［例13］　I want these sending off（ = to be sent off）by the first train.

第四，有些动词，由于本身的词汇意义的缘故，其现在分词作状语，有时可以用主动形式表被动意义。如：

［例14］　Profiting by modern technology, students are able to learn foreign languages faster and faster.

这里 profiting 相当于 being profited，但由于 profit 有 cause to be profited 的意思，因此，可以用主动形式表被动意义。下面一句用法相同：

［例15］　Benefiting from（or：by）this novel, he decided to read more novels.

4．在主动句中表被动意义的其他结构。

上面我们讨论了动词的谓语形式和非谓语形式（动词不定式、动名词和现在分词）的主动形式表被动意义的情况。此外，在主动句中，还有一些固定结构也可以表示被动意义。

第一，以 -able、-ible 结尾的形容词大多具有被动意义。如：

［例1］　The fruit is eatable.（ = The fruit may be eaten/is capable of being eaten.）

[例2] The tree is discernible from a fair distance. （＝ The tree may/can be discerned from a fair distance.）

这类形容词很多，常见的有 bearable、eatable、acceptable、preferable、punishable、saleable、debatable、pitiable、available、dependable、desirable、dispensable、laughable、reliable、respectable、audible、contemptible、credible、divisible、flexible、legible、permissible、visible 等。这些形容词往往可用被动态形式加以解释。如：

bearable = that can be borne or endured

eatable = fit to be eaten

audible = that can be heard

visible = that can be seen

但是，有些以 -able 结尾的形容词没有被动意义，如 comfortable、reputable、reasonable、suitable。如：

[例3] Smith is quite comfortable now.

史密斯现在很舒服。

第二，某些介词短语可以表示被动意义，用以替代现在分词的被动态。如：

[例4] The matter in dispute is the ownership of a house. （＝The matter being disputed is the ownership of a house.）

[例5] The machine is in process of repair. （＝The machine is being repaired.）

[例6] The highway is in couse of construction. （＝The highway is being constructed.）

[例7] The house under repair is our classroom building. （＝The house being repaired is our classroom building.）

［例 8］　Grapes from Xinjiang are on sale.（＝Grapes from Xinjiang are being sold.）

［例 9］　Your suggestion is still under discussion.（＝Your suggestion is being discussed.）

第三，有时名词词组含有被动意义，可用被动结构替代。如：

［例 10］　His trousers were the talk and admiration of the British residents.（＝His trousers were talked and admired by the British residents.）

［例 11］　Lord Reading had a wonderful reception on his arrival in New York.（＝Lord Reading was wonderfully received on his arrival in New York.）

［例 12］　If you consider rightly of the matter, Caesar has had great wrong.（＝If you consider rightly of the matter, Caesar has been greatly wronged.）

综上所述，英语中某些主动句可以表示被动意义，但这是有条件的。弄清楚这些条件对我们来说是不无好处的，这样，我们就能准确地运用主动表被动这一语法形式，避免出现像"※The house needs being cleaned."" ※The book is worth being read."" ※The door is easily locked."" ※I want a book to be read."之类的病句或不合习惯的句子。

引导状语从句的 as[*]

as 的用法极为复杂。它可以用作副词、介词，可以跟在动词后面作为动词不可分离的部分，可以作关系代词和关系副词引导定语从句，可以作连接词引导状语从句、表语从句和同位语从句，还可以跟别的词结合构成各种习语。刘重德在《英语 AS 的用法研究》一书中列举了 146 个含有 as 的谚语和成语，可见 as 用法之广。就使用频率来讲，as 仅次于 and、which、that、what、it 等词。本文不打算就 as 的用法作全面的探讨，只想谈一谈 as 引导状语从句的问题。

as 引导的状语从句按其作用来分，可以表示下列 8 种概念。

1. 表示时间。如：

[**例 1**]　I saw him as he was getting off the bus.

他下公共汽车时我看见他。

[**例 2**]　She dropped the glass as she stood up.

她起身时把玻璃杯打破了。

[**例 3**]　As we talked we laughed.

我们边谈边笑。

＊　本文原发表于《福建外语》1984 年第 3 期。

　　as 引导的时间状语从句所表示的动作与主句的动作具有同时性，有时还表示动作的持续性（如例3）。as 引导的表示时间的结构常可采用省略形式。如：

[例4]　As（he was）a child, he joined the Red Army.

还是小孩子的时候，他就参加了红军。

　　此外，as long as、as soon as、as often as 也可引导时间状语从句。如：

[例5]　As soon as he comes, I'll tell him about it.

他一来，我就告诉他这件事。（主句的动作紧接在从句的动作之后）

[例6]　We will fight for the cause of communism as long as we live.

我们活一天，就要为共产主义事业奋斗一天。（限制主句中动作或状态的时间）

[例7]　As often as he's tried to go there, he's always failed.

他每次想到那里去都没有去成功。（as often as = whenever = each time that，意为"每次，每当"）

　　2.　表示原因。如：

[例1]　As he was not well, I decided to go without him.

因为他身体不好，我决定独自去。

[例2]　As it has rained, the air is cooler.

因为下了雨，空气凉爽了。

　　as 引导的原因状语从句所说明的原因一般都是比较明显而且为大家所公知的，是以既成事实作为理由，并没有"不好"或"勉强"的含义，语气远没有 because 那么强。在回答

why 的问题时，只能用 because，不能用 as，通常也少用其他表原因的连词。如：

[例 3]　　—Why do they study so hard?

　　　　　—Because they study for the revolution.

—他们为什么学习这么努力？—因为他们为革命而学习。

3. 表示方式。

as 常用来引导方式状语从句，指出主句中主要动词所表示的动作或状态的方式。如：

[例 1]　　Do in Rome as the Romans do.

入乡随俗。

[例 2]　　He writes about China as he sees it.

他照他亲眼看见的样子描述中国的情况。

[例 3]　　State the facts as they are.

如实地陈述事实。

as 引导方式状语从句时，前面可加 just 以加强语气。如：

[例 4]　　Most plants need sunlight just as they need water.

大多数植物需要阳光，恰像它们需要水一样。

as if、as though 也常用来引导方式状语从句。从句中用虚拟语气和过去时表示臆想的，但实际上并不存在的事情；如果主句中的动词为现在时，从句中也可用现在时表示依据判断实际上可能存在的事情；用将来时表示将来可能发生或存在的事情。如：

[例 5]　　You talk as if I were under an obligation to him.

照你这么说，好像我受过他的恩惠似的。

[例 6]　　He talks as if he is drunk.

从他谈话的样子来看他似乎醉了。

［例7］　It looks as though we shall have to do the work our-selves.

看来，这工作得由我们自己来干了。

as if、as though 引导的表示方式的结构也可采取省略形式。如：

［例8］　He is walking up and down as if in search of some-thing（＝as if he was in search of something）.

他在走来走去，好像寻找什么似的。

4. 表示比较。如：

［例1］　It is quite as good as I thought.

这和我所预想的一样好。

as 也可用于不同事物的比喻结构中。如：

［例2］　Cultivation to the mind is as necessary as food to the body.

学习对于头脑，如同食物对于身体一样不可缺少。

［例3］　Air is to man as water is to fish.

空气之于人犹如水之于鱼。

5. 表示程度。如：

［例1］　Please read as clearly as you can.

请念得尽可能清楚点。

此外，还有一种 as 引导的从句，其性质是与主句的性质同步增长的。如：

［例2］　As one grows older, one grows wiser.

一个人随着年龄的增长，会越来越聪明。

6. 表示让步。如：

［例1］　Deep as her sympathy was, words stopped on her lips.

尽管她深表同情，但她仍然无话可说。

[例2]　Rashly as he acted, he had some excuse.

他虽然行动鲁莽，但还是不无理由的。

[例3]　Child as he is, he knows English well.

他虽然还是个孩子，但却精通英语。

as 引导让步状语从句时，相当于 though 或 although，但语气比 though 或 although 强，且需要倒装语序。作表语的如果是单数可数名词（如例3），前面不能有冠词。

7．表示条件。

as 一般不能单独用来引导条件状语从句，但 as long as 和 so long as 等 as 词组可引导条件状语从句。如：

[例1]　We can surely overcome these difficulties so long as we are closely united.

只要我们紧密地团结一致，就一定能克服这些困难。

[例2]　As long as you persevere, you will succeed in the end.

只要你坚持下去，你就终究会得到成功。

此外，as … so 用作对比连词，表推论条件，相当于 since。如：

[例3]　As you make your bed, so you must lie on it.

自作自受。

8．表示限制。如：

[例1]　As far as I know, he is a good doctor.

据我所知，他是一个好医生。

[例2]　That is all right, so far as I am concerned.

就我来说，这就很好。

也可以只用 as 来表示 as far as 的意思。如：

[例3]　As boys go, he is polite.

就孩子而论，他是有礼貌的。

以上是几种常见的 as 引导的状语从句；除此外，可能还有一些，譬如说，as 引导的从句可以表示地点，相当于地点状语从句。如：

[例4]　It is right in front of you as you cross the bridge.
(= It is right in front of you where you cross the bridge.)

它就在你过桥那地方的正前面。

不过这类从句毕竟不多见，这里我们就不多述了。

引导定语从句的 as[*]

1. as 作关系代词，可以引导限制性定语从句，主要用于 the same 和 such 之后；as 在从句中可以作主语、宾语和表语等。如：

[例1] I should like to use the same textbook as is used in school. （as 在定语从句中作主语）

我想使用你们学校里所用的那种教科书。

[例2] He uses the same book as I use. （作宾语）

他使用的就是我使用的那一本书。

[例3] He is not the same man as he was before. （作表语）

他已不再是过去的他了。

有时也可以用于 so 和 as 之后。如：

[例4] He is as remarkable a person as ever came here.

他是到这里来的最出色的人物。

[例5] Here is so big a stone as no man can lift.

这里是一块没有人搬得动的大石头。

---

* 本文原发表于《福建外语》1992 年第 3、第 4 期。

2．as 也可作关系副词，引导限制性定语从句，as 在从句中作状语，相当于 in（or：on）which 或 with which。如：

[例1]　I live in the same room as he does.（＝…in which he lives.）

我和他住在同一间房里。

[例2]　He is solving the problem with the same method as（＝with which）they solved it.

他正在用他们曾用过的相同的方法来解这道题。

[例3]　I shall use the instrument in such a way as（＝in which）he used it.

我们将按照他使用的方法来使用这架仪器。

3．在 the same…as 结构中，作关系代词的 as 有时可以由 that 取代，表示的意义稍有不同。试比较：

[例1a]　This is the same bag as I lost yesterday.

这个书包和我昨天丢失的相似。

[例1b]　This is the same bag that I lost yesterday.

这正是我昨天丢失的那个书包。

例1a 用 as 指的是同类事物，意为"相似"（resemblance）；例1b 用 that 指的是同一事物，意为"同一的"（the very）。因此，如果只表示"相似"含义，则 as 不能被 that 取代。

[例2]　She has the same fair hair and blue eyes as her mother had.（不说：※…that her mother had.）

她和她母亲一样有着金色的头发、蓝色的眼睛。

as 作关系副词时，也可由 that（指时间、地点、方式）或 where（指地点）等取代。如：

［**例3**］　I went out <u>the same</u> way that/as I got in.

我沿着进来时的路走出去。

［**例4**］　We met at <u>the same</u> place where/as I saw him last.

在上次我见到他的地方，我们又见面了。

such…as 引导的定语从句，有时具有状语从句的含义，表示程度或结果。如：

［**例5**］　We'll each of us give you <u>such</u> a thrashing <u>as</u> you'll remember.（＝…<u>such</u> a thrashing <u>that</u> you'll remember it.）

我们每人都将痛打你一顿，以便你记住。

初学者常将它与 such…that（如此……以致）混淆，其实，二者之间的差别是很大的。试比较：

［**例6**］　I never heard <u>such</u> stories <u>as</u> he tells.

我从来没听过像他讲的那种故事。

［**例7**］　He made <u>such</u> an excellent speech in defence of his friend <u>that</u> every one admired and respected him.

他做了这样卓绝的演讲来为他的朋友辩护，以致人人都仰慕他、尊敬他。

such…as 表示"同一"或"相似"关系，意为"像……这样的"，as 是关系代词，引导定语从句，修饰 such 后面的名词；而 such…that 表示程度或结果，意为"如此……以致"，that 是连词，引起结果状语从句，表示 such 后面的形容词所达到的程度，而不是修饰 such 后面的名词。

4．as…as 结构除可引导限制性定语从句外，也常可表示比较或比喻，引导比较状语从句。其句式为："主语＋谓语＋as＋形容词或副词＋as＋被比较对象"。如：

［**例1**］　It is quite <u>as</u> good <u>as</u> I thought.

这和我所预想的一样好。

[例2] He drove as fast as he could.

他尽可能快地开车。

as…as 引导定语从句和 as…as 引导状语从句，形式上相似，其实差别很大。试比较：

[例3] He is as remarkable a person as ever came here.

[例4] It is quite as good as I thought.

例 3 中的第二个 as 是关系代词，在从句中作主语，修饰其先行词 a person；例 4 中的第二个 as 为连接词，含有"比、如同"的意思，引导比较状语从句，常采用省略形式。不过，对"as + many（much）+ 名词 + as"结构的分析，语法学家的看法却不尽相同。如：

[例5] There are as many books as are needed.

凡是所需要的书都有了。

[例6] You may use as much as you need.

你需要多少就可以用多少。

Jespersen 认为，例 5 和例 6 中第二个 as 所引导的都是定语从句，as 在从句中分别作主语或宾语；而 Curme、Quirk 等则认为，该 as 引导的是比较状语从句，只是从句中省略了某一成分。上面两句分别为下列两句的省略式：

[例5b] There are as many books as（they）are needed.

[例6b] You may use as much as you need（it）.

Curme 还认为省略的主语经常是代词 what，如：

[例7] He never reads as much as（what）is required of the class.

他从来没有读过要求全班读的那么多。

这两种观点都不无道理。Curme 等着眼于意义，而 Jespersen 强调的是结构。我们认为，看作定语从句较为妥当，因为语法分析自然应强调语法结构；这种句型或者可以称为"表示状语意义的定语从句"。

5．as 引导非限性定语从句。

如前所述，只有在与 the same、such、so 等连用时，as 才能引导限制性定语从句，as 单独一般不能引导限制性定语从句。如不能说：

［例1］　※I know a man as has a horse.

这个句子应改为"…who has…"。as 单独使用，可以引导非限制性定语从句，as 修饰主句中某一个名词、某一概念或整个主句。如：

［例2］　He seemed a foreigner, as in fact he is.（as 指 a foreigner，在从句中作表语）

他似乎是外国人，事实上，他也是外国人。

［例3］　This problem is not easy to solve, as indeed it is.（as 指主句中的 not easy to solve，在从句中作表语）

这道题不易解，确实如此。

［例4］　He was not sick, as some of the other passengers are.（as 指 sick，在从句中作表语）

他没有病，其余的乘客有些人倒是病了。

［例5］　He is late, as is often the case.（as 指主句 he is late 所说明的现象，在从句中作主语）

他迟到了，这是经常的事。

［例6］　The machine, as might be expected, has stopped operation.（as 指整个主句，在从句中作主语）

正如所料，这台机器已停止运转。

[例7] As all know, practice is the only yardstick of truth. (as 指整个主句的意思，在从句中作宾语)

众所周知，实践是检验真理的唯一标准。

从以上例句我们可以看出，as 引导非限制性定语从句时，as 在从句中可作主语、宾语或表语等；从句的位置也比较灵活，可以位于句首、句中或句尾，一般都用逗号与主句隔开。此外，as 引导非限制性定语从句时，有时还可以采用省略形式。如：

[例8] As announced in the papers, our country has launched another man-made satellite. (= As is announced…)

报上宣布，我国又发射了一颗人造卫星。

[例9] The author was brought up in a small village, as recounted in some of his stories (= as is recounted…).

正如在他的一些小说中所描述的那样，作者是在一个小村子里长大的。

注意在例8和例9中，as + 过去分词是定语从句，as 是关系代词，而不是连接词，as 在从句中作主语。因此，不能再加 it。上面两句都不能改为：※As it is announced…；※…as it is recounted…

[例10] Nucleus is heavy as compared with electrons. [= …as (if, when) it is compared…]

和电子相比，核就较重。

[例11] Summer days were then as now. (= …as they are now)

那时的夏天就和现在一样。

as 作连词时和 when、if、though、although 等连词一样，如果所引导的从句中的主语与主句的主语相同，而句中谓语部分又含有系动词 to be，则可以采用省略形式，即将主语和系动词一并省略。但不能只省略其中的一个，如不能说：※The city as is seen from the top of the mountain is a wonderful sight. 引导非限制性定语从句的 as 是关系代词，所修饰的是整个主句，as 在从句中作主语，自然从句中不能再加 it。as 作关系代词修饰整个主句时，as 一定属于单数，而 as 引导的状语从句的省略句时，as 是单数或复数应根据其主句中的主语而定，它完全可以是复数，如例 11。

6. as 和 which 都可以用来引导非限制性定语从句，其先行词通常都是整个主句。

as 和 which 在从句中都可作主语、宾语。如：

［例 1］　　He comes early, <u>as/which</u> is always his habit.

他总是来得早，这是他的习惯。

［例 2］　　He saw the girl, <u>as/which</u> he hoped he would.

他见到了这个姑娘，这是他所希望的。

也可以作表语，其先行词通常是主句中某一名词或形容词所表示的概念。如：

［例 3］　　He was not sick, <u>as/which</u> some of the passengers were.

他没有病，其余的旅客倒是有些病了。

但是，as 和 which 在引导非限制性定语从句时，也有许多不同之处。

第一，as 引导的非限制性定语从句位置比较灵活，可以放在句末、句中或句首，而 which 引导的非限制性定语从句只能放在主句之后。如：

　　［例4］　He saw the girl, <u>as/which</u> he hoped he would.

　　［例5］　<u>As</u> he hoped he would, he saw the girl. （但不说：※Which he hoped he would, he saw the girl.）

　　［例6］　Electrons, <u>as</u> one knows, are minute negative charges of electricity. （但不说：※Electrons, which one knows, ...）

　　第二，as 和 which 均可以在从句中作主语，但用法不同。as 作主语时，其谓语通常是系表结构、被动语态或不及物动词，而不能是及物动词加宾语结构；也就是说，as 不能作及物动词动作的发出者，which 则无此限制。如：

　　［例7］　He married her, <u>as/which</u> was natural.

　　［例8］　The ships were frozen, <u>as/which</u> not infrequently happens in those regions.

　　［例9］　He saw the girl, <u>which</u> delighted him. （但不说：※He saw the girl, as delighted him.）

　　此外，当句子破坏 as 本身所具有的语义，即不表示"正如""像……那样"时，即使是系表结构，也只能用 which，而不能用 as。如：

　　［例10a］　He married her, which was disgraceful.

　　他与她结了婚，这是不光彩的事。

　　［例10b］　※He married her, as was disgraceful.

　　例10a 正确，10b 则不通，因为这里是表示语气的转折，而不是表示"正如""像……那样"，因而不用 as。

　　第三，which 在从句中还可以作定语和介词的宾语，而 as 不能。如：

　　［例11］　He admires Mrs. Brown, <u>which</u> fact surprises me.

［**例 12**］ *Reader's Digest*, <u>to which</u> we have just sub-scribed, has an enormous circulation.

第四，as 引导的非限制性定语从句常可采用省略形式，即省略系动词，只保留作表语的过去分词或形容词。如：

［**例 13**］ He came very early this morning, <u>as</u>（was）usual.

［**例 14**］ The author was brought up in a small village, <u>as</u>（is）recounted in some of his stories.

［**例 15**］ The electrons, <u>as</u>（is）shown in Fig. 5, are very light.

如图 5 所示，电子是非常轻的。

而 which 引导的非限制性定语从句不能用省略式。以上各句中的 as 均不能改为 which。

英语疑问句的一个用法——不表疑问[*]

疑问句通常用来提出问题，表示疑问，如：

[例1]　　Is he a teacher?

[例2]　　How many students are there in your class?

[例3]　　Are you an Englishman or American?

[例4]　　These tools are very useful, aren't they?

以上几句都是疑问句。例 1 是一般问句（general question），例 2 是特殊问句（special question），例 3 是选择问句（alternative question），例 4 是附加问句（tag question）。它们有一个共同的特点，即都是提出问题，要求听话人作出答复。但是，从语义功能上看，并非所有的疑问句都是真正的提问。有些疑问句并不表示疑问，而只是一种修辞手段，用来表示惊异、委婉、暗示、确认、双关、申辩、否定等感情色彩，如：

[例5]　　—Look at this picture, Li Ping.

　　　　　—Oh, it's an old picture. Who's this man?

　　　　　—He's my father.

　　　　　—Oh, your father?

很显然，这里的"your father?"虽然具有疑问句的形式，

＊　本文原发表于《福建外语》1991 年第 3、4 期。

但并不表示疑问，也不要求回答，因为 A 已经明确地告诉了 B "他是我的父亲"，无须再问。这里用疑问句只是表示 B 对 A 所陈述的事感兴趣。

在下列情况中，疑问句不表示疑问。

一、 修辞疑问句

修辞疑问句（rhetorical question）形式上是疑问句，但在意义上相当于一个强调的陈述句，它不要求回答，而是用来表达特殊情感和意味。肯定形式的修辞问句表示强烈的否定意义，否定形式表示强烈的肯定意义，如：

[例 1]　Who would have believed it possible?（= Nobody would have believed it possible.）

谁能相信会有这样的事？（谁也不相信会有这样的事。）

[例 2]　Didn't I tell you he would spoil it?（= You know I told you he would spoil it.）

我不是给你讲过他会把事情搞糟的吗？（我给你讲过他会把事情搞糟的。）

二、 感叹疑问句

感叹疑问句（exclamatory question）是用疑问句的形式来表示感叹的一种方法，通常表示对美好事物的赞叹，一般用否定形式。如：

[例 1]　Isn't it a beautiful lake?　= What a beautiful lake it is!

那湖真美啊！

［例2］　Wasn't it a marvellous concert?（＝What a marvellous concert it was!）

多么美妙的一个音乐会呀!

感叹疑问句并不提出问题，实际上是感叹句，因而可以用感叹号（而且多数情况下用感叹号），一般念降调，不念升调。如：

［例3］　Hasn't it been warm today!

三、　祈使疑问句

祈使疑问句（imperative question）形式上是疑问句，实际上是祈使句，同一般祈使句一样，可以表示请求、建议、邀约等。祈使疑问句可分以下几种情况：

1. 以"Will you…"或"Would you…"开头的祈使疑问句。如：

［例1］　Will you please lend me five dollars?（＝Please lend me five dollars.）

请借给我五块钱。

［例2］　Will you be as quick as possibly can, please?（Please be as quick as you can.）

请尽可能快一点。

［例3］　Would you open the window, please?（＝Please open the window.）

请打开窗户。

正因为这种问句是表示请求，而不是疑问，所以，不用疑问号，用句号也是可以的，特别是带有一个很长的分句时。如：

[例4]　　Will you please complete the enclosed form and return it to us, when we will examine the matter further and let you know whether we think it is possible to take any further action.

有时不能用疑问号。美国现代作家阿瑟·黑利（Arthur Hailey）写的小说 *Hotel* 中有一章描写克罗伊敦（Croydon）公爵夫妇驱车外出时撞死一个小孩，但他们不去投案，竟绕道回旅馆，装作无事，以为别人不知道。不料被旅馆侦探长奥格尔维察觉。奥格尔维想乘机讹诈一大笔钱。他来到公爵夫妇的房间时，目空一切，嘴边竟叼着一支烟。对此公爵夫人十分反感，于是她说："My husband and I find strong smoke offensive. Would you kindly put that out."（"我和我丈夫都讨厌浓烟味，请把烟灭掉。"）这里"Would you kindly put that out."用句号，念降调，表示公爵夫人傲慢、轻蔑的态度。她在对比她地位低下得多的侦探长说话时，简直是在下命令。如果用疑问号，那表示的是一种有礼貌的请求，与原文不合。

2．以"Why not…"开头的祈使疑问句，表示请求或劝告。如：

[例1]　　Why not try again?（Please try again.）

何不再试一下？（请再试一下。）

[例2]　　Why not speak to the Dean about it?（= Please speak to the Dean about it.）

为何不同系主任谈一下？（请和系主任谈一下。）

也可以用"Why don't you…"。如：

[例3]　　—My girl-friend's in a bad mood.

　　　　　—Why don't you give her some flowers?

—我的女朋友情绪不好。

—为什么不送给她一些花呢？

3．以"How about…"或"What about…"开头的祈使疑向句表示建议，征求对方意见等。如：

[例1]　How about playing badminton now? (= Please play badminton.)

现在来打羽毛球吧？

[例2]　How about a drink，Bill? (= Please have a drink，Bill!)

比尔，来喝一杯。

[例3]　What about a game of tennis?　(= Let's have a game of tennis.)

来打一盘网球!

祈使疑问句和祈使句都表示请求、建议等，但前者的语气较后者婉转得多。

四、 答语疑问句

在对一个陈述句作答时，我们常用简短的疑问句，这种疑问句叫答语疑问句（reply question）。其实它并不表示疑问，而是表示说话人对所陈述的内容的态度，如表示兴趣、关心、惊奇、愤怒等。如：

[例1]　—I've got a headache.

　　　　—Have you，dear? I'll get you an aspirin. （关切）

—我头疼。

—真的吗，亲爱的? 我去给你拿片阿司匹林。

[例2]　　—It wasn't a very good film.

　　　　　　—Wasn't it? That's a pity. （遗憾）

—这部影片不太好。

—不好吗? 真遗憾。

在一定的语言环境中，也可以没有陈述句，而单独用简短的疑问句。如当你找某人找了很久没有找到，突然在某个地方看见了他，你可以说："What! Are you here?"（怎么，你在这里?）既然看见了，还说"Are you here?"，很显然，这不是提问，而是表示惊讶的感情。

五、 共感疑问句

有一种附加疑问句，其陈述部分和疑问部分或者同是肯定式，或者同是否定式，用于向对方讲出自己对某种言行的看法，表示怀疑、讥讽、反感等感情，通常不需回答。我们把这种附加疑问句叫作共感疑问句（sympathetic question）。如：

[例1]　　"You want to fool me, do you?" he warned the landlord. （愤怒）

"你想欺骗我，好!"他警告那个地主。

[例2]　　"So I've found you at last, my beauty, have I?" He began. （高兴）

"我的美人儿，我终于找到了你呀!"他说。

[例3]　　He is Tom, is he? （惊奇）

真想不到他是汤姆呀!

六、 问候语

"How do you do?"（你好!）是见面时用的寒暄语，虽具有疑问句的形式，却丝毫没有疑问的意思，而且对方也必须说"How do you do?"，不需要说"I'm quite well，thank you."等答语。这也说明"How do you do?"并不表疑问。

以上我们列举了几种不表疑问的疑问句。这些句子从一个侧面告诉我们，在阅读中我们不仅要注意句子的形式，更要注意它的内容。疑问句固然主要是表示疑问，但不表疑问而作为一种修辞手段来表达某种感情色彩的，也不乏其例，只有从形式和内容两方面都加以注意，才能加深我们的理解。

连词 when 用法上的几个特点 *

英语中 when 可以算得上一个多义词。它可以是疑问副词，用以构成特殊疑问句，在句中作时间状语；可以是连接副词，引导主语从句、宾语从句和表语从句；可以是关系副词，引导定语从句；还可以是连词，引导状语从句。when 引导状语从句时主要表时间，但间或也可以表示其他意义。下面谈一谈连词 when 用法上的几个特点。

一、when 引导时间状语从句时，从句动作和主句动作的时间关系

when 引导的时间状语从句用来修饰主句中的动词，说明动作发生或进行的时间。从句动作和主句动作的时间关系是多种多样的，可以是同时发生，也可以是先于或后于主句的动作发生，即我们通常所说的同时性、先时性和后时性。

1. 同时性。

在以下几种情况中，从句的动作和主句的动作同时发生。

第一，主句或从句的谓语是由系词加表语构成，表示一种

＊ 本文原发表于《教学研究（洛阳外国语学院学报）》1984 期第 3 期。

状态时。如：

[**例 1**]　When we reached home，it was already dark.

我们到家时，天已经黑了。

[**例 2**]　It was ten o'clock when I went out.

我出去时，已经十点了。

[**例 3**]　I will come when I am ready.

我准备好了就来。

第二，从句的谓语是动作动词（doing verb）的一般时，主句的谓语动词是进行时，作为从句谓语的动作发生的背景。如：

[**例 4**]　When I went downstairs，they were eating breakfast.

我下楼去的时候，他们正在吃早餐。

[**例 5**]　When my cousin came yesterday，I was playing volleyball.

昨天我表哥来时，我正在打排球。

在上面几句中，when 从句的动作发生时，主句的动作正在进行。

第三，从句的谓语是持续动词（durative verb）一般时。如：

[**例 6**]　When I lived in the countryside I learned a lot from the peasants.

我在农村时，向农民学到了很多东西。

[**例 7**]　James pretended to be deaf when I spoke to him.

我和詹姆斯讲话时，他假装耳聋。

表示同时性的 when 从句，如果从句的主语和主句的主语一致，或从句的主语是 it 时，从句往往可以采取省略形式。如：

[例8] When (he was) a boy, he liked to wander about the fields and the woods.

他小时候喜欢在田野树林里漫游。

[例9] I'll do that only when (it is) necessary.

只是有必要时，我才做那事。

2. 先时性。

第一，从句用完成时，表示从句的动作在先，主句的动作在后。如：

[例1] When the storm had passed, we continued our way.

暴风雨过后，我们继续前行。

[例2] When he had walked about ten miles, he took a few minutes' rest.

他走了十里后，停下来休息了几分钟。

[例3] He will go when he has finished his dinner.

他吃过饭就去。

第二，如果从句谓语是非持续动词（non-durative verb），也可以用一般时表示从句的动作在先。这时主句中的动词不能是进行时。如：

[例4] When I pressed the button the radio stopped.

我按了电钮收音机就停了。

[例5] When he returned from work, his wife cooked dinner.

他下班回家后，妻子做了饭。

注意：例5中，主句如果用进行时则表示同时性。试比较：

［例5］　When he returned from work，his wife was cooking dinner.

他下班回家时，妻子正在做饭。

如果在主句中有 at once，则强调从句的行为一经发生，主句的行为立即发生，意为"一当……便立即"。如：

［例6］　When the cock crowed，we got up at once.

鸡一叫，我们便起床了。

表示先时性时，when 相当于 after，上述前两句中的 when 都可改为 after。

3．后时性。

主句中如果用完成时，表示主句的动作在先，从句的动作在后。如：

［例1］　When he came back，the whole question had already been settled.

他回来时，问题已经完全解决了。

［例2］　When I got home，all my brothers had already gone.

我到家时，我兄弟都出去了。

表示后时性时，when 相当于 before，上述各句中的 when 可改为 before。如果要表示从句的动作是紧接着主句的动作发生的，在主句中常用 hardly、scarcely、barely 等含有否定意义的词。如：

［例3a］　I had hardly reached the station when the train started.

我刚一到车站，火车就开了。

［例3b］　Hardly had I reached the station when the train

started.

[**例4a**]　We had scarcely gathered in the grain when it be-gan to rain.

我们刚把粮食收进就下雨了。

[**例4b**]　Scarcely had we gathered in the grain when it be-gan to rain.

二、以 when 引导的时间状语从句和主句之间意义的关系

1. 从属关系。

以 when 引导的时间状语从句通常处于从属地位，说明主句动作发生的时间，相当于主句中的时间状语。如：

[**例1**]　I began to go to school when I was seven.

我七岁时开始上学读书。

这里 when I was seven 可以用时间附加语 at the age of seven 来代替，因而 when I was seven 处于从属地位。

有一种 when 从句虽然在形式上也处于从属地位，但在意义上却处于主导地位，是句中最重要的部分。如：

[**例2**]　Beryl was in the living-room when Stanley ap-peared.

贝丽尔在起居室时，突然斯坦利来了。

很显然，在文意上 when 引导的从句 Stanley appeared 处于主导地位，而主句 Beryl was in the living-room 反而处于从属地位，用作背景。Wood 把这种结构叫做"倒装从属"（inverse subordination）。下面几句都是这种"倒装从属"关系：

［例 3］　He was 17 when he was enrolled as a postgraduate at Harvard University.

他十七岁就考取哈佛大学研究生了。

［例 4］　The last man was emerging from the escape tunnel when a distant shout signalled its discovery by the guards.

当最后那个人从坑道出口出来时，在远处的卫兵们发现了，大声叫喊起来。

这种结构有以下一些特点。

第一，从形式上看，同一般的时间状语从句与主句之间的关系并无区别，实则刚好相反，语义上从句为主，主句为从。如果将主句和从句的位置倒置，句子仍然成立，且意义不变。如：

［例 2a］　Beryl was in the living-room when Stanley appeared.

［例 2b］　Stanley appeared when Beryl was in the living-room.

第二，从时间关系上看，主句动作和从句动作具有同时性。

2．并列关系。

此外，还有一种 when 分句形式上是从句，实际上不表从属关系，而表并列关系。如：

［例 1］　He remained in the army till the end of the war, when he was demobilized.

战争结束以前他一直在军队里，战争一结束他就复员了。

［例 2］　We'll go to the countryside at the beginning of June, when the summer harvest will start.

我们六月初下乡去，那时夏收即将开始。

[**例3**]　The Queen will visit the town in May, when she will open the new hospital.

女王将于五月访问该城，届时她将主持一所新医院的开幕式。

上述各句中的第一个分句（主句）都已经有了时间状语 till the end of war、at the beginning of June、in May，因此，when 分句（从句）不可能是时间状语从句。从意义上看，我们也绝不能说"他复员了"是"他在军队里"的时间状语。这里的 when 不是从属连词，而是并列连词，连接两个并列句。这种结构的特点是 when 分句通常放在句尾，而且要用逗号与前面的分句隔开，when 相当于 and then、just then。when 不能译为"当……时"，而要译为"那时""届时"等。

三、when 从句不表时间而表强调

有一种 when 从句并不真正表时间，而表强调。如：

[**例1**]　When he talked, it was with eloquence of the entire frame.

他讲话时，全身都绘声绘色地富于表情。

[**例2**]　When he met the new politicians, it was a good match.

他与这些新政客会见，真是沆瀣一气。

[**例3**]　When Fuller laughed, it was with very alien jaws.

富勒总是皮笑肉不笑。

上述句中的 when 从句形式上是时间状语从句，而实际上

只是起一种强调作用。它们分别是下列各句的强语势：

[例 1a]　He talked with eloquence of the entire frame.

[例 2a]　His meeting with the new politicians was a good match.

[例 3a]　Fuller laughed with very alien jaws.

when 从句表强调时，主句的主语通常是代替从句内容的 it 或 that。此外，下句中肯定形式的 when 从句表示强否定：

[例 4]　I'll believe you when hell freezes over.

我决不相信你。

这里的 when hell freezes over 等于 never，这句话相当于"I'll never believe you."。

四、when 从句表示其他意义

when 从句除了表示时间，引导时间状语从句外，还可以表示条件、让步、原因、对比、方面等意义。

1. 表条件。如：

[例 1]　When it rains he doesn't go out.（＝If it rains, he doesn't go out.）

要是下雨，他就不出去。

[例 2]　There can be no freedom in the world when men must beg for jobs.

如果人们必须乞求得到职业的话，世界上是不会有自由的。

[例 3]　No one can make a dress when they haven't learnt how.

人们如果没学会做衣服，他就做不了衣服。

2．表让步。如：

[**例1**]　He usually walks when he might ride. （He usually walks though he might ride. ）

虽然有车可坐，他通常总是步行。

[**例2**]　He keeps on talking when he knows it annoys us.

他虽晓得饶舌使我们不快，却仍然继续喋喋不休。

[**例3**]　We sometimes expect gratitude when we are not entitled to it.

有时候我们总希望别人感激我们，尽管我们并不是受之无愧的。

3．表原因。如：

[**例1**]　How can we convince him when he will not listen? （ ＝How can we convince him since he will not listen?）

既然他不听我们的话，我们怎么能说服他呢？

[**例2**]　Why use metal when you can use plastic?

既然能用塑料，为什么要用金属呢？

4．表对比。如：

[**例1**]　They have only three copies when we need five. （ ＝They have only three copies whereas we need five. ）

他们只有三本，可是我们需要五本。

[**例2**]　You are idle when all the comrades are so busy.

同志们都很忙，而你却在这里无所事事。

还有一种 when 从句用来补充纠正主句所表达的某一想法和说法，也有对比的含义，相当于 whereas。如：

[**例3**]　Thus many indulge themselves in the conceit that

they are cultivating their minds, when they are employed in the humbler occupation of killing time.

这样，许多人就心安理得地自以为他们是在学习提高，实际上他们只不过是在消磨时间。

由于这种 when 从句是对主句加以补充说明，因而总是放在主句后面，且常用逗号分开。

5．表方面。如：

［例1］　Your aunt spoke the truth, when she said you were a strange girl.

你姑妈说你是个古怪女孩，确实不错。

［例2］　Be careful when you choose your companions.

选择友人须慎重。

上面两句中的 when 从句与其说是起主句中时间状语的作用，不如说是起方面状语作用。它们分别相当于：

［例1b］　In saying that you were a strange girl your aunt spoke the truth.

［例2b］　Be careful in choosing your companions.

下面两句中的 when 从句也表示方面意义：

［例3］　Joe is not good in sports, but when it comes to arithmetic he's the best in class. (= Joe is not an athlete, but he is very good at arithmetic.)

乔不擅长运动，但在算术方面，他是班上最好的。

［例4］　The school has very good teachers, but when it comes to buildings, the school is poor. (= The school has very good teachers, but as buildings are concerned, it is poor.)

几组英语状语从句辨异[*]

同一个连接词可以引导不同的状语从句，需要注意辨别。

1. if 引导的状语从句。

if 引导状语从句时，主要表示条件，但也可以表示其他意义。试比较：

[例1] If you ask him, he will help you.

[例2] If he is poor, at least he is honest.

例 1 中 if you ask him 是条件状语从句。换句话说，你不向他请求，他就不会帮助你。if 引导条件状语从句时，从句中的谓语动词要用一般现在时表一般将来时。

例 2 中 if he is poor 显然不是条件状语从句，因为 he is honest 绝不可能以 he is poor 为前提。"穷"可以说是不好的，而"诚实"却是一种美德，因此，"穷"和"诚实"在意义上是相反的。所以 if he is poor 是让步状语从句，if 相当于 though。

[例3] If you mix yellow and blue you get green. （表时间）

if 从句表时间时，从句和主句的时态可以是相同的。

---

* 本文原发表于《山东外语教学》1985 年第 1 期。

［**例4**］ If you want to be a qualified teacher, you must study hard. （表目的）

if 从句表目的时，从句中常含有表"意愿"的动词，主句中通常有 must、should、need、ought to 等情态动词。

［**例5**］ If you don't like your job, why don't you change it? （表原因）

例 5 中的 if 在意义上等于 seeing、seeing that 或 since，表原因。

有时 if 从句还可以陈述一种事实，而主句却是这种事实发生的原因。如：

［**例6**］ If I have made some progress it is because of the help the Party has given me.

这里"我取得一点进步"的原因是"党对我的帮助"，说话者强调的不是"取得一点进步"的这种事实，而是产生这种事实的原因。

［**例7**］ If anybody likes to speak English, it is Comrade Li. （表强调）

这句是"Comrade Li likes to speak English."的强语势。if 从句用来表强调时一般要放在主句前面，且主句的主语通常是代替从句内容的 it、that 等。

［**例8**］ If you allow me to say so, I am afraid you are not qualified. （表委婉）

这里的 if 从句只不过是一种客套，叫作评注性状语从句或插入语，它的作用是缓和语气，表示委婉。

［**例9**］ If I was a bad carpenter, I was a worse tailor. （= I really was bad as a carpenter, but worse as a tailor.） （表对比）

从上面例句中，我们还可以看出，"if 从句要用一般现在时表将来"这条规则只有当 if 从句表条件时才适用，表其他意义时都不行。

2. when 引导的状语从句，可表示时间、让步、条件、原因、对比、强调等。

［例 1］　I went to school when I was seven.

例 1 中的 when 引导时间状语从句，说明主句动作发生的时间，在这里 when 从句处于从属地位。表时间的 when 从句通常处于从属地位，但有时候在意义上却是全句最重要的部分，起主句的作用。

［例 2］　Beryl was in the living-room when Stanley appeared.

贝丽尔在起居室里时，斯坦利来了。

很显然，在意义上 Stanley appeared 处于主导地位，而 Beryl was in the living-room 处于从属地位。但形式上却刚好相反，前者是从，后者为主。Wood 把这种结构叫"倒装从属"（inverte subordination），表示所发生的事是出乎意料之外的。

此外，还有的 when 从句形式上是从句，实际上也不表示从属关系，而表并列关系。如：

［例 3］　We were about to start when it began to rain （ = just then it began to rain）.

句中 when 是并列连词，相当于 just then、and then。

［例 4］　He usually walks when he might ride.

例 4 中 when 从句形式上是时间状语从句，但意义上讲不通，"他可以坐车"不可能是"他步行"的时间。这里的 when 相当于 though（although），when 从句表示让步。

when 引导状语从句时，除表示时间和让步意义外，还可表示下列意义：

［例5］　There can be no freedom in the world when men must beg for jobs（＝if men must beg for jobs）.（表条件）

［例6］　How can I help them to understand when they won't listen to me（＝since they won't listen to me）.（表原因）

［例7］　They have only three copies when we need five.（表对比）

［例8］　When he talked, it was the eloquence of the entire frame.（表强调）

例8 的 when 从句表强调，该句是"He talked with the eloquence of the entire frame."的强语势。when 从句表强调时，主句的主语是代表 when 从句内容的 it。

［例9］　Your aunt spoke the truth, when she said you were a strange girl.

例9 中 when 从句，与其说是主句的时间状语，不如说是起方面状语的作用。本句相当于"in saying that…"。这句在意义上等于"In saying that you were a strange girl your aunt spoke the truth."。

3. in case 引导的状语从句。

in case 引导的从句通常看作条件状语从句，表示"在……情况下"，多指一种偶然遇到的情况。

［例1］　You'd better take a raincoat with you in case it rains.

［例2］　She explained again and again in case her comrades should misunderstand her.

例 1 在 in case 后面加上 that 也是可以的，但通常不加。有的语法学家如依拉德斯认为，把 in case 引导的这种从句看作条件状语从句是不妥的，因为讲话人要对方带雨衣，显然不是以天要下雨为前提的，而是考虑有下雨的可能性，因此，他认为把它看作偶然状语从句（a clause of contingency）为宜。这种看法不是没有道理。但是，把状语从句分得过细反而不利于初学者掌握。笔者认为，这种从句仍可看作条件状语从句。

此外，in case 还可以引导目的状语从句，如例 2。

"她一再解释"的目的是"唯恐同志们发生误会"，也就是说，为了"不让同志们发生误会"，"她一再解释"。in case 引导的目的状语从句中谓语动词通常要用虚拟语气，这种虚拟语气可以用"should + 动词原形"或动词原形。如：

[例 3]　Please remind me of it again tomorrow, in case I (should) forget.

in case 引导的目的状语从句是一种反面目的句，因为它本身已含否定意义，所以，从句一般不再用 not 等否定词。

in case 所引导的究竟是条件状语从句还是目的状语从句，主要应根据意义而定。从结构上看，如果能将 in case 换成 in order not to 而意义不变的话，则是目的状语从句，否则是条件状语从句。如例 2 可改为：

[例 2b]　She explained again and again in order not to let comrades misunderstand her.

又如：

[例 4a]　Be quiet in case you should wake the baby.

[例 4b]　Be quiet in order not to wake the baby.

此外，据 Quirk 等人的看法，"He will come in case he's

wanted." 在美国英语中是 "He will come only if he is wanted." 的意思，in case 引导的从句是条件状语从句；而在英国英语中，是 "He will come because he may be wanted." 的意思，in case 引导的从句是原因状语从句。

4. that 引导的状语从句。

[例1]　Have you nothing to do, that you are sitting there idle?

对例1中 that 从句属于什么从句的看法，存在分歧。Poutsma 认为是原因状语从句，依拉德斯对此表示异议，认为"句中所指的那个人闲坐在那里的这种情况绝不会是他没有事干的原因"。笔者认为，依拉德斯的看法是正确的。这里的 that 从句不可能是原因状语从句。依拉德斯认为把它看作"论据从句"（clause of motivation）为宜，因为"从句所要表明的是说话人赖以作出假设或推断的一种论据"。这种看法无疑是有道理的，然而，它并没有把主句和从句之间的关系说得十分透彻。笔者以为不如把它看作结果状语从句，因为我们可以说"那个人闲坐在那里"是"他无事可做"的一种结果，而"他无事可做"正是"他闲坐在那里"的原因。因为这是疑问句，表明说话者对产生"他闲坐在那里"这种结果的原因作出推断，提出是不是"无事可做"的疑问。这种"因果"关系，主句为"因"，从句为"果"，正是结果状语从句的特点。最近出版的《新编英语语法》就把类似的句子"Have you finished all your homework that you are now sitting idle here?"看作结果状语从句。that 引导结果状语从句并不罕见，下面几句中的 that 从句都是结果状语从句：

[例2]　What have I done that you should cut me?

[例3]　There must be something wrong that he hasn't arrived yet.

[例4]　Have you lost your money that you look so sad?

此外，that 从句还可以是原因状语从句，如例5。

[例5]　They rejoiced that they had scored fresh victories in their socialist construction.

例5中，rejoice 常用作不及物动词，后接 in、at、over 等介词引导短语或不定式，表示高兴的原因，作原因状语。有时也可接 that 从句，也是表示高兴的原因。因此 that 从句是原因状语从句。

that 用来引导原因状语从句常见于下列三种情况：第一，某些表示情感的不及物动词（如 rejoice、grieve、delight）后的 that。第二，be + 表示情感的形容词和分词（如 glad、sorry、thankful、afraid、surprised、ashamed、disappointed、annoyed、pleased、delighted、hurt、satisfied、content、proud 等）后的 that 从句。如：

[例6]　I am glad that he came.

第三，在"形容词（名词）+ that + 主语 + 系词"的结构中，如：

[例7]　Tom, curious little rogue that he was, must need go and see what it was.

汤姆因为是个好奇的淘气包，所以非去看个明白不可。

英语介词 in 用法三则*

in 是一个用途非常广泛的介词，本文不打算对它进行全面论述，仅就其中的三个问题发表一点浅见。

这三个问题是：表示地点时，in 和 at 的区别；表示位置时，in 可以表示"在……上"；in 与表示时间长度的名词连用时的含义。

一、表示地点的 in 和 at

介词 in 和 at 都可用来表示地点。如：

[例1]　He was standing <u>in</u> the room.

他站在房间内。

[例2]　My house is <u>at</u> the third crossroad after the bridge.

我家就在过了桥的第三个路口。

从上面两个例句我们可以看出，in 和 at 在表示地点时，其用法是不相同的。in 表示"在……里"，强调的是位置的立体概念（有长、宽、高）；at 表示"在……上"，强调的是位置的某一点。这是它们的基本区别。实际上它们的用法比这要

＊　本文原发表于《山东外语教学》1986 年第 3 期。

复杂得多，有时并不是很容易就可以区分的，需仔细揣摸。下面我们就来谈谈它们的区别。

1. 一般说来，在与表示地点的名词连用时，in 用于较大的地方，如国家、省和大城市；at 用于较小的地方，如村、镇和小城市。如：

[例1]　They live <u>in London</u>.

他们住在伦敦。

[例2]　He was born <u>at Bath</u>.

他在巴思出生（Bath 英国一市镇，以温泉著名）。

不过"大小"是相对的，例如上海是大城市，因此，我们通常说"He arrived in Shanghai."。但是，与中国相比，上海就小多了，因此，我们要说"He arrived at Shanghai in China."。一个人的家乡，虽说是个很小的地方，但在他的心目中似乎总是大的，因此可以用 in，如：I was born in Longhua.（我在龙华出生）在许多情况下，"大小"并非是决定用 in 或 at 的唯一因素，也不是决定性的因素。请看下列例句：

[例3]　He lives <u>in Manchester</u>.

他住在曼彻斯特。

[例4]　Passengers for Liverpool, change <u>at Manchester</u>.

到利物浦去的旅客，请在曼彻斯特换车。

在上面两句中，同样一个地名 Manchester，分别与 in 和 at 连用。可见，并无"大小"之分。例4用 at，是把 Manchester 这个地方当作旅途中的一个"点"（point），着眼点是这个地点（the place regarded as a point, with a distinctive association "address"），并不关心这个地方的形状与大小。也可以说，这里的 Manchester 指的是"the railway station"。例3用 in Manchester，是把 Manchester 看作一个地区（an area），联想的是它的外貌、大小（the place regarded as an area，with an association of its appearance）。又如：

[例5]　He arrived at New York on Saturday and will arrive in Washington on Sunday.

他星期六到达了纽约，并将于星期日抵达华盛顿。

New York 比 Washington 要大，但由于只把它看作旅途中的一个地点，所以用 at。Washington 虽比 New York 小，但它是此行的目的地，因此，用 in。由此可见，起决定作用的是把一个地方看作一点还是一个区域，看作一个点时用 at，看作一个区域时用 in。任何一个大城市（包括伦敦、纽约在内），如果只把它看作与别的城市相对的地图上的一个点的话，都用 at，而不用 in。

[例6]　Our aeroplane stopped at London for an hour and then flew to New York.

[例7]　On our trip we stopped at New York and stayed two days in Chicago.

葛传椝先生认为"在 London 前通常用 in，不用 at"，似乎是片面的。

2. 当一个地名第一次提到时，往往用 at；再次出现时，用 in。如：

[例1]　The news from India continues to be very gloomy. The plague spreads at Bombay. —It would be just as well to describe the horrors of the plague in Bombay.

[例2]　Labour demonstration at Bristol—one of the largest Labour demonstrations ever held in Bristol—took place on Saturday.

在上述两句中，Bombay 和 Bristol 在第一次出现时，用 at，因为表示的是地理概念，强调的是"点"；再次提到时，这个概念已不存在，因此用 in。

3．在谈到如娱乐场所、餐馆以及工作和学习的地点时，往往把它们看作一个"点"，用 at；但如果看作一个"地区"（an area），仍用 in。试比较：

［例1］　I'll be at the theatre at 8：30.

我八点半到戏院去。

［例2］　There are two thousand seats in the theatre.

4．与名词所有格连用，表示在某人家里或某家商店里，用 at，而不用 in。如：

［例3］　—Where's Jane? Is she at the hairdresser's again?

　　　　　—No, she's at her mother's.

—珍妮在哪里？又到理发馆去了吗？

—没有，她到她母亲那儿去了。

5．有一些名词，当它们不表示具体的地理位置，而表示与之有关的活动或作用的抽象概念时，常用 at。如：

［例1］　Mary is at the cinema. （She is there to see a film, or because she works there. ）

玛丽在看电影。

［例2］　Mary is in the cinema, not outside in the street, so she won't get wet.

玛丽在电影院，没有在街上，因此，身上不会淋湿。

［例3］　I was at school from 1947 to 1954；I was at university from 1956 to 1961；after that I worked at a private school for several years.

从 1947 年到 1954 我在中小学读书，1956 年到 1961 年念大学，后来在一家私立学校教了几年书。

常见的这类 at 词组有：at（the）bank/cinema/hotel/office/university/etc.，at church/school/sea/etc.，at one's post，at the court of a king/emperor，at a（football）match.

但有些名词前，习惯用 in，如 in class/bed/prison/hospital。church 和 school 前也可用 in。如：

[例4]　You won't find Helen here. She is in class.（i. e. She is busy at her classwork.）

在这里你找不到海伦，她在上课。

[例5]　Fred is in prison for stealing a bicycle.

弗雷德因为偷了一辆自行车而坐牢。

二、表示位置的 in 和 on

in 和 on 都可用来表示位置，其主要区别在于：in 表示的位置是一个立体的地方，意为"在……里"（within the limits of）；而 on 表示的位置是一条线或一个平面（on the surface of），意为"在……上"。试比较下面两句：

[例1]　There is a book in the desk.

桌子里面有一本书。

[例2]　There is a book on the desk.

桌子上面有一本书。

但是，表示"在……上"并非总是用 on。相反，有时不能用 on，而要用 in。试比较下面两组例句：

[例3a]　There is a picture on the wall.

墙上有一幅画。

［例3b］　There is a hole in the wall.

墙上有一个洞。

［例4a］　I can see something floating on the sea over there.

我看见那边海上飘着什么东西。

［例4b］　John is swimming in the sea.

约翰在海上游泳。

例3的两个句子，汉语意思都是"在墙上"，但例3a用的是 on the wall，例3b用的是 in the wall。例4的两个句子都表示"在海上"，但例4a用 on the sea，4b用 in the sea. 为什么例3b表示"在……上"也可以用 in 呢？只要稍加分析，就不难知道其中的道理。例3a"墙上有一幅画"，表示"画"在"墙"的表面上，自然用 on。例3b"墙上有一个洞"，虽然也是"墙上"，但着眼点不是它的表面那个地点，而是洞深入墙内的事实，表示不仅是"面"，而且有一定的"深度"（depth），这里实际上包含"在墙里面"的意思，因此，要用 in。同样，例4a中 on the sea "在海上"是表示在表面上（on the surface of the water），而例4b中的 in the sea 表示在"水中"（under water），因此，用 in 也是显而易见的。但是，在更多的情况下，并非这么容易就可以看出来，需要我们仔细琢磨。试比较下列几组例句：

［例5a］　John is lying on his bed.

约翰在床上。

［例5b］　John is in bed with a cold.

约翰患感冒在床上睡觉。

［例6a］　On his face was a happy smile.

他脸上露出幸福的微笑。

[例6b]　He was wounded in the face. 他脸上受了伤。

[例7a]　He is sitting on a chair. 他坐在一张椅子上。

[例7b]　Come and sit in this chair. It is more comfortable than the one which you are on now.

　　到这张椅子上来坐，比你坐的那一张要舒服些。

　　例5a 的 on his bed 只表示约翰"躺在床上"这回事，并未说在睡觉，这里 bed 是可数名词，前面有限定词修饰，表示具体的床。例5b 用 in bed，表示约翰"因病在睡觉"，他身上盖了被褥之类的东西，他的身体就在被褥里面（He was covered by bed-clothes.），这里的 bed 是可数名词用作不可数名词，表示抽象的概念，而不表示具体的床，因此前面不能有限定词。这与 go to bed（去睡觉）的用法相同。例6a 中的 on his face，讲的是面部表情，因此用 on。凡是讲人的身体的表面，都用 on，又如：

[例8]　She had blood on her forehead.

　　她的前额有血。

　　例6b 讲的是面部受伤，从绝对意义上讲，"伤"自然有一定的深度，因此，用 in。在谈到身体内部的部位受伤时，用 in 更是不言而喻的，如：

[例9]　He was wounded in the shoulder.

　　他的肩膀受了伤。

[例10]　I've got a pain in my head.

　　我的头有点疼。

　　例7a 中的 chair 指的是一般的椅子，而例7b 中的 chair 指的是有扶手之类的椅子，如围椅（arm-chair），人好像是坐在里面似的，因此，用 in。有些东西粗看起来，似乎只有表面，而无深度，但也可以与 on 和 in 连用，表示不同的意思。如：

[例1a] There is some dust on that photograph.

那张照片上有些灰尘。

[例1b] Are you in this photograph?

这张照片上有你吗？

[例2a] Be careful! There is a glass on the newspaper.

小心！报纸上有一个玻璃杯。

[例2b] There is an important article in today's newspaper.

今天报上有一篇重要文章。

例 11a 中，（something）on the photograph（picture）表示该东西不是它的一部分，只是在它的表面上（for something which is not part of it, but only on its surface），而例 11b 中的 in the photograph 表示该人或物是照片中的一部分（for persons or things portrayed in it）。同样，例 12a 中的 on the newspaper 只表示"在它的表面上"，而例 12b 中的 in the newspaper 表示文章刊登在报纸上。因此，如果谈到某件东西在一条线上，而且这件东西实际上构成这条线的一部分，就要用 in。又如：

（13）There's a misprinting in the sixth line on page 22.

在第 22 页第 6 行有一个印刷错误。

表示在一个平面的位置，如果这个平面周围有墙、篱笆等，通常用 in，否则用 on。试比较：

[例14a] I last saw her in the car park.

我最后一次是在停车场看见她的。

[例14b] I last saw her on the beach.

我最后一次是在沙滩上看见她的。

例 14a 表示"停车场"不是一块空坪，而是被围起来的，而例 14b 表示在空旷的沙滩上。因此，我们常说：in the garden、in the marketplace、in the square、in the field，on the lawn、on the moor、on the common、on the farm。注意下面几组句子中 in 和 on 的区别：

[例 15]　There is a temple on the mountain. （When you are near or on the peaks, you are on the mountains.）

山上有一庙宇。

[例 16]　We made our way up the mountain and lost our way in the mountains. （When the peaks rise around you, you are in the mountains.）

我们向山上走去，在山中迷路了。

[例 17]　Was John on the train today? （on introducing a means of transport）

约翰今天坐火车来的吗？

火车、公共汽车等公共交通工具，可以用 on，也可以用 by；用 by 时须不用冠词，即 by train/ bus 等。

[例 18]　He came in a car.

他坐轿车来的。

小汽车、出租汽车、卡车、小船等具有密闭空间的交通工具，通常用 in。

[例 19]　What is going on in your mind?

你在想些什么？

in 表示"在……之内"，与 your mind 搭配，表示"在头脑里想"。

[例 20]　There are a lot of problems on his mind.

209

他思想里有一大堆难题。

on 表示"在……上面",与 mind 搭配,含有"严重问题的"意思,表示问题压在他的头脑上面,造成他精神上的负担。

[例21] The men were walking in the fields.

那些人在田野间散步。

[例22] Tom lost his life on the field.

汤姆在战场上丧了命。

三、in 与时间长度名词连用

介词 in 与表示时间长度的名词(length of time)连用,具有两种不同的含义:"在……以内"(during the time of);"在……以后"(after the time of)。试比较:

[例1] The work was done in a week.

这工作在一星期内就完成了。

[例2] I'll come and see you again in a week.

一星期后我再来看你。

例 1 中的 in a week 表示"在一周以内",例 2 中的 in a week 表示"在一周之后"。究竟什么时候表示"在……以内",什么时候表示"在……以后"呢?我们先看一看上面两句中谓语动词的时态:例 1 用的是一般过去时 was done;例 2 用的是一般将来时 will come and see。是否可以得出结论:当句中谓语动词是过去时时,in 表示"在……以内";当谓语动词是将来时时,in 表示"在……以后"呢?请看下面两组例句:

［**例 3a**］　　He will learn another foreign language in three years.

三年内，他将学会另一门外语。

［**例 3b**］　　He learnt English in three years.

他三年内学会了英语。

［**例 4a**］　　The lecture will begin in five minutes.

演讲五分钟后就开始。

［**例 4b**］　　The bull-fight was to commence in twenty minutes.

斗牛二十分钟后开始。

例 3a 和例 3b 的谓语动词都是 learn，例 3a 为一般将来时，例 3b 为一般过去时，但 in three years 都表示"在三年以内"。例 4a 和例 4b 的谓语动词都表示"开始"意义，例 4a 是将来时 will begin，例 4b 是过去时 was to commence，但 in 都表示"在……以后"。可见问题并不在于时态，或者说主要不在于时态。那么问题在哪里呢？我们觉得，决定的因素在于动词的体性。

我们知道，根据其本身的词汇意义，英语动词可分为限界动词（terminative verbs）和非限界动词（non-terminative verbs）。限界动词表示动作有一个终极的限界，到了一定的限界，动作便无法继续下去了，它包括瞬间动词和一部分持续动词；非限界动词表示动作是在持续过程中，它包括状态动词和没有目的或界限的持续动词。

一般说来，in 短语与非限界动词连用时，in 就作"在……以内"解。例 3a 和例 3b 中的 learn 是非限界动词，因此，两句中的 in 都作"在……以内"解。in 短语与限界动词连用时，in 通常表示"在……以后"，例 4a 和例 4b 中 begin、commence 都是表示开始意义的限界动词，因此 in 都表示"在……以后"。

［例 5］ He <u>will graduate</u> from the university <u>in two years</u>.

过两年他就大学毕业了。

［例 6］ It's two o'clock. <u>I'll come in an hour</u>. (= at three o'clock)

现在是两点，我过一小时回来。

但是，in 短语与表示完成意义的瞬间动词，如 complete、finish、accomplish、fulfill 等连用时，in 不作"在……以后"解，而作"在……以内"解。如：

［例 7］ All this <u>was accomplished</u> <u>in a year</u>.

这一切都是在一年之内完成的。

［例 8］ I'll <u>finish</u> the work <u>in two days</u>.

我将在两天内完成这项工作。

［例 9］ Can you complete the work in an hour?

你能在一小时内把事情做完吗？

有些动词，如 see、hear 既可作非限界动词，又可作限界动词。当它们作非限界动词时，in 表示"在……以内"；作限界动词时，in 表示"在……以后"。试比较：

［例 10］ I shall see him again <u>in a week</u>.

我一星期后再见他。(see 作限界动词)

［例 11］ I shall see him several times <u>in a week</u>.

我一星期之内将要见他几次。 （因为用了 several times，see 作表持续动作的非限界动词)

有些非限界动词在一定的上下文中可以转化为表示动作或

状态的开始的限界动词，这时，in 表示"在……以后"。如：

［例 12］　I am（= shall become）50 in a year.

一年后我就五十岁了。（不是"一年内我就五十岁了"）

［例 13］　My son will be（= will come）here in a fortnight.

我儿子两星期后到这儿来。

［例 14］　In an hour there was（= came）a telegram back.

一小时后回了电报。

［例 15］　I shall be back（= return）in a few days.

我过几天回来。

［例 16］　I'll be ready（= get ready）in a minute.

过一会儿我就准备好了。

与 no，not 连用时，即在否定句中，in 表示"在……以内"，因为在否定句中，不管谓语动词是非限界动词还是限界动词，都是表示持续的状态。如：

［例 17］　Rome was not built in a day.

罗马非朝夕建成。（build 是限界动词）

［例 18］　He hasn't had a good meal in a week.

他一个星期没有好好吃过一顿饭了。（have 是非限界动词）

［例 19］　I have not slept in several days.

我几天没睡觉。（sleep 是非限界动词）

此外，在与最高级，以及 only、first 等词连用时，in 表示"在……以内"，这是因为它们都需要有表示范围的状语的缘故。如：

［例 20］　It is the first time I've seen her in two years.

两年来我第一次见到他。

［**例 21**］　Long skirts were the <u>only</u> thing to wear <u>in those days</u>.

在那些日子里，唯一能穿的只有长裙。

综上所述，一般说来，in 短语限界动词（表完成意义的限界动词除外）连用，以及在一定的上下文中非限界动词用作限界动词连用时，表"在……以后"；与非限界动词、限界动词的否定式、形容词最高级以及 only、the first 等连用时，表"在……以内"。

Since 表时间用法几则

一、since 作副词

since 是一个常用来表时间的词，它可以作副词，意为
"从那时起"（from a specified time in the past to a later time or
till now），作副词的 since 常与现在或过去完成时连用。如：

[例1]　Her husband died ten years ago but she's remarried
since.

她丈夫十年之前去世了，但从那时起，她就改嫁了。

[例2]　The town had been destroyed by an earthquake ten
years earlier and had since been rebuilt.

这小城在十年前为地震所毁，后来曾予以重建。

作副词的 since 前还可以用 ever、long 等表示强调。如：

[例3]　He went to Beijing in 1950 and has lived there ever
since.

他在 1950 年去北京，此后一直住在那里。

[例4]　Bows and arrows has long since been out of use.

弓箭早已不用了。

除用作副词外，since 更多用作介词和连词。

二、since 用作介词

1．since 作介词时，后面接名词或动名词作它的宾语，句子的谓语动词一般用完成时态。如：

［例1］　He has lived with us since his return.

他自从回来后就跟我们住一起。

［例2］　Since last seeing you I have been ill.

上次见到你以后，我就病了。

［例3］　Since living in Paris we have visited Brussels and Amsterdam.

自从离开巴黎后，我们参观了布鲁塞尔和阿姆斯特丹。

［例4］　He had spoken to her only once since the party.

自从那次聚会以后，他仅对她讲过一次话。

since 后面也可以接 then、when 或介词短语。如：

［例5］　I've always been on my guard since then.

从此，我总是警惕着。

［例6］　Since when have you been living in this country?

从何时起你住在这个国家?

［例7］　He had been there since before the war.

战前他就在那里。

2．强调动作的延续时，与 since 短语连用的谓语动词也可以用完成进行时。如：

［例1］　She has been working in a bank since leaving school.

自从离校以来，她一直在一家银行工作。

有时也可以用一般时态甚至现在进行时态，如：

［例2］　It's a year now <u>since</u> the party. （表时间长度）

自上次聚会到现在已经一年了。

［例3］　<u>Since</u> when <u>do</u> you read newspapers？（强调现在的情况）

从什么时候起你开始读报？

［例4］　She <u>had</u> no photograph of herself taken since her marriage. （since 引起的状语修饰过去分词 taken）

自从结婚以来，她没有照过相。

［例5］　Next year, it <u>will be</u> ten years <u>since</u> my coming here.

到明年，我来这儿就满十年了。

［例6］　He <u>is working</u> with us <u>since</u> the 1970s. （强调这动作将持续下去）

从20世纪70年代起，他就同我们一起工作。

从以上例句我们可以看出，与 since 词组连用时，句中的谓语动词通常是表持续动作或状态的持续动词或状态动词，如上述各例中的 live、visit、speak、work、be、have。非持续动词或者短暂动词，如 open、close、leave、miss、find、lose、get 等一般不可与 since 词组连用。如不能说：

［例7］　※I have opened the door since ten minutes ago.

3．但是非持续动词的现在完成时，在下列情况下可以与 since 连用：

第一，非持续动词的否定式。如：

［例1］　I <u>have not heard</u> from him since writing last.

自上次写信以来，我没有收到过他的信。

217

［**例**2］　He has never touched beer since last month.

上个月以来，他没有喝过啤酒。

第二，非持续动词表重复的动作或状态。如：

［**例**3］　I have met him every day since last month.

上个月以来，我每天都见到他。

［**例**4］　Since my last letter I have heard from him twice.

自从我上次写信给他以后，我已经收到他两封信了。

［**例**5］　Since the end of 1981, over 5 billion trees have been planted all over China.

1981 年年末以来，全中国已经栽了 50 亿株树。

第三，有时非持续动词表示的动作虽已结束，但其影响还存在，这时其现在完成时可以与 since 连用，以强调动作的过程和结果。如：

［**例**6］　I have changed my address since last year.

自去年起，我的地址改了。

薄冰教授认为，此句中的 have changed 与现在有关，它不但表示该动作已经结束，而且意味着句中的主语现在的地址仍是去年所变换的那个地址，这就是所谓的现在完成时的影响或结果。①

第四，当非持续动词后面接有表示持续动作或状态的非谓语动词形式时。如：

［**例**7］　I've got to know him since 1980.

从 1980 年起我就认识他。

---

① 薄冰：《英语语法札记（第三集）》，外语教学与研究出版社 1995 年版，第 109 页。

[例8]　I have become converted to his ideas since hearing him speak.

听了他的发言后，我就赞成他的观点了。

上面两句中的 get、become 虽然都是非持续动词，但由于它们后面接了持续动词 to know 和表状态的过去分词 converted，使人们感到的不是动作的结束，而是动作的结果以及持续的过程，因而它们的现在完成时可以与 since 连用。

此外，薄冰教授认为，有些表短暂动作的非持续动词与具体时间或日期连用时，其动作性特别强，只能表动作的结束，不能表过程和结果，因而不能与 since 连用。如不能说：

[例9]　※I have graduated from college since 1985.（应改为：I graduated from college in 1985.）

但是如果不与具体时间或日期连用，则可以。如可以说：

[例10]　Since then I have graduated from college.

上面讲的是 since 作介词时与之连用的谓语动词的时态选择问题。下面我们来看看 since 的宾语问题。

4．作介词 since 宾语的一般是名词或动名词。

如果是表示时间的名词，必须是确定的"时间点"（a point of time），而不能是"一段时间"（a period of time）。如可以说：

[例1a]　I have been waiting for you since four o'clock.

但不能说：

[例1b]　※I have been waiting for you since four hours.

不过如果在表一段时间的名词后，加上 ago 使之变成"时间点"，则可以。如例1b 可以改为：

[例1c]　I have been waiting for you since four hours ago.

　　有时有些名词本身就包含一段时间，如一场战争可以经历几年，一次运动也可以进行数月或数年，当这些名词与 since 连用时，它所表示的时间通常是从这一段时间的结束而不是从它的开始算起。如：

　　[例2]　Since the War of Resistance Against Japan，Old Lin has been living in Changsha.

　　抗日战争结束后，老林就一直住在长沙。

　　这里 since the War of Resistance Against Japan 指的是"抗日战争结束以来"。如果要表示"从抗日战争一开始"，要说"since the beginning（或 start）of…"。又如如果在 1996 年，回答"How long is it since the 'Cultural Revolution'?"，这个问题正确的答案应该是"It is twenty years since the 'Cultural Revo-lution'."。但是如果某个运动或战争尚未结束，则要从它的开始算起。如在 1970 年回答"How ling is it since the 'Cultural Revolution'?"的问题，就可以说"It is four years since the 'Culture Revolution'."。当然，为了更加清楚明白，最好更改为"since the beginning of the 'Cultural Revolution'"。

　　三、since 作连词

　　since 作连词引导时间状语从句，表示从过去某一时刻到现在或从过去某一时刻到过去另一时刻为止的一段时间，与其连用的主句中的谓语动词多用完成时态，其用法与 since 作介词时句中的谓语动词用法相同，这里不赘述。下面要讨论的是 since 从句中谓语的动词用法的几个问题。

1．从句中的谓语动词，一般用非持续性动词的一般过去时。如：

［例1］　We've been friends since we left school.

我们从学校毕业后一直是朋友。

［例2］　Where have you been since I last saw you?

自从我上次见到你以后，你到哪里去了？

动词的过去式表示动作的完成，而非持续的动词，特别是像 see、come、leave 这样一些短暂动词，其动作的发生和结束，都是在瞬间完成的，因而，动词的词汇意义和语法意义具有一致性。从句所表示的时间从谓语动词表示的动作完成时算起，这一点不会造成理解上的困难。

2．从句中的谓语动词，也可以是持续动词或状态动词的一般过去时。如：

［例1］　I have written to her since she lived in London.

自从她离开伦敦以来，我还没给她写过信。

［例2］　Two years has passed since I smoked.

我戒烟已经两年了。

［例3］　He has written to me frequently since I was ill.

我痊愈之后，他经常给我写信。

上述句中的 lived、smoked 是持续动词的一般过去时，was 是状态动词的一般过去时。前者表示 lived、smoked 这一动作的完成，即"不居住""不抽烟"了，后者表示 was ill 的状态的结束，即不生病了，因此 since 从句中的谓语动词如果是持续动词或状态动词的过去时，since 从句所表示的时间一般也应从动作或状态结束时算起，因此，其含义与动词的词汇意义刚好相反，具有否定意义，这一点必须特别注意。

3．如果表示动作或状态延续至今，那就要用持续动词或状态动词的现在完成时。如：

［例1］　I have met him often <u>since</u> I <u>have lived</u> here.

自从我在这里住下之后，我常看见他。

［例2a］　I have not written to her <u>since</u> I <u>have been</u> home.

自从我回家以来，一直没给她写信。

［例2b］　I have not written to her since I was home.

自从我离开家，一直没给她写信。

since 从句中用持续动词或状态动词的现在完成时，其词汇意义和语法意义一致，不会造成理解上的困难，这时，since 相当于 while，通常可以用 while 代替，如前面两句可改为：

［例1b］　I have met him often <u>while</u> I have lived here.

［例2c］　I have not written to her <u>while</u> I have been home.

但是在特定的上下文或特定的情景中，持续动词或状态动词的一般过去时也可表示延续动作或状态的起点，这时多用 ever 强调 since 的语义。如：

［例3］　We have enjoyed the beautiful scenery around us <u>ever since</u> we stayed here.

自从我们待在这儿以来，饱尝了周围美丽的景色。

［例4］　The bell has been out of order <u>ever since</u> I was here.

我来这儿以后，这铃一直是坏的。

状态动词 be 在 since 从句中有时由于表语的意义限定，不能表示延续意义，因此不能用现在完成时而要用一般过去时，时间的起点可以从动作发生之时算起。如：

［例5］　I've lived here <u>since</u> I <u>was</u> a boy.

我还是孩子时就住在这里。（不说 "...since I have been a boy."，因为不可能总是孩子，不长大）

［例6］　I have not found a wife though I have been looking for one <u>ever since</u> I <u>was</u> twenty.

虽然从 20 岁起我就一直在找对象，但至今尚未找着。（不说 "...ever since I have been twenty."，因为不可能总是 20 岁）

4. since 从句中有时也可以用非持续动词的现在完成时，相当于一般过去时，时间的起点也是从动作完成的那一刻算起。如：

［例1］　He has learned to shoot <u>since</u> he <u>has joined</u> the army. (= ...since he joined the army.)

他参军后一直在学习射击。

现在完成时和一般过去时都表示在说话前动作已完成 (the act was completed at some time before the time of utterance)。因此，这两种时态在表示动作时间方面并无多大区别，所以都可以用于 since 从句，只是一般过去时更简便，因此人们都用一般过去时。

5. since 从句中的谓语动词，有时也可以用一般现在时。如：

［例1］　I have had such impression <u>since</u> I <u>can</u> remember. (= ...since the beginning of the time I can remember.)

从我能记得时起，我就有这种印象。

值得注意的是，当 since 从句中谓语动词为过去时时，从句所表示的行为都发生在主句谓语动词所表示的行为以前，而不是以后。如：

［例2a］　I <u>have had</u> no news of him <u>since</u> he left home.

［例2b］　I had had no news of him since he left home.

以上两句都译为"自从他离开家以后，我一直都没有得到他的消息"。很显然，从句中 left 所表示的行为先于主句中 have had、had had 所表示的行为，只不过前者是以现在为时间参考点，后者是以过去某一时刻为时间的参考点，但是与 since 从句不同的是，一般来说，过去完成时所表示的行为发生在过去时所表示的行为之前。如：

［例3］　The rain had stopped and the air was cleaned.

雨停了，空气很清新。

［例4］　When we got there the basketball match had already started.

我们到那里时，篮球赛已经开始了。

四、"it is + 时间 + since"结构

这种结构与带有 since 从句的其他结构用法基本相同，since 从句多用一般过去时，表示动作或状态的完成，时间从动作或状态完成时算起。如：

［例1］　It is four years since he was in New York.

他离开纽约已经四年了。

它与下面两句意义相同：

［例1a］　He was in New York four years ago.

［例1b］　He has not been in New York for four years.

但这种结构与带有 since 从句的其他结构也有不同之处，主要表现在以下两个方面。

1．在带有 since 从句的主句中，通常用完成时态，虽然偶尔也可用一般时态，而在"it is ＋时间 ＋since"结构中，主句用一般时态比用完成时态普遍一些。如：

［例1］ It is/has been five years since he came back.

他回来已经五年了。

［例2］ It was years since I had seen her.

我多年不见她了。

这时，主句中的谓语动词除 be 外，还可以用 seem、feel like 等。如：

［例3］ It seems a long time since we last met.

我们似乎很久没见面了。

［例4］ It feels like ages since I was last here.

我离开这里似乎很久了。

2．since 从句中可以用非持续动词的现在完成时，也可以用非持续动词的一般过去时，时间的起点都是从动作完成的那一刻算起，在"it is ＋时间 ＋since"结构中非持续动词的用法与此相同。如：

［例1］ He has learned to shoot since he has joined the army. （ ＝…since he joined the army.）

［例2a］ It is three years since I saw Bill.

［例2b］ It is three years since I have seen Bill.

我已经三年没见比尔了。

［例3a］ It is two months since Tom smoked a cigarette.

［例3b］ It is two months since Tom has smoked a cigarette.

汤姆已经有两个月不抽烟了。

当然，since 从句中的现在完成时与一般过去时的细微差别是有的。用一般过去时，说话人似乎是意识到动作发生的具体时间；用现在完成时，其动作发生的时间在说话人的心目中就不那么具体确切了。不过，这种差别通常均忽略不计。由于用一般过去时更简便，因而，用完成时态不多见。

但是如果是持续动词或状态动词，情况就不一样了。在带有 since 从句的其他结构中，从句中用持续动词或状态动词的现在完成时态通常表示动作或状态的持续，如例 4 和例 5。

［例 4］　I have been reading <u>since</u> I <u>have been</u> here.

我到这儿以来一直在读书。

［例 5］　I have learned a lot since I <u>have worked</u> in the factory.

我在工厂工作以来，学到了很多东西。

但是在"it is + 时间 + since"结构中，持续动词或状态动词的现在完成时在从句中并不表示动作或状态的延续，而是和非持续动词或持续动词的一般过去时一样，表示动作或状态的结束。如 Crume 认为，例 6a 和例 6b、例 6c 等值，Jespersen 认为例 7a 和例 7b 等值，例 8a 和例 8b 也含义相同。

［例 6a］It is four years now since I <u>have studied</u> this question.

［例 6b］　It is four years now since I <u>studied</u> this question.

［例 6c］　I haven't studied this question for four years.

我已经四年没有研究这个问题了。①

［例 7a］　It is an age since you <u>have been</u> here.

---

① Geurge O. Curme：*Syntax—A Grammar of the English Language*, 1931, p. 190.

［例 7b］　It is an age since you <u>were</u> here.

你离开这里已经很久了。

［例 8a］　It is four years since he <u>has lived</u> in Shanghai.

［例 8b］　It is four years since he <u>lived</u> in Shanghai.

他离开上海已经四年了。

又如:

［例 9］　Remember it is six years since I <u>have been</u> there— I want to go back again. And I can do it, with your help.

我记得离开那儿已经六年了,我想回去。有你的帮助,我就能做到。

上面例 6 ～例 9 中的 have been、have lived 等都表示动作或状态的结束。如要表示延续,则要用"it is + 时间 + that"结构。试比较:

［例 10a］　<u>It is</u> four years <u>that</u> he has lived in Shanghai.　= He has lived in Shanghai (for) four years.

他在上海已经住了四年了。

［例 10b］　<u>It is</u> four years <u>since</u> he has lived in Shanghai. = He hasn't lived in Shanghai for four years.

他离开上海已经四年了。

人称代词用法札记

一、I 和 we

英语中当讲话者或写作者所指的是他自己时，要用单数第一人称代词 I（我）。与其他人称代词不同的是，I 在任何情况下都要大写，不管是否在句子开头。如：

[例1]　I think，therefore I am.

我思故我在。

[例2]　John told me I needn't wait.

约翰告诉我不必等了。

前面我们说 I 总是大写，似乎是有点"唯我独尊"的味道。其实不然，英语民族很讲究绅士风度，在 I 与其他人称代词或名词并列使用时，习惯上总是把 I 说在别人的后面，以示谦逊。如：

[例3]　Jane and I have already eaten.　（不说：※I and Jane…）

简和我已经吃过了。

[例4]　That's for you，Tom and me.

这是为你、我及汤姆好。

但是，在承认错误时，同样出于礼貌，往往先说 I，以示有错误自己首先承担。如：

［例 5］　I and he are to blame.

该由我和他负责。

当然，在谈到大人和小孩时，因为不存在礼貌问题，可把 I 放在前面。如：

［例 6］　I and my little two daughters went to the movies last night.

昨天晚上，我同两个小女儿去看了电影。

I 只是单数形式，we 并非与它相对应的复数形式，we 并不意味着"两个或两个以上的 I（我）"，而是 I（我）和 you（你、你们），或"I and he（or she）"（我和他/她），或"I and all these other people"（我和所有其他这些人）。如：

［例 7］　Let's go to the cinema tonight, shall we?

咱们今晚去看电影，好不好？（we 包括听话人在内，相当于汉语的"咱们"）

［例 8］　We want to have a chat with you.

我们想同你谈一谈。（we 不包括听话人，指说话人和另外一个或多个其他人）

有时，we 可用来代替 I，常见于以下几种情况。

第一，报刊编辑、作者或演讲者，在提出自己的意见时，往往用 we，不用 I，以示谦虚或表示他是代表整个编辑部，而不是代表个人。这种用法的 we 称之为"editorial we"。翻译时，"editorial we"仍然译为"我们"，但从语义的角度来看，we 实质上相当于 I。如：

［例 9］　In this chapter, we shall describe the relations of

language to society.

在本章，我们将叙述语言与社会的关系。

教师讲课时，也常用这种 "editorial we"。如：

［例10］ We'll now explain the text.

现在我们讲解课文。

第二，与 "editorial we" 相类似的还有 "royal we"，即国王、女王等统治者讲话，或正式的皇家布告都喜欢用 we 代替 I，可译成 "朕" 或 "寡人"。如：

［例11］ We are not interested in the possibilities of defeat.

朕对失败的可能性不感兴趣。

第三，在通俗的口语中，特别在祈使句中，us 有时也当作 me 用。如：

［例12］ Give us （＝me）a kiss，love.

吻我一下，亲爱的。

［例13］ Tell us （＝me）what he said.

告诉我他说了什么。

we 除可以用来表示 I 外，还可以代替 you。如医生对病人、大人对小孩、老师对学生常用 we 代替 you，以示亲切。这种用法的 we 称之为 "paternal we"。如：

［例14］ How are we feeling today，Mr. Smith?

史密斯先生，您今天感觉怎样？

［例15］ Oh，little darling! We are a nice boy，and don't make a noise.

哦，小乖乖，你是个好孩子，别吵了。

这种用法的 we，有时表示挖苦。如：

［例16］ How touchy we are!

（你）脾气可不小哩！

此外，在口语中，we 也可以用来指单数第三人称 he 或 she，如秘书常用 we 来指其老板。如：

［例17］　We're in a bad mood today. （＝ He is in a bad mood today.）

他（老板）今天情绪不好。

二、人称代词并非一定指人

顾名思义，人称代词的主要用法是指代人。we、I、you 和 they 没有性的区别，而 he、she、it 有性的区别，he 代表阳性，she 代表阴性，it 代表中性，指非生物或下等动物。但是，我们这里所讲的人称代词是就语法上的"人称"而言，它们并非仅仅指人。人称代词也常可以用来指物。例如，当我们亲切地谈论到船只、汽车、火车、飞机等时，常把它们看作阴性，用 she 来指代。如：

［例1］　That's the Queen's yacht, Britannia. She's a beautiful ship.

那是女王的游艇，"不列颠号"，她是一艘很漂亮的船。

［例2］　My car's not fast, but she does 50 miles to the gallon.

我的汽车不快，但她每加仑汽油能跑50英里。

在谈论自己的国家、城市、学校等时，人们往往有一种自豪感。因而，也常用 she 来指代。如：

［例3］　China will always do what she has promised to do.

中国是说话算话的。

[**例4**] Oxford taught me as much Latin and Greek as she could.

牛津大学尽她最大的努力把拉丁语和希腊语教给我。

当然，如果不赋予感情色彩，只是就事论事，只是把它作为一个物体，仍然要用 it。如：

[**例5**] Japan is an island country in the Pacific. It lies to the east of China.

日本是个岛国，在中国的东方。

此外，在具体的语言环境中还可以直接用人称代词来指代商店（shop）、旅馆（hotel）、剧院（theatre）、车辆（car）、船只（ship）以及私人物品（one's belongings）等。譬如，你问一家商店什么时候关门，你完全可以说"What time do you close?"（不一定要说"What time does your shop close?"），商店老版也完全可以回答为"I close at 5：30."。这里 you 代表 your shop，I 代表 my shop。类似的如：

[**例6**] We have sprung a leak.

我们船漏水了。

[**例7**] At last we are packed.

我们的行李终于收拾好了。

[**例8**] I am fast.

我的表快了。

[**例9**] How much petrol does she use?

这车消耗多少汽油？

三、表泛指意义的人称代词

人称代词，如 we、you、they、he 等可以表示泛指意义，即不仅仅是表示其本身的词汇意义，而是泛指"人们"（people in general）或"所有的人""任何人"。表示泛指意义的人称代词作主语的句子，译成汉语时，可以译成无人称句，将主语省略不译，或译成"人们""人人"，或根据具体的语言环境，使用不同的词。如：

[例1] We eat to live, not live to eat.

吃饭是为了活着，但活着不是为了吃饭。

这句中的 we 指的是 anyone、every one（任何人、每个人），因此最好译成无人称句。当然，有时仍然将 we 译成"我们"，也未然不可，因为汉语中的"我们"含有所有的人的意思。如：

[例2] We have shortcomings as well as good points.

我们都有优点，也有缺点。（人人都有优点，也有缺点。）

you 表示泛指意义时，通常译成无人称句。如：

[例3] Look before you leap.

三思而后行。

[例4] You are always to knock before you enter.

进屋前先敲门。

有时可以活译，如：

[例5] You never know what may happen.

谁也不知道会发生什么事。

[例6] Gravity is what makes you weigh what you weigh.

地心引力使人们（或"我们"）称得自己的重量。

They 表泛指意义时，常与 say 连用。如：

［例 7］　They say a new steel works is being planned.

据说正在计划建造一个新的钢铁厂。

［例 8］　They say（＝People say）oil prices will be going up soon.

人们说油价快要上涨了。

在某些谚语中，he 可表示泛指意义。如：

［例 9］　He who hesitates is lost.

当断不断，必受其患。

此外，one 作人称代词时，常表示泛指意义。如：

［例 10］　World trade is improving, but one cannot expect miracles.

世界贸易正得到改善，但是人们不能期望出现奇迹。

［例 11］　One can't be too careful in matters like this.

在这样的问题上，越谨慎越好。

one 作主语时，其附加疑问句的主语可以用 one（正式文体）、you（非正式文体）或 he（非正式文体，只适用于美国）。如：

［例 12］　One can't be too careful in matters like this,
$$\begin{cases} \text{can one?} \\ \text{can you?} \\ \text{can he?} \end{cases}$$

此外，在口语中，当作者或说话者希望谦虚地提到他自己时，one 有时可以代替 I。如：

［例 13］　I've been shadowed for a long time; one gets used

to that.

很长一段时间我被跟踪了，对此，我已经习惯了。

［例 14］　One likes to have one's breakfast in bed now and again.

本人时不时喜欢在床上吃早饭。

［例 15］　One doesn't like to be treated that way.

我不喜欢受到那样的待遇。

汉语中也有类似的情况。如："不要打扰我，人家很忙嘛。"这里"人家"相当于英语中的 one，指的是"我"（I）。

四、用 he 还是 they？

与别的语言譬如俄语不同的是，英语的名词绝大多数在词形上是没有"性"的标志的，属于所谓的共性名词，如 person、teacher 既可以是男性，也可以是女性。英语中的不定代词，如 anyone、everyone 等也是如此。而且英语中没有一个对男、女都适用的单数第三人称代词。因此，当先行词是这些共性名词或不定代词时，究竟用什么人称代词来指代就成了问题。按照传统语法，要用 he，如：

［例 1］　If anyone calls while I'm out, ask him to call back later.

我外出时，要是有人来电话，叫他过一会再打来。

但是，自 20 世纪 60 年代以来，这种用法遭到了女权运动倡导者们的极力反对，她们将它抨斥为"男性主义"。她们认为，既然 anyone 也包括女性，用 he 来指代，岂不是可笑吗？所以，从那时起越来越多的人在正式场合说"If anyone calls when I'm out, ask him or her to call back later. "。这样一来，女权主义者满意了。但这种结构重复使用时显得啰唆、不精练。如下面一句听起来总觉得有些别扭：

[例2] If I ever wished to disconcert anyone, all I had to do was to ask him or her how many friends he or she had.

因此，这种用法为语言学家所反对。于是，用 they（them、their）来指代先行词为共性名词或不定代词这种别具一格的方法应运而生了："If anyone calls when I'm out, ask them to call back later. "这种用法在口语中非常普遍，听起来似乎比用 he or she 或 he 更符合习惯。而且，在附加疑问句中，通常要用 they。如：

[例3] Everybody has got a ticket, haven't they?
大家都有票吧!

五、人称代词的主格和宾格

英语人称代词有主格和宾格之分。主格通常在句中作主语或主语补语，宾格则作宾语。如：

[例1] I am very busy.

[例2] He is always making jokes about me.

但是，事情并非如此简单。有时，在本该用主格的时候却用了宾格；反之，在该用宾格的时候又用了主格。请看下面两例：

[例3] This is me, Winston Churchill, speaking to you....

我，温斯顿·丘吉尔，向你们说话……

[**例4**]　It is a wonderful moment for my husband and I after nearly six months away to be met and escorted by ships of the Home Fleet.

离开（英国）差不多6个月后，受到内海舰队的迎接和护送，这对我和我的丈夫来说确是一个美好的时刻。

例3是英国前首相丘吉尔几十年前访问美国时所做的一次讲演的开场白，例4是英国女王伊丽莎白二世1954年在结束她的英联邦之行返回英国后的一次广播讲话中的一句。按照传统语法，上面两例中无疑都有语法错误。"This is me"应改为"This is I"，因为I在句中作主语的补语（或称表语），应该用主格，而不是宾格；"for my husband and I"应改为"for my husband and me"，因为me在句中作介词for的宾语，要用宾格，而不是主格。难怪在听到丘吉尔的讲话后，美国有些人乘机抨击丘吉尔，说他的语法太差了。但是，请注意，丘吉尔是一位擅长辞令、口若悬河的著名的政治家、文学家；而女王讲的更是the Queen's English①，他们既然这么说，是不会没有道理的。正如哥伦比亚大学一位教授在为丘吉尔解围时所说的那样："这是通俗英语（informal English）。"

通俗英语，即非正式英语（或称"口语"）。在口语中以人称代词宾格代替主格的情况俯拾皆是。几十年前如此，现在更加是这样。现在几乎人人都说"It's me"，而没有人说"It is I"了。正如C. E. Eckersley所指出的那样，"没有一个人，甚至没有一个教师，会去使用更加符合语法的I"（No one—not even a teacher—would use the more grammatical "I".）。

---

①　the Queen's English 通常译为"标准英语"。

1. 人称代词以宾格代替主格，常见于以下几种情况。

第一，在日常会话中，在 be 后面一般使用宾格形式，不用主格。如：

[例 1]　—Who is it?

　　　　—It's me（him, her, us, them）.

—是谁呀？

—是我（他、她、我们、他们）。

第二，主格代词通常不单独使用，也不用在有 not 的简短回答中。这时要用宾格形式。如：

[例 2]　—Who wants a ride on my bike?

　　　　—Me!（Not me!）

—谁想骑骑我的自行车？

—我!（我不想!）

第三，在表示惊奇、反问、否定、轻蔑、不满等感情色彩的没有谓语动词的感叹句中。如：

[例 3]　—You are a very beautiful woman, aren't you?

　　　　—Me beautiful? No, dear!

—你是一个漂亮的女人。

—我，漂亮? 不，亲爱的。

[例 4]　He's got to repay the money. Poor him.　（= ….Isn't he unlucky!）

他必须赔偿这笔款。他真倒霉!

当作主语的人称代词与不定式连用时，通常也用宾格形式，以起强调作用。如：

[例 5]　—You can tell him.

　　　　—Me tell him? Not likely!

——你可以告诉他。

——我告诉他？不可能的事！

［例6］　What! Me (to) play him at chess? No!

什么！我去和他下棋？我才不呢！

［例7］　What! Me (to) fight a big chap like him?

什么！要我跟他这样的大个儿斗？我可不干。

这种句式虽为肯定形式，但暗含有强烈的否定意义，表示某种不愉快的感情。

第四，在表示补充说明或意义上转折的独立主格结构中。如：

［例8］　We had to wade across the street——and me in my best suit.

我们得踩着泥水过街，而我却穿着最好的衣服。

［例9］　I was hungry and tired, and me without a cent to my name.

我又饿又累，而且身无分文。

第五，在 there（here）be 句型中作主语的人称代词出现在句尾时。如：

［例10］　There's only me.

只有我一人。

［例11］　There was little me, astride on his bare back.

这里用宾格 me 代替 I 还可以从语音的角度得到解释，因为 I 是双元音，不像单元音 me 容易念，而且可以延长。这也就是为什么人称代词的宾格代替主格这种现象多见于第一人称单数，而少见于其他人称代词的原因。但是，在"It is（was）…who（that）…"这种强调句式中，大多数语法学家都认为要用主格形式。Quirk 等在其《当代英语语法》一书中指出：带先行词 it 的结构中，一般用主格形式，并举有一例：

[例 12]　　It was he who came.

不过，在该书"主谓一致"一章（第 367 页）中他们也举过下面两例：

[例 13]　　It is I who am to blame.

[例 14]　　It's me who's to blame.（informal English）

并作了以下说明：在分裂句，作主语的关系代词后面的动词，通常与主语的先行词一致。但是（在非正式语体中），在用宾格代词 me 时，动词通常与第三人称单数一致。

在该书第 592 页"分裂句"部分，作者又举有一例"It's he/him that is a genius."，并指出，用 him 是非正式语体。章振邦等人在《新编英语语法》（上册，第 153 页）中指出："如果作为主语补语的人称代词后面跟有关系分句，并在分句里作主语时，一般用主格。"该书并未谈到可以用宾格的问题。但他们在随后出版的《新编英语语法教程》中明确指出：在非正式文体中，用作主语补语的人称代词出现在句尾，通常采用宾格形式。并举有两例：

[例 5]　　It was them who saved the drowing girl.

[例 6]　　It was me that did it.

笔者认为，在"It is（was）…who（that）…"这种强调句式中，如果被强调的是主语，通常还是用主格形式；但在非正式英语文体中，也可以（并非"必须"）用宾格形式。这时谓语动词要用单数第三人称，即与 it 一致。但是，"It was I""It was he"这种结构听起来总有些不自然。因此，通常避免使用，而用其他表达方式代替，如：

［例 17］　He was the man who came.

［例 18］　—Who cut down the cherry tree? —I did.

第六，在以 than、as 等引导的比较状语从句中，当从句的其他成分都省略时，作主语的人称代词可用宾格代替。如：

［例 19］　She draws better than me.　（= She draws better than I.）

她画得比我好。

［例 20］　She's as old as me.　（= She's as old as I.）

她的年纪和我一样大。

上面两句中，人称代词用主格和宾格都可以。用主格，则 than 和 as 为连词；用宾格，则为介词。

上面我们讲了人称代词宾格代替主格的情况。下面讲一下主格代替宾格的情况。

2. 用主格代替宾格的情况多出现在并列宾语中；由于前一个宾语是没有格的变化的名词或 you，后面的代词也就不变为宾格了。如：

［例 1］　It made Dad and I laugh.

弄得爸爸和我都笑了。

［例 2］　He says she saw you and I last night.

他说她昨晚看见我们俩了。

［例 3］　I am deeply honored that so many of you should have come down to welcome Mrs. Eisenhower and I back to Washington.

你们这么多人赶来欢迎我和我的夫人回到华盛顿，我深感荣幸。

其实，这种用法早在几个世纪前就已出现了。1971 年，由 James A. H. Murry 编纂的 *The Oxford English Dictionary* 就转引了以下二例：

[例4]　To give you and I a right understanding.（1649）

[例5]　Leave your lady and I alone.（1710）

Quirk 等也认为，这种用法在非正式谈话中是很常见的。you and I 已被看作一种固定的搭配形式。前面我们所引用的英国女王伊丽莎白二世和美国总统艾森豪威尔所说的 "for my husband and I" "Welcome Mrs. Eisenhower and I" 更证实这种用法已具有普遍性。当然，这种结构中的第一个词必须是 you 或没有格的变化的名词。没有人会说 "between him and I"，更不至于说出 "between he and I" 了。

英语 There 存在句研究

第一章　引言

英语中表示存在的意思可以用两种句型：一种是 there be 句型，另一种是 I（you，they...）have 句型。如：

[例1a]　There are more than 6000 students in our university.

[例1b]　We have more than 6000 students in our university.

我校有六千多名学生。

这两句表示的基本意思相同，经常可以换用，但略有差别。前者强调客观，后者强调主观。因此，在表示某处存在某人或某物时，常用 there be 句型。这种句型通常称为 there 存在句（*there*-existential sentences）。对 there 存在句，历来的语法学家都进行过大量的研究，在许多问题上取得了一致或基本一致的看法。例如，大多数语法学家，不论是传统语法学家、结构语法学家还是转换生成语法学家，都认为 there 存在句中的 there 是虚词（empty word），而不是表示地点意义的副词；there 在句中起引导词的作用，作形式主语；there 存在句中的谓语动词除 be 外，还可以是其他表示存在或类似存在的动词。如 exist、remain、happen、occur、stand、seem、appear 等。但是，在不少问题上，人们看法却不尽相同。例如，there 存在句中跟在动词后面的名词词组究竟是看作真正主语还是谓语的一部分，名词词组后面的分词的句法功能问题等。还有一些问题有待进一步探讨。例如，there 存在句中名词词组限定词的选择问题。一般语法书都认为，there 存在句中作真正主语的名词词组通常是表示不确定的人或物，因而，只能和不定冠词、零冠词以及其他表示"不确定"含义的限定词如 no、some、any、many、much、few、little、several 等连用，而不能与表示"确定"含义的限定词 the、this、that、my 等连用。但实际情况是怎么样的呢？事实上，there 存在句中的名词词组与定冠词以及其他表示"确定"含义的限定词连用的现象却俯拾皆是。下面略举几例：

[例2]　Indeed there is the common saying "as rich as a Jew".

确实有这么句俗语："富似犹太人。"

[例3]　There was the sound of a man striking the door three times.

传来了一个人的敲门声，砰砰砰一连三下。

[例4]　A phrase began to beat in my ears with a sort of heady excitement："There are only the pursued and the pursuing, the busy and the tired. "

一个警句开始在我耳中令人兴奋地激动鸣响："世界上只有被追求者和追求者、忙碌的人和疲倦的人。"

可见，问题不在于 there 存在句中的名词词组能否与表示确定意义的限定词连用，而在于如何对它进行解释：是否有什么规律可循？

本文旨在对 there 存在句和 have 存在句进行较为系统、全面的研究；对一些有争论的问题，参酌不同语法学家的意见提出一些粗浅的看法；着重讨论一些悬而未决的问题，以期抛砖引玉，激起对这些问题的进一步探讨。

第二章　There 的词性和功能[①]

there 这个词，通常作表示地点意义的副词，意为"在那里，往那里"或"在那点上"；这时，需重读（stressed），念[ðeə(r)]。它在句中的位置比较灵活，可以放在句首，也可以放在句尾。如：

[例1]　There Scott wrote all his best novels. (= Scott wrote all his best novels there.)

斯科特的名著就是在那里写的。

[例2]　I'm on my way there.

我正在往那里去。

[例3]　There (= on that point) I agree with you.

在那一点上我同意你的意见。

但在 there 存在句中，there 不是表地点意义的副词，而是个虚词，或称为"功能词"（function word）、"结构词"（structural word），在句中不重读（unstressed），念[ðə(r)]，通常位于句首。如：

[例3]　There's a man at the door.

---

①　本章内容曾发表于《苏州大学学报（哲学社会科学版）》外国语教学专辑中，此处略有修改。

门边有个人。

[**例 4**]　　There were six people in the room.

房里有六个人。

有时副词 there 和功能词 there 可用在同一个句子里。如：

[**例 5**]　　There were many people there.

那里有许多人。

这句中，句首的 there 是功能词，句尾的 there 是副词。据 Michael West 的调查，there 作副词只不过占其总数的 23% 左右，而作功能词却占 77% 左右[①]。这就是说，there 的主要功能在于引导存在句。

一、there 的性质

在 there 存在句中，there 是功能词或结构词。但不同的语言学家可能使用不同的名称。如 Jespersen 称之为"预备词"（preparatory）、Curme 称之为"前在词"（anticipative），Quirk 等称之为"表示存在的词"（existential），Partridge 把它叫作"引导词"（introductory），还有的把它叫作"先行词"（anticipating）、"前行词"（anticipatory）、"小品词"（particle），"虚词"（empty）、"形式词"（formal）或"填空词"（expletive），等等。名称繁多，不胜枚举。所有这些名称虽然有异，却都在某种程度上说明了 there 存在句中 there 的特性：there 纯属一个语法词，并无多少实在意义。因此，这些名称都是可以接受的。但是，Erades（依拉德斯）认为，称 there 为"引导词"

---

① 见 Michael West：A General Service List of English Words p512.

是观察错误，因为它并非永远在句首；它可以出现在句中，甚至句尾。称它为"预备词""先行词"等回避了句法作用。称之为"表示存在的词"，则只适用于动词是 to be 的场合，而不适合表示发生、出现等其他动词。他认为，称它为"虚词"和"形式词"最为恰当。我们认为，Erades 的看法是不无道理的，称它为"虚词"或"形式词"似乎更恰当一些。虚词是只有语法意义或功能意义而没有完整的词汇意义的词，它与"形式词""功能词""结构词"或"语法词"（grammatical word）表示的是同一个意思，通常可以替换。本书将使用"虚词"这一术语，同时也使用"引导词"这个术语。因为，尽管 there 并非总是位于句首，但是，在绝大多数情况下，它确实位于句首，引导一个表示"某处存在某物或某人"的存在句。这个术语一目了然，便于读者见其形就知其义。

也有人认为 there 是代词。其理由有二：其一，因为它以音素［ð］开始。英语里以［ð］开始的词只有代词和冠词。there 存在句中，there 不可能是冠词，因为它后面没有名词，所以，只可能是代词。其二，在附加疑问句中，there 可与一般代词起相同作用。如：There is a boy outside，isn't there?

我们以为这种看法似乎不太妥当。其一，英语里以［ð］这个音素开始的词，除代词、冠词外，还可以有副词和名词，如 than、then、thereabout、thisness、though 等。there 这个词本身也可以是副词。其二，在附加疑问句中，there 确实可以起代词的作用，这是 there be 句型的特殊之处。但是，起某种词作用的词，并非一定是那种词。例如，在 "To see is to be-lieve." 一句中，to see 和 to believe 都起名词词组的作用，但它们不是名词，而是动词不定式，这一点不是显而易见吗？

二、there 的句法功能

there 在 there 存在句中作什么成分的问题，语法学家的看法并不一致。不少人只把 there 看作引导词，引起一个句子，不把它看作句子成分；有的语法学家，如 C. T. Onions 把它和 be 一起看作谓语。国内的语法学家，如张道真先生，在《实用英语语法》中明确地把 there 看作谓语的一部分。张先生引了下面一个例句：

[例1]　To make the matter worse，there is a strong wind.
更糟糕的是起了一阵大风。

在该书中，张先生用"＿"代表主语，"～"代表谓语。可见张先生是将 there 看作谓语的一部分。不少语法学家把 there 看作形式主语（formal subject）。著名的荷兰语法学家 P. A. Erades 列举了六条理由来证明 there 的"形式主语"的地位，现沿引如下：

1. 在附加疑问句中，there 起代词的作用。如：

[例2]　There is no brandy in the house，is there? 家里没有白兰酒，是吗？

（比较：It is not heavy for you，is it?）

2. 在带动词 to be 的问句中，紧跟在动词之后，相当于作主语的名词词组或代词。如：

[例3]　Is there any difficulty in this? 干这事有困难吗？

（比较：Is this difficult to understand?）

3．在独立主格结构中，there 和名词词组或代词一样可以位于-ing 分词之前。如：

［例4］ She was at a loss what to do，there being no one else at home. 因为家中无人，她不知怎么办。

（比较：She was at a loss what to do，she being alone in the house.）

4．在句首为否定状语的句子中，there 和名词词组或代词一样要与作用词倒装。如：

［例5］ Nowhere was there any trace of Henry Jekyll. 哪里都见不到亨利·吉基尔的影子。

（比较：Nowhere was the child to be found.）

5．和名词词组或代词一样，there 可以作动词不定式的逻辑主语。如：

［例6］ I should be sorry for there to be any more trouble on my account. 如果因为我而造成更多的麻烦，我将感到歉意。

（比较：I should be sorry for your beautiful carpet to be spoiled.）

6．在修饰作表语的名词的定语从句中，there 和名词词组或代词一样可以位于分句之首。如：

［例7］ This is all there is. 所有的全在这里。

（比较：A common thief，that's all he is.）

Erades 认为，这六条理由足以说明 there 的主语地位。为了进一步证实这一论点，他继而又提出了两条他认为无可争辩的理由：

第一，there 的句法功能与在各方面都具备主语性质的 it 的用法完全一致。试比较：

252

［**例8**］ There blew a great gale.

［**例9**］ It blew a great gale.

刮了一阵大风。

第二，当作表语的是 you、we 等复数意义的人称代词时，谓语动词一概与 there 保持数的一致，用单数。如：

［**例10**］ There is you—and here is the rest of the universe.

有你——而且，还有世上其他人。

［**例11**］ In the intervals, Walter darling, there's you.

［**例12**］ There is but me two.

只有我们两人。

Quirk 等认为，在大多数情况下，there 是作分句的主语，他们提出了三条理由：

第一，在 there 存在句中，即使"真正的主语"是复数，谓语动词也可以用单数。如：

［**例13**］ There's some people in the waiting room.

候诊室里有一些人。

（与"There are some people in the waiting room."并列使用）

第二，在 yes-no 疑问句和附加疑问句中作主语。如：

［**例14**］ Is there any more soup? 还有汤吗？

［**例15**］ There's something wrong, is there?

出了毛病，是吗？

第三，在不定式或-ing 分词的非限定分句中作主语。如：

［**例16**］ I don't want there to be any misunderstanding.

我不希望产生任何误解。

［**例17**］ He was disappointed at there being so little to do.

他对没有多少事情可做感到失望。

[**例18**]　There having been trouble over this in the past，I want to treat the matter cautiously.

对这些事，以前曾有过麻烦，因此，我想小心为之。

因此，把 there 看作主语是不容置否的了。只不过它与常见的"首位主语"（starting-point subject）有所不同，它是"形式主语"，或称为"表层主语"（surface subject）。"语法主语"（grammatical subject）即没有多少语义的主语。谓语动词后面的名词词组才是"真正主语"（real subject）或实义主语（notion subject）。

第三章　There 存在句中的谓语动词和 There 存在句的分类

一、there 存在句中的谓语动词

能够用于 there 存在句中的动词，大多是能够表示"存在"意义的动词。动词 to be 是最典型的表示"存在"和"处所"意义的动词。因此，"there be + NP"就成为存在句最普通的结构。用于 there 存在句中的动词 to be 可以是一般现在时、一般过去时或一般将来时。如：

[**例 1**]　There is a good reason for doing all this.

有充分理由做这一切。

[**例 2**]　There are some pictures hanging on the wall.

墙上挂着几张画。

[**例 3**]　There was very little work done that day.

那天做完的工作很少。

[**例 4**]　There will be many problems with this.

这将有许多问题。

也可以是现在完成时、过去完成时或将来完成时。如：

[**例 5**]　There have been many such incidents.

［例 6］　　Nearby there have been a fight in full progress.

［例 7］　　Earlier there will have been many false starts.

也可以是情态动词加动词不定式。如：

［例 8］　　There must be very few cities that are not threatened by pollution.

很少有城市不受污染的威胁。

［例 9］　　There can be very little doubt about his guilt.

对他的罪行不会有多少疑问。

［例 10］　　There must be drinks if you wait a bit.

如果你等一会儿，可能会有酒。

［例 11］　　There should be a stronger light on the staircase.

楼梯上的电灯还应该强一点。

［例 12］　　There used to be a cinema here before the war, isn't there?

战前这儿曾有一座电影院，是吗？

也可以是情态动词加不定式的完成式。如：

［例 13］　　There may have been a handful of tanks, but an army there was not.

可能有过一些坦克，但是一支陆军却是不曾有的。

［例 14］　　If the police hadn't reached quickly, there could have been a bad accident.

要不是警察来得快，本来会发生严重车祸的。

［例 15］　　There can't have been much traffic so late at night.

这么晚了，路上不可能有多少车辆了。

［例 16］　　There must have been a mistake.

这一定是个错误。

[例 17] Oh, it wasn't so bad, only there ought to have been a little more cabbage.

哦，味道不坏，只是应该多放点卷心菜。

也可以是跟助动词加不定式 be。如：

[例 18] There's going to be a test on Friday.

星期五有个测验。

[例 19] There's to be an investigation.

必须进行调查。

[例 20] There's sure to be some rain tonight.

晚上一定会下雨。

[例 21] There's likely to be a large audience.

观众会很多。

[例 22] You mark my words, there's got to be war with Turks.

你记住我的话，会跟土耳其人打仗的。

[例 23] There seems to be no doubt about it.

对此似乎无可怀疑。

[例 24] There appears to be something wrong with the engine.

发动机似乎出了故障。

但是，be 通常不用于进行时。如不说：

[例 25] ※There is being a book on the desk.

除动词 to be 外，其他一些动词也可用于 there 存在句。如：

[例 26] There rose in his imagination grand vision of a

world empire.

[例27]　　Presently there came in a young man with thin, black hair, an enormous nose, and a face so long that it reminded you of a horse.

[例28]　　There followed the 1914 – 1918 war.

[例29]　　In the cottage there lives a family of six.

[例30]　　There sprang up a wild gale that night.

[例31]　　There took place an elaborate ceremony in honor of the visiting dignitaries.

[例32]　　There entered a strange figure dressed all in black.

用于 there 存在句中的动词，大都表示"存在""到达""坐落""发生""出现"等意义。这些动词可以分为以下三类。

第一，表示运动的动词（verbs of motion），如：arrive、arise、appear、approach、blow、come、enter、fall、flow、follow、grow、pass、ride、rise 等。

第二，表示开始或发生的动词（verbs of inception or happening），如：emerge、spring up、take place、happen、occur、flash 等。

第三，表示位置或状态的动词（verbs of stance），如：exist、live、remain、stand、lie 等。下面几点值得注意。

第一，这些动词通常都是不及物动词。及物动词一般不用于 there 存在句。如不说：

[例33]　　※There took a man a walk.

Quirk 等人对下面两句的可接受性表示怀疑：

［例 34］　？ There struck me a sudden idea.

［例 35］　？ There then addressed the meeting the new lead-er of the party.

不过，Jespersen 认为 there 存在句中的谓语动词是及物动词在以前并非罕见（formerly were not at all rare），如：

［例 36］　There met us at Bruges they whom…

Pontsma 也认为有时可以是及物动词，并举有一例：

［例 37］ Among the rest，there overlook us a little elderly la-dy.

可见，there 存在句中的谓语动词并非绝对不能是及物的，只是一般是不及物的。如果是由及物动词变来的不及物动词，当然可以。如：

［例 38］ There took place between him and his son a violent and painful scene.（take place = happen）

［例 39］ If there crossed her path a man with a strong protec-tive arm，he was whisked away.（cross her path = come）

如果及物动词用于被动语态，则是可以接受的，因为被动态表示一种状态；如果这种状态含有"存在"的意义，则可以用于 there 存在句。如可以说：

［例 40］ And days went on there was born a boy.

［例 41］ From the instant that the lips of the old lady touched Jill's，there was sealed a bond.

［例 42］ The school only took her mornings and for the after-noon there was proposed to her the teaching the little Baxeendales.

如果被动语态不含"存在"意义，则也不能用于 there 存在句。如不能说：

［**例 43**］ ※There were snatched quite a number of very valuable jewels.

there 存在句中的被动语态结构常用"there + be + NP + -ed 分词"来代替。试比较：

［**例 44a**］　There was presented by the mayor a gold medal.

［**例 44b**］　There was a gold medal presented by the mayor.

［**例 45a**］　There never was written such a story.

［**例 45b**］　There never was such a story written.

上面 a、b 两种用法都可以，只不过，后者用得更广，有时只能用后者，如：

［**例 45**］　There's a parcel come.

［**例 46**］　There's a new history of Indonesia published.

与例（45）和例（46）相应的不带 there 的句子分别为：

［**例 45a**］　A parcel has come.（不是 is come）

［**例 46b**］　A new history of Indonesia has been published.（不用 is published）

第二，在 there 存在句中，这些动词可以用于进行时态。如可以说：

［**例 47**］　There were standing in the rain a dozen hungry people.

但常见的是将 ing 分词放在名词词组后面，如：

［**例 48**］　There were a dozen hungry people standing in the rain.

通常的情况是：如果作真正主语的名词词组较长的话，就采用前者，否则就采用后者。试比较：

［**例 49**］　There were arising in Germany forces which were not in accord with what we conceived to be the democratic ideal.

［例50］　　I noticed that already there are some fish lying in the pond.

第三，并非所有的不及物动词都可以用于 there 存在句，通常只有前面讲过的三类动词才可以用于这种句型，其他动词，如描写动作的动词以及表示"消失""离开"的动词都不能用在 there 存在句。下面几句都不对：

［例51］　　※There sneezed a man.

［例52］　　※One night there broke out a fire.

［例53］　　※There complained a King.

［例54］　　※There coughed a welder near me.

［例55］　　※There disappeared ship after ship.

［例56］　　※There sailed away a ship.

应将 there 去掉，分别改为：

［例51a］　A man sneezed.

［例52a］　A fire broke out one night.

［例53a］　A King complained.

［例54a］　A welder near me coughed.

［例55a］　Ship after ship disappeared.

［例56a］　A ship sailed away.

但是，有些不表示"存在"意义的动词，间或也可以用于 there 存在句。如：

［例57］　　As the organization grew more complex there developed the necessity for keeping up the supply of officials.

［例58］　　On Dec. 28，1859 there died at Holly Lodge，Campden Hill，Thomas Babington，Lord Macaulay.

有些动词能否用于 there 存在句中，不同的语法学家看法并非相同。例如，Bruce L. Liles 认为"There grew wild flowers in the garden." 一句是错误的，应改为"Wild flowers grew in the garden."; 而 G. Scheurweghs 认为"There grew up around the hall a number of huts." 是对的。事实上，grow 用于 there 存在句是完全可以的。如可以说"There grew a tree.", 这里 grew 相当于 was。Rokert Krohn 在 *English Sentence Structure* 一书中举有一例：

[例59]　We hadn't seen many forests in Southern California north of San Francisco; there grew large forests of tall trees.

二、there 存在句的分类

根据其结构，there 存在句可以分为以下五类。

1. 带有状语的 there 存在句。

大多数 there 存在句都带有状语。我们可以用下列公式来表示：

there + be + NP + A

A 代表状语（adverbial）。

一般语法书认为 there 存在句必须要带地点状语（adverbial of place）。其实，除地点状语外，还可以是"时间状语"（adverbial of time）、"方式状语"（adverbial of manner）或其他状语。因为它不仅可以表示"在某处存在某人或某物"，而且还可以表示"在某个时候存在某人或某物"或"某物以某种方式或为什么而存在"。如：

[例1]　There is a man in the room.

房里有个人。

［例2］　There are fifteen students in my class.

我们班有十五个学生。（地点状语）

［例3］　There were several parties last night.

昨晚有几个聚会。（时间状语）

［例4］　There was a storm like a hurricane.

有过一场飓风一样的风暴。（方式状语）

［例5］　There is truth in what you say.

你讲的话中有道理。（方面状语）

有时，可以同时有两种或两种以上的状语，如：

［例6］　There weren't many students here yesterday.

昨天这里没有很多人。（here 地点状语，yesterday 时间状语）

［例7］　There has never been anybody like you here.

这里从来还没有像你这样的人。（never 时间状语，like you 方式状语，here 地点状语）

2．带有其他附加成分的 there 存在句。

这种 there 存在句虽不带状语，但带有其他附加成分，如 -ing 分词、-ed 分词、形容词、动词不定式、定语从句等。如：

［例1］　There was someone looking for you.

有人找你。

［例2］　There must be no more time wasted.

再不能浪费时间了。

［例3］　There won't be time enough.

时间不太够。

［例4］　There were about fifty persons present.

出席的大约五十人。

［例5］　There is nobody to type these letters.

没有人打这些信。

［例6］　There is a thermostat that constrols the temperature.

有一种恒温气可以控制温度。

3．无修饰存在句。

这种存在句仅说明某人或某物的存在，它是由"there + be + NP"组成，不带任何状语或其他附加成分。如：

［例1］　Is there any other business?

还有别的事吗？（会议主席在会议结束时所讲）

［例2］　There must be a more direct route.

一定会有更直达的路。

Quirk 等认为这种无修饰存在句实际上是上述两种存在句省略了最后一个成分而来的。这或者是由于上下文已清楚，省略不会引起误解；或者是由于说话人仅仅提到某物的存在，无须表示具体的时间或地点。上面两句均可理解为以下两句的省略形式：

［例1a］　Is there any other business（for the committee at this meeting）?

［例2a］　There must be a more direct route（than the one we're discussing）.

下面例3形式上像是"无修饰存在"句，实际上不是：

［例3］　There have always been wars.（Wars have always existed.）

Quirk 等在1972年出版的 *Grammar of Contemporary English* 一书中把这句看作"无修饰存在"句。但在1985年出版的 *A Comprehensive Grammar of the English Language* 一书中作了修改，

认为它是 SVA 存在句，即我们前面讲的带状语的存在句。只不过因为 always 是中位状语，位于句中而不在句尾而已。

4. 地点状语位于句首的 there 存在句。

有一种 there 存在句可以将地点状语放在句首，即 "A + there + V + S"。如：

[例1]　In the garden there was a sundial. (= There was a sundial in the garden.)

园子里有个日晷。

[例2]　On the hill there stands a tall tree. (= There stands a tall tree on the hill.)

山上有一棵大树。

[例3]　In front of the village there flows a stream. (= There flows a stream in front of the village.)

村子前面有一条小溪流过。

因为状语位于句首时，句中的主谓语通常必须倒装，因此，上述各句中的 there 可以省略：

[例1a]　In the garden was a sundial.

[例2a]　On the hill stands a tall tree.

[例3a]　In front of the village flows a stream.

在例1—例3 中，有无 there 意义上差别不大。但省略 there 的现象多见于书面语，在口语中以不省略较为自然。此外，用 there 是提供一种新信息，省略 there 只是具体地把事物提到人们面前。因此，主语特指某一具体事物而不提供新信息时，there 常省略。如：

[例4]　In the garden lay his father (John/the old lady) fast asleep.

265

此外，位于句首的可以是时间状语。如：

［例5］　That night there sprang up a wild gale.

那天晚上刮起了一阵狂风。

［例6］　In the afternoon there occurred an accident.

下午出了事故。

5．以动名词作主语的 there 存在句。

这种存在句的结构为"there + be + not + -ing"。如：

［例1］　There is no knowing whether we shall be able to get enough materials.

无法知道我们是否能够弄到足够的材料。

［例2］　There's no getting over it.　这是躲不了的。

［例3］　There is no denying the seriousness of the situation.

形式的严重性是无法否认的。

这种存在句中作主语的动名词必须是否定式，不能是肯定式。如不能说：

［例1a］　※There is knowing whether we shall be able to get enough materials.

这是一种表示强烈否定意义的结构，意为"It is impossible…"。上面几句分别相当于：

［例1b］　It is impossible to know whether we shall be able to get enough materials.

［例2a］　It is impossible to get over it.

［例3a］　It is impossible to deny the seriousness of the situation.

因此，这种句式实际上并非存在句。此外，还有一种表示否定的 there be 句型，其结构为"there is no use + （in）

-ing"。如：

　　［例4］　There is no use crying over spilled milk.

覆水难收。

　　［例5］　There's no use asking her—she doesn't know any-thing.

问她毫无用处——她什么都不知道。

这种结构实际上是"It is no use + -ing"结构的变体，而且"It is no use…"更为常见：

　　［例4a］　It is no use crying over spilt milk.

　　［例5a］　It is no use asking her—she doesn't know any-thing.

与"there is no use + -ing"结构类似的结构还有"there is no sense in + -ing"和"there is no point in + -ing"结构。如：

　　［例6］　There is no sense in making him angry.

惹他生气是没有道理的。

　　［例7］　There is no point in talking about it again.

没有必要再提这个。

这种句式实际上不是存在句。

第四章　There 存在句与基本句型的
转换关系

一、英语七种基本句型及其与 there be 句型的转换

英语的句子千变万化，但其基本句型也只不过七种。它们是：

1. SVC，如：

[例1]　Something must be wrong.

2. SV，如：

[例2]　A bus is coming.

3. SVA，如：

[例3]　Nobody was around.

4. SVO，如：

[例4]　A few people are getting promotion.

5. SVOC，如：

[例5]　Two bulldozers have been knocking the place flat.

6. SVOA，如：

［例6］　　A boy is putting the book on the bookshelf.

7. SVoO，如：

［例7］　　Something is causing her distress.

根据 Quirk 等人的意见，这七种基本句型如果符合以下两个条件，就都可以转换为 there 存在句。

第一，有一个不定特指的主语（indefinite subject）；

第二，谓语动词是动词 to be 的某种形式。上面七句都符合这两个条件，因此可分别转换为 there 存在句：

［例1a］　　There must be something wrong.

［例2a］　　There is a bus coming.

［例3a］　　There was nobody around.

［例4a］　　There are a few people getting promotion.

［例5a］　　There have been two bulldozers knocking the place flat.

［例6a］　　There's a boy putting the book on the bookshelf.

［例7a］　　There's something causing her distress.

被动语态也可以进行这种转换，如：

［例8a］　　A whole box has been stolen.

［例8b］　　There has been a whole box stolen.

［例9a］　　No shop will left open.

［例9b］　　There'll be no shops left open.

带定语从句的 there 存在句是由相应的基本句型转换而来的，如：

［例10a］　　There is a thermostat that controls the temperature.

［例10b］　　A thermostat controls the temperature.

二、关于转换的几个问题

1. 根据存在句的真正主语应是不定特指的名词词组的原则，基本句型中作主语的名词词组如被定冠词 the 或其他表示有定特指意义的限定词所修饰时，一般不能转换为 there 存在句。如：

[例1]　　The intruder is in the garden.

[例1b]　　※There is the intruder in the garden.

[例2a]　　The door was open.

[例2b]　　※There was the door open.

[例3a]　　James was at the party.

[例3b]　　※There was James at the party.

有时，虽然是受不定冠词（a 或 an）所修饰，但如果表示的不是不定特指，而是类指（generic reference），也不能直接转换为 there 存在句。对此，Jespersen 早就有所论述。他指出，如果主语受不定冠词的修饰，常用 there 存在句结构，除非这个不定冠词具有"类指"的意义（except when this is meant as the generic article designating the whole species）。试比较下列两组句子：

[例4a]　　A cow was crossing the road.

[例4b]　　There was a cow crossing the road.

[例5a]　　A plant needs light and water.

[例5b]　　※There is a plant that needs light and water.

例4 中的 a cow = a certain cow，表示不定特指，因而可以转换为 there 存在句；例5 中的 a plant = any（every）plant，表

类指，是指植物类的任何一株，而不是某一株，译成汉语时，应为"植物需要光和水"，而不是"有一株植物需要光和水"，因此，不能转换为 there 存在句。"There is a plant that needs light and water." 一句本身不错，只是与原句语义相差甚远，因而不能视作转换。但例 5a 可转换为：

　　[例 5c]　　There is no plant that doesn't need light and water.

这句意为"没有植物不需要光和水"，即"凡植物都需要光和水"，因而是正确的。

2. 同不定冠词一样，零冠词表示不定特指时，可转换为 there 存在句；表类指时，不能转换。试比较：

　　[例 1a]　　Weeds must have been growing in the garden.

　　[例 1b]　　There must have been weeds growing in the garden.

　　[例 2a]　　Water will soon be flooding the street.

　　[例 2b]　　There will soon be water flooding the street.

　　[例 3a]　　Tigers are dangerous animals.

　　[例 3b]　　※There are tigers that are dangerous animals.

　　[例 4a]　　Water is composed of hydrogen and oxygen.

　　[例 4b]　　※There is water that is composed of hydrogen and oxygen.

零冠词是表示不定特指还是类指，其检验的方法是借助于 some。如果以 some 替代零冠词，句子仍然成立的话，是不定特指；如果加 some 后，句子不成立的话，则是类指。上面例 1 和例 2 中的 weeds、water 都表不定特指，因为加 some 后原句仍成立，因此，可转换为 there 存在句：

［例1c］　　Some weeds must have been growing in the garden.

［例2c］　　Some water will soon be flooding the street.

在例 3 和例 4 中，tigers、water 表类指，因为加上 some 后
原句不成立：

［例3c］　　※Some tigers are dangerous animals.

［例4c］　　※Some water is composed of hydrogen and oxygen.

**3. 表示某处存在某人某物，如果作主语的是不定特指的
名词词组的话，常用 there 存在句。一般语法学家都认为下面
两句尽管在语法上是对的，但不合习惯：**

［例1a］　　A desk is on the platform.

［例2a］　　Some books were on the shelf.

习惯上要说：

［例1b］　　There is a desk on the platform.

［例2b］　　There were some books on the shelf.

也有的语法学家认为前者是错误的。如 Michael Swan 把
"A hole is in my tights." 之类的句子当作典型错误；我国学者
张其春先生在《简明英汉辞典》中把 "A tree is in the garden." 当作病句，认为只能说 "There is a tree in the garden."
还有的认为两种用法都可以，只是用 there 存在句表示强调。
如美国语言学家 Jeanne H. Herndon 在 *A Survey of Modern Grammar* 一书中指出："A fire is across the street." 一句，fire 放在
句首，就不太着重，因而也就不太强调。如果是一场大火，人
们就会把 fire 放在更加强调的位置，因此会说 "There's a fire
across the street."。用 there 与否，虽然并不一定表示"火"有

大小差别，但是 there 句型表示强调却是千真万确的，因为它符合末端中心（end focus）的原则。

我们同意大多数语言学家的看法，像"A desk is on the platform."之类的句子，符合语法，但不大符合习惯，因此，通常以"There is a desk on the platform."代替。因为被不定冠词所修饰的名词词组很显然是传递新信息，而新信息通常不位于句首的位置，因此，常需要借助 there，而将它置于谓语之后。但是，例外是有的。

首先，如果带不定冠词的名词词组带了一个分裂的后置修饰语，则是可以的。试比较下列两组句子：

[例 3a]　　A bird is in that tree.

[例 3b]　　There is a bird in that tree.

[例 3c]　　A bird is in that tree which I've never seen around here before.

[例 4a]　　An idea is in his head.

[例 4b]　　There is an idea in his head.

[例 4c]　　An idea is in his head that the rest of us are against him.

其次，不定冠词表示类指时，不用 there 存在句，如：

[例 5a]　　A tree is a living organism.

[例 5b]　　※There is a tree that is a living organism.

当句子的主语是 some、any、no、somebody、anybody、nobody、something、anything 或 nothing 时，常用 there 存在句。如：

[例 6]　　There are some people outside.

外面有些人。

［**例7**］　Is there anybody at home?

有人在家吗?

［**例8**］　There is nothing in the fridge.

冰箱里一点东西也没有。

有时只能用 there 引导。如:

［**例9**］　There was no wind. (不说: ※No wind was.)

4. 谓语动词是进行时或被动语态的句子,转换为 there 存在句时,原句中的-ing 分词和-ed 分词通常转换为名词词组的后置修饰语。如:

［**例1a**］　A girl was water-skiing on the lake.

［**例1a**］　There was a girl water-skiing on the lake.

一个女孩子在湖上滑水。

［**例2a**］　More Americans have been killed in road accidents than in all the wars since 1900.

［**例2b**］　There have been more Americans killed in road accidents than in all the wars since 1900.

自1900年以来,在交通事故中死去的美国人比在所有战争中死去的美国人还多。

但间或也有因修辞的需要把-ing 分词和-ed 分词置于名词词组之前。如:

［**例3a**］　Quite a number of very valuable jewels were stolen.

［**例3b**］　There were stolen quite a number of very valuable jewels.

很多贵重的珠宝被盗了。

例3中,由于名词词组较长,若将 stolen 放在句尾会显得头重脚轻,使句子失去平衡。

5．在基本句型 **SVC** 中，只有当 **C** 是不表示固有特点（**permanent property**）的形容词时，才能转换为 **there** 存在句。如：

　　［例1a］　Something is wrong.

　　［例1b］　There is something wrong.

　　［例2a］　Several students were ill.

　　［例2b］　There were several students ill.

如果 C 是表示固有特点的形容词，则不能转换。如：

　　［例3a］　Several students were tall.

　　［例3b］　※There were several students tall.

6．基本句型中的谓语动词是除 **to be** 以外的其他动词时，有时也可以转换为 **there** 存在句。如：

　　［例1a］　A thunder storm came.

　　［例1b］　There came a thunder storm.

　　［例2a］　A dozen hungry people were standing in the rain.

　　［例2b］　There were a dozen hungry people standing in the rain.

　　［例2c］　There were standing in the rain a dozen hungry people.

　　［例3a］　Many great changes have occurred in Beijing since 1949.

　　［例3b］　There have occurred many great changes in Beijing since 1949.

　　［例4a］　Nothing more healthy exists than a cold shower.

　　［例4b］　There exists nothing more healthy than a cold shower.

7. 除基本句型以外，还有一种没有动词的揭示语（**block language**），以及广播评论中的省略句，它们表示存在的意思，因此，可以转换为 there 存在句。如：

［例1a］　　Danger!

［例1b］　　There is danger!

有危险!

［例2a］　　Men at work overhead.

［例2b］　　There are men at work overhead.

上面有人在操作。

［例3a］　　No way out.

［例3b］　　There is no way out.

毫无办法。

［例4a］　　No exit.

［例4b］　　There is no exit.

不得通行。

［例5a］　　No arrest without warrant.

［例5b］　　There must be no arrest without warrant.

没有证据不得实施逮捕。

［例6a］　　Two players wounded.

［例6b］　　There are two players wounded.

两个球员受了伤。

揭示语和广播评论的省略句短小精悍、言简意赅。尽管语义上相当于一个存在句，实际上，一般无须作这种转换。

此外，with（或 without）词组，有时也会有"存在"的意思，因此，也可以转换为 there 存在句。试比较下面几句：

［例7a］　　With a taxi soon available, Dr. Lowes was able

to catch the train.

[**例**7b]　　There was soon a taxi available and Dr. Lowes was able to catch the train.

[**例**7c]　　There soon being a taxi available，Dr. Lowes was able to catch the train.

很快就打上了出租车，洛斯博士赶上了火车。

第五章　There 存在句中谓语动词后的
名词词组的功能

在第二章里，我们谈到 there 存在句中 there 的词性和句法功能。我们认为 there 是虚词，在句中置于主语的地位，作"形式主语"（formal subject）。既然确定了 there 的"形式主语"的地位，就不难确定动词后面的名词词组的"真正主语"（real subject）的地位。绝大多数语法学家都认为动词后面的名词词组是"真正主语"或"实义主语"（notion subject）。但是，也有的语法学家主张把这种名词词组归入谓语部分。其理由如下。

第一，there 存在句中的谓语动词并非总是与后面的名词词组保持数的一致。在许多场合下，即使后面的名词词组是复数形式，谓语动词也可用单数形式。如：

［例1］　There is five shillings to pay.

要付五先令。

［例2］　There is some paper, a dictionary and two note-books on the desk.

桌上有一些纸、一部词典和两个笔记本。

［例3］　There's some people（that）I'd like you to meet.

我想要你会见一些人。

第二，"形式主语"之后不一定总是带有"实义主语"，只有"形式主语"或"虚词主语"而没有"实义主语"的句子是极其寻常的。如：

[例4]　　It is raining.

[例5]　　It is five o'clock.

[例6]　　It's getting dark.

[例7]　　It's me.

因此，there 存在句也可以只有"形式主语"，而没有"实义主语"。

第三，主语通常表示已知信息（known information），谓语则表示新信息（new information），新信息最重要的部分通常出现在句尾，因此，there 存在句中的名词词组应看作谓语的一部分。

以上看法是从句子的语义结构（semantic structure）着眼，有一定道理。但是，从整体上看，还是把它看作"真正主语"或"实义主语"为好，其理由如下。

第一，尽管 there 存在句中的动词有时可以不与其后面的名词词组保持数的一致，这或者是由于"概念上的一致"原则，或者是由于"邻近一致"原则（principle of proximity），或者是由于习惯，在口语中，说话人还没有来得及考虑后面的主语是单数还是复数时，就说出了 there is 的缘故。如：

[例8]　　There is some magazines here.

这里有几本杂志。

[例9]　　There is a pen, a few envelops and some paper on the desk.

桌上有一支笔，几个信封和一些纸。

但是，在大多数情况下，there 存在句中的谓语动词必须与其后面的名词词组保持数的一致。

此外，主谓不一致的情况的存在并不能改变名词词组的主语功能。我们知道，英语主谓语不一致现象不仅在 there 存在句中存在，而且在其他场合也存在。试比较：

［例 9］ What she said is correct.

她说的话是对的。

［例 10］ What he left me are but a few old books.

他给我留下的只是几本旧书。

［例 11］ What I saw was two books.

我见到的是两本书。

［例 12］ What they want are promises.

他们要的是许诺。

what 从句作主语时，谓语动词通常用单数，因此，用的是单数 is 和 was。在例 10 和例 12 中，虽然也是 what 从句作主语，但由于受作表语的复数名词的影响，谓语动词用复数 are。我们并不因为其谓语动词与其后的复数意义的名词一致，而将复数意义的名词词组看作主语。在口语中，同 there's 一样，where's 也可以带复数主语。试比较：

［例 13］ There's some children at the door.

门口有几个孩子。

［例 14］ Where's those records I lent you?

我借给你的那些唱片在哪儿？

难道，where 也看作主语吗？

第二，there 存在句中的 there 与 it 确实有相似之处，如例 15 和例 16 所表示的意思相同：

[例15]　There blew a great gale.

[例16]　It blew a great gale.

刮了一阵大风。

但严格来说，这两句的结构不相同。例 15 中的 blew 是不及物动词，a great gale 是主语，为了强调，用 there 来引导，引起主谓语倒装。例 16 中的 blew 虽然也是不及物动词，但是，它带了一个意义与之相近的 a great gale 作同源宾语，it 是主语。英语中，it 这个词的用法很多，其中之一就是作无人称主语，表示时间、天气、距离等，如 "It is raining." "It is five o'clock." "It's getting dark." 三句都是这种用法，it 是代词，作主语，并非形式主语。只有当 it 作先行词，代替后面由不定式、动名词或从句表示的主语时，it 才是"形式主语"。由此可见，既然有"形式主语"，就必然有"真正主语"。it 是如此，there 也不例外。

第三，英语句子中，主语通常表示已知信息，谓语表示新信息，新信息通常出现在句尾。这叫作"末端重心"（end focus）。因此，谓语通常在主语的后面。但是，为了强调，也可以把主语后移。如：

[例17]　It's no use warning him.

警告他是没有用的。

句中用 it 作形式主语，而把"真正主语" warning him 后移，放在句尾，达到强调的目的。there 存在句也就是用 there 作先行词，而把"真正主语"后置的一种强调手段。其作用就是为了吸引听者或读者的兴趣与好奇，到句末才说出主要内容。

第四，有一类将地点状语位于句首的 there 存在句，there

往往可以省略，而全句意义不变，这时，后置名词词组作主语更是显而易见的了。如：

[例18] About a mile away from us (there) was a railroad bridge across a deep, narrow valley.

在离我们一英里远的地方，有一座铁桥横跨过峡谷。

[例19] At the foot of the mountain (there) stood a temple.

在山脚下有一座庙宇。

第五，从转换语法角度看，there 存在句都是由基本句型转换而来的，是将作主语的名词词组移至动词后面，再在原来的空位上插入一个虚词 there。这样，there 就成了"形式主语"，后移了的名词词组成了"真正主语"。试比较：

[例20a] A boy is outside.

[例20b] There is a boy outside.

[例21a] Nothing is wrong.

[例21b] There is nothing wrong.

因此，我们认为，there 存在句中谓语动词后面的名词词组应看作"真正主语"或"实义主语"。

第六章　There 存在句中的主语[*]

一、there 存在句的主语可以是具有确定意义的名词词组

当代大多数语法学家都认为，there 存在句中的主语通常应该是表示不确定的人或物，即作主语的名词词组通常被不定冠词、零冠词及 another、no、some、any、many、much、few、little、several 等表示不确定意义的限定词所修饰。如：

[例 1]　　There is a book on the desk.

[例 2]　　There's ice on the lake.

[例 3]　　There are no children in this house.

[例 4]　　There is someone at the door.

[例 5]　　Was there any soap in the bathroom?

[例 6]　　I don't know how many people there are for lunch.

[例 7]　　There is much truth in what he says.

there 存在句中的主语能否是表示确定意义的人或物？也

---

*　此章以《试论 There 存在句中的主语》为题发表在《现代外语》1989 年第 2 期，pp. 51 – 56，收入本书稍有改动。

就是说，there 存在句中谓语动词后面的名词词组能否被定冠词 the 或 my、this、that 等表示确定意义的限定词所修饰呢？不少语法书对此持否定态度，认为当一个句子有一个肯定的主语时，一般不用 there is。如不说：

[例8]　　※There was the door open.（应为：The door was open.）

章振邦主编的《新编英语语法》（1983）也认为，"作为 there 存在句真正主语的名词词组一般都是泛指的"。有的语法书对此避而不谈，但所举例则全是表示不确定的人和物，如张道真的《实用英语语法》，薄冰、赵德鑫的《简明英语语法手册》。是否 there 存在句中的主语真的不能是表示确定的人或物呢？请看下列例句：

[例9]　　—Have we any loose cash in the house?

　　　　　—Well，there's the money in the box over there.

[例10]　　I said to myself："There's the kind of man you'd like to take home and introduce to your mother and sister."

[例11]　　Well，we'll think about it，and then we'll look through his bits of things and make a list of them：There's all the furniture in his room.

[例12]　　Then there awoke in me the wish to build shops of my own.

[例13]　　There is the need for a local bath house that is now being met.

[例14]　　Almost before I had grasped her meaning there was the flutter of a dress and the crunch of leather boots and Tom and Daisy were back at the table.

[**例15**]　Then there shot through Philip's mind the recollection of the money he had seized.

[**例16**]　There was，too，his habit of not coming up until quite late.

[**例17**]　There's John；he might be interested.

[**例18**]　—Who else should we invite?

　　　　　—Well，here's John，and the people upstairs.

例 9 ～例 17 各句中的主语都是确定的人或物，即作主语的名词词组带有一个表示确定意义的限定词 the、his 或者本身是专有名词。可见问题不在于表确定意义的人或物的名词词组能否在 there 存在句中作主语，而在于什么情况下可以作主语。

二、表示确定意义的名词词组作 there 存在句的主语的三种情形

Quirk 等 1972 年出版的 *A Grammar of Contemporary English* 一书中注意到表示确定意义的名词词组可以作 there 存在句的主语这一现象。在肯定存在句的主语应是表不确定意义的名词词组的同时，在不同的地方指出了三种例外情况。

第一，对表示存在的疑问句作答时。如：

[**例1**]　—Is there anyone coming to dinner?

　　　　　—Yes，there's Harry and here's also Mrs. Jones.

—有人来吃饭吗?

—有。有哈里，还有琼斯夫人。

第二，there 存在句中作主语的名词被形容词最高级所修饰，表示感叹的意味时。如：

［例2］ There's the oddest-looking man standing at the front door!

一位样子非常古怪的人站在门口。

第三，名词词组受到动词不定式修饰时。如：

［例3］ There's the man next door to consider.

隔壁那一位应加以考虑。

随后，在1985年出版的另一巨著 *A Comprehensive Grammar of the English Language* 中，Quirk 等基本上仍持此观点，只是作了一些修改。在第一种例外中加进了"当确定的名词词组传递新信息时"，将"There's the oddest-looking man standing at the front door!"一句中的感叹号改为句号，并指出这里的定冠词 the 相当于不定冠词 a。全句等于：

［例2a］ There's a man of the oddest appearance standing at the front door.

这些修改使得他们对 there 存在句中作主语的名词词组什么时候能够表示确定的人或物的观点更趋明确：

第一，在回答表示存在的问题，如果名词词组能够传递新信息时；

第二，名词词组受形容词最高级所修饰，这时 the 相当于 a，而且并不一定表示感叹意味；

第三，名词词组受动词不定式所修饰时。

此外，Quirk 等还增添了一个例句：

［例4］ There are several animals commonly depicted in heraldry, for instance, there is the lion.

他们并未指出句中的 the lion 的用法。不过，很明显，这里的 the 是表示一个类型或一个例子。美国语言学家 Evans 在

A Dictionary of Contemporary American Usage 中指出，there be 句型中的主语用 the、this、my 等词修饰是作为一个类型、一个例子提出的。

上述这些提法解决了 there 存在句中可以用表示确定意义的人或物的名词词组作主语的大部分问题，但不是全部。前面例 9～例 12 可作此解释，但例 13～例 18 却无法用此观点解释。

究竟如何解释这类现象？there 存在句中作主语的名词词组什么时候可以被 the 等表示确定意义的限定词所修饰？这有待于我们进一步研究，特别需要探讨一下英语冠词——不定冠词 a(n)、定冠词 the 以及零冠词——的用法，因为它与 there 存在句作主语的名词词组能否是确定的人或物有直接关系。

三、there 存在句的主语与名词词组冠词的用法

我们知道，there 存在句中最重要部分是句尾的名词词组，它是句子的核心，是句子所要传递的新信息。因此，there 存在句中作真正主语的名词词组必须符合传递新信息的特点。只要能传递新信息，名词词组不论被什么限定词所修饰，都可作 there 存在句中的主语。因此，我们首先要讨论一下冠词的含义。

英语冠词有两个主要用法：一个是表示类指（generic reference），另一个是表示特指（specific reference）。我们先看看表示特指的用法。特指又可分为不定特指（indefinite specific reference）和有定特指（definite specific reference），不定特指通常是由不定冠词 a(n) 或零冠词表示的，表示"某一个"

或"某一些"的意思，通常用来指前面没有提到过的人或事，具有新信息的特点，因此，常用于 there 存在句中。如：

［例1］　There is a cherry tree in my garden.

［例2］　There are roses in the flower beds.

例 1 中的 a cherry tree = a certain cherry tree；例 2 中的 roses = some roses。

有定特指主要是由定冠词 the 表示的。表示有定特指时，the 有以下含义。

第一，后照应（cataphoric reference），即照应上文已经提到的人或事。如：

［例3］　John bought a TV and a video recorder，but he returned the video recorder.

句中 the video recorder 指的是前面已经提到的那同一台录像机，the 是从后面照应上文已出现的 a，因而叫做后照应。这里被照应的对象 video recorder 在上文中是直接出现的，因而是直接后照应（direct cataphoric reference）。有时，被照应的对象并非直接出现，而是间接出现，即根据常识进行推论而出现的，这叫作间接后照应（indirect cataphoric reference），如：

［例4］　John bought a bicycle，but when he rode it，one of the wheels came of.

句中上文并未提到"车轮"，但是提到"自行车"，而"自行车"必然有车轮，这是不言而喻的，因此，the wheels 是间接后照应。

第二，前照应（anaphoric reference）。与后照应相反，前照应是从前面照应后面的，即 the 照应名词中心词后面的修饰语。如：

[例5]　　John returned the radio he bought yesterday.

[例6]　　The President of Mexico is to visit China.

[例7]　　The girls sitting over there are my cousins.

前面我们所讨论的间接后照应实际上是前照应的一种省略结构：

[例4a]　　John bought a bicycle, but when he rode it, one of the wheels（of the bicycle）came off.

第三，情景照应（situational reference），即指说话当时听、说双方定会知道的事物。如：

[例8]　　Close the door, please. （指这房里未关上的那扇门）

[例9]　　What is the climate like? （指正在谈论的那个地区的气候）

[例10]　　I declare that the meeting is over. （指正在开的这个会）

第四，定冠词 the 还可以用在一些公用事业名称的名词前，如 the radio、the television、the telephone、the paper、the theater、the post、the mail、the train 等。Quirk 称之为 sporadic reference，姑且译为"单个照应"。此外，同不定冠词、零冠词一样，定冠词还可以表示类指。试比较：

[例11a]　　The bull terrier makes an excellent watchdog.

[例11b]　　A bull terrier makes an excellent watchdog.

[例11c]　　Bull terriers make an excellent watchdog.

上面三句中，定冠词 the、不定冠词 a 和零冠词都表示类指，意义基本上相同，因此，三例都可译为"短毛狼是最好的看门狗"。当然，细微的差别是有的：the 强调整个这一类，把它作为一个整体；a 表示这一类中的任何一个；零冠词强调这一类中的所有的个体。

四、定冠词修饰的名词词组作 there 存在句的主语时须注意的几个问题

一般语法书说 there 存在句中的主语通常不能被 the 修饰，恐怕指的只是当 the 表示后照应时。the 表示后照应时，确实不能用来修饰 there 存在句中的主语。如不能说：

[例1]　　※There's the book on the desk.

[例2]　　※There's the pen in the bag.

例 1 和例 2 中的 the book、the pen 一定是上文已经提到过的特定的书和笔，因而，是已知的信息，不是新信息，自然不能充当 there 存在句中的主语。

至于其他含义的 the，则完全可以用来作 there 存在句中主语的限定词。请看下列例句：

[例3]　　Then there awoke in me the wish to build shops of my own.

然后我产生了一种自己开店的想法。

[例4]　　There is the possibility of what is said of him being false.

有关他的说法可能是假的。

[例5]　　There are the eggs all broken.

所有的蛋都打碎了。

[例6]　　There was the time when minister of the local

church had seen a school boy creeping into the church late one eve-ning.

　　有过那么一次，教长在一天夜里看见一个男孩爬进了教堂。

　　例 3 中用了 the wish，正如 Quirk 所说，是因为其后有动词不定式作后置修饰语。例 4 ～ 例 6 的 the possibility、the eggs、the time 虽无动词不定式修饰，却分别受介词短语、-ed 分词或定语从句所修饰，因而成了有定特指。这几句中的 the 都不是后照应，而是前照应，照应名词中心词后面的定语（动词不定式、介词短语或分词）或定语从句。the 实际上表示不确定的意义，相当于 a；之所以用 the，完全是由于它后面的修饰语的缘故，而不是指前面已提到的事物，因而它传递的是新信息。有时，表示前照应的 the 可以采用省略形式，即省略被照应的对象。如：

　　[例 7]　There's the man next door (to consider).

　　[例 8]　—Have we forgotten anyone?

　　　　　—Yes, there's the man with a stick (that we have forgotten).

　　再请看下列例句：

　　[例 9]　The window was so wet I couldn't see, so I ran down stairs as I was and slipped out the back into the garden and there was the poor fellow at the end of the garden, shivering.

　　窗子湿得我没法看见外头，所以我来不及再披件衣服，急忙下楼，冲出后门，跑进花园里，可怜的人就在那儿，在花园到头的地方，冷得打哆嗦。

　　[例 10]　There is the difficulty.

这就是困难所在。

例 9 中的 the poor fellow 和例 10 中的 the difficulty 是指说话人和听话人都清楚的"那个人""那种困难",是情景照应,而不是后照应。这里,"那个可怜的人""那种困难"虽然是已知的,但提醒它们的存在却具有新信息的性质。

定冠词 the 表示类指时,完全可以用来修饰 there 存在句中作主语的名词词组,如:

[例 11] A phrase began to beat in my ears with a sort of heady excitement: "There are only the pursued, the pursuing, the busy, and the tired."

一个警句开始在我耳中令人兴奋地激动鸣响:"世界上只有被追求者和追求者,忙碌的人和疲倦的人。"

[例 12] There's the kind of man you'd like to introduce to your mother and sister.

有一种人你是愿意向你母亲和妹妹介绍的。

[例 13] There are several animals commonly depicted in heraldry; for instance, there is the lion.

在纹章学中通常描绘几种动物,如狮子。

例 11 中的 the pursued、the pursuing、the busy、the tired 很显然是表示类别,是指整个那一类人。定冠词 the 加在某些形容词、-ed 分词或-ing 分词的前面,可以表示类别。例 12 中的 the kind of man,例 13 中的 the lion 也不是特指某个人、某头狮子,而是指一类人、整个狮子类。因此,也是类指。the 表示类指时也不是指前面已经出现过的人或物,因此是新信息,可以充当 there 存在句的主语。值得注意的是,不定冠词 a(n)和零冠词表示"类指"时,反而不能用来修饰 there 存在句中的主语。如不能说：

[例14]　　※There is a plant that needs light and water.

[例15]　　※There are tigers that are dangerous animals.

因为表示类指时，a(n) 意为"某类人或物之中的任何一个"，零冠词意为"类别中的许多个体"，而 there 存在句中作主语的"a + 名词词组"表示"某一个"，零冠词表示"某一些"，不可能是"任何一个"或"许多个体"。如：

[例16]　　There is a boy in the room.

例16 中的 a boy 只能是某个具体的男孩，而不可能表示"任何一个男孩"。因此，表示类指的 a(n) 和零冠词不能用于 there 存在句是可想而知的。我们再来看看下面例子：

[例17]　　There's the oddest-looking man standing at the front door.

一位样子非常古怪的人站在前门边。

[例18]　　When, at last, she stopped there followed the strangest silence.

当她最后停住时，接着便是一片非常奇怪的寂静。

[例19]　　There's the first day of summer.

夏季的第一天。

[例20]　　There's the last supper.

最后的晚餐。

[例21]　　There were the same frantic changes of policy and format.

上面几句中，名词词组被 the 所修饰，都是语法结构的需要。例17 和例18 是因为形容词最高级之前必须要用定冠词，最高级可以用来起强调的作用。又如：

［**例 22**］　Isn't she the most beautiful woman （ ＝ an extremely beautiful woman ＝ a most beautiful woman）？

因此，例 17 和例 18 中的 the 相当于 a，可改为：

［**例 17a**］　There's a man of the oddest appearance standing at the front door.

［**例 18a**］　When, at last, she stopped there followed a very strange silence.

例 19 ～例 21 中用 the 是因为在序数词（包括表示次序的词，如 last、next 等）及 same 前通常要用 the。另据 Jespersen 的看法，that 和 those 有不定特指意思（indefinite meaning），that ＝ something, those ＝ some people, 因此，可以作 there 存在句中的主语。又如：

［**例 23**］　There was that in her manner which prepared us for what was coming.

［**例 24**］　There are those who believe it, though others are more sceptical.

that 还可以加在表示人的名词前。如：

［**例 25**］　Jacob, there is that old gentleman at our house with Mary.

［**例 26**］　There's that Lily, I'm sure I don't know what has come over her lately.

有时，表示举例说明某种情况或存在什么问题，这种情况和问题对听话者来说，具有新信息的作用，因而可以作 there 存在句的主语。如：

［**例 27**］　Many children like to play football. There is the child next door for example.

294

很多小孩喜欢踢足球。比方说，邻居的孩子就是一个。

［例28］　　Anyhow there's his insurance money.

还有他的保险金的问题。

例27是举例说明某种情况，具有新信息的性质，句中 for example 可有可无。例28表示"有什么问题"，是一种省略结构，这句相当于：Anyhow there's the question of his insurance money.

在特定的语言环境中，如 Quirk 等所说的在回答表示存在的问题时，there 存在句中作主语的还可以是专有名词，甚至是人称代词。如：

［例29］　　—Is there anyone in the office?（＝or Is it empty?）

　　　　　　—Yes，there's Harry.

［例30］　　…there is you—and there is the rest of the universe.

此外，据 Thomson 的意见，在 there 存在句中，有时虽然并不传递新信息，只是提醒对方回忆起某人或某物，以免忘记，因而具有新信息的作用。如：

［例31］　　—Who else should we invite?

　　　　　　—Well，there's John，and the people upstairs.

有时，当说话人向对方提出某种建议或说出自己的想法时，这种建议或想法对对方来说，无疑是新信息。如：

［例32］　　There's the family next door; we mustn't forget to invite them.

［例33］　　There's John; he might be interested.

［例34］　　There's also that new man, Johnson; have you seen him yet?

上述各句的含义为"What about trying…?",或"I have suddenly thought of…"。

综上所述,there 存在句中,作主语的名词词组不但可以被不定冠词、零冠词或其他表示不确定意义的限定词所修饰,而且也可以被定冠词 the 及其他表示确定意义的限定词所修饰。定冠词 the 只有当它表示后照应时,因为是指上文已经提到过的人或物,所传递的是已知信息而不是新信息,才不能用来修饰 there 存在句中的主语。而定冠词 the 的其他用法,包括前照应、情境照应、单个照应以及类指等,只要意义许可,完全可以用来修饰 there 存在句中作主语的名词词组。本来,传统语法学家并没有认为 there 存在句中作主语的不能是表示确定意义的名词词组。Poutsma、Jespersen、Curme 等在肯定大多数情况下 there 存在句的主语应是表示不确定的名词词组的同时,也都举了不少表示确定含义的例句。只是从 20 世纪 60 年代起,由于受转换语法的影响,一些语法学家才把 there 存在句的主语应是不确定的名词词组作一规则定下来。即使如此,也有不少语法学家具有不同意见,如 G. Scheurweghs、A. J. Thomson 都明确表示 there 存在句中作主语的名词词组可以是表示确定意义的。Quirk 等在 1972 年和 1985 年出版的两部巨著中均列举了不少例外的现象,实际上也就认为表确定意义的名词词组在 there 存在句中作主语的可能性。通过上面的分析,我们认为 there 存在句中的主语为确定的人或物大体上可归纳为以下几种情况:

其一,当主语被一后置定语所修饰,即 the 表示前照应时;

其二,当主语表示一种类型,即 the 表示类指时;

　　其三，当主语被形容词最高级、序数词或其他表示次序意义的词所修饰时；

　　其四，在回答"表示存在的问题"时；

　　其五，在"表示有什么问题"，或作为举例时。

第七章 There 存在句的主谓一致问题

英语中主语和谓语的一致关系是个非常复杂的问题。一般说来，主语为单数形式，谓语动词也采用单数形式；主语为复数形式，谓语动词也采用复数形式。如：

［例1］ The teacher is in the classroom.

老师在教室里。

［例2］ The students are doing their exercises.

学生们在做练习。

上述两句中的主语和谓语是从语法形式上取得一致，叫作语法一致（grammatical concord）。这是主谓一致关系中最重要的原则，我们通常讲的一致关系，就是指的这种语法一致。此外，还有概念上的一致原则（notional concord）和邻近一致原则（principle of proximity）。如：

［例3］ My family are all fond of playing table tennis.

我全家都爱打乒乓球。

［例4］ Four thousand dollars is more than she can afford.

她付不起四千美元。

［例5］ A needle and thread was given her, but she could not sew the button on.

给了她针线，可是她不会把纽扣缝起来。

例 3 中的 my family 尽管从语法上看是单数，但从意义上看是复数，因为它指的是"我家的家庭成员"，因此，谓语动词用复数 are。例 4 中的 four thousand dollars 从语法上看是复数，但从意义上看是单数概念，是看作一个总数，即一笔钱，因而谓语动词用单数 is。例 5 的 a needle and thread 看作同一件东西"针线"，是单数概念，因此，谓语动词也用单数 was given。

[例 6]　Where is your wife and children to stay while you are away？

你不在这儿的时候，你爱人和孩子在哪儿待呢？

[例 7]　On the left of each person is a table-napkin and a plate with a roll on it.

每个人的左边放着一块餐巾和一个盘子，上面放着一个花卷。

例 6 中的主语 your wife and children，例 7 中的主语 a table-napkin and a plate with a roll on it 明明都是复数，但由于靠近谓语动词的名词 your wife、a table-napkin 是单数，因此，谓语动词也用单数，这符合邻近一致的原则。

这三个原则对 there 存在句都适用，而且在 there 存在句中，不但有作真正主语的名词词组，而且还有一个作形式主语的 there 的问题，因此，there 存在句中的主谓一致关系问题变得更为复杂。不过，在大多数情况下，特别是在正式文体中，语法一致仍然起主导作用。下面例 8a、例 9a 正确，例 8b、例 9b 则不符合语法。

[例 8a]　There is a cherry tree in my garden.

我花园里有一株樱桃树。

［例9a］　　There are roses in the flower beds.

花圃里有许多种玫瑰花。

［例8b］　　※There are a cherry tree in my garden.

［例9b］　　※There is roses in the flower beds.

但是，在非正式文体中，用单数形式的 there is 或 there's 代替复数形式 there are 的情况却屡见不鲜。归纳起来有以下几种情况。

第一，当作真正主语的是表示度量、时间、钱数等复数名词时，往往把这些复数名词看作一个整体，谓语动词采用单数形式。如：

［例10］　　There is five pounds to pay to clear this debt.

要付 5 英镑才能偿还这笔债。

［例11］　　There's only a few handfuls of rice left.

只剩下几把米了。

［例12］　　There is only another two miles to go.

还要走两里路。

当然，如果把这些复数名词看作一个个的个体，谓语动词也可用复数形式。如：

［例13］　　There were three quarters of milk in the refrigerator.

冰箱里有 3 瓶四分之一磅的牛奶。

第二，用 and 连接的单数并列主语，如果在意义上指同一人、同一物、同一事或同一概念时，谓语动词采用单数形式。如：

［例14］　　There is a journalist and author waiting to see you.

有一个新闻记者兼作家要见您。（指同一人）

［例15］　　There is a watch and chain on the table.

桌上有一只上了链条的表。(指同一物)

[例 16]　There's a concert and dancing at school last night.
我们学校昨晚有音乐舞蹈会。(指同一事)

[例 17]　There was much laughing and joking at the party.
晚会上充满着嬉笑声。

[例 18]　There is more leisure and money about, so travel has become available to many people.

有更多的空闲和钱, 因此, 旅游对许多人来说就成为可能的事了。(同一概念)

这时, 即使两个并列成分中有一个为复数形式, 谓语动词也可用单数形式。如:

[例 19]　There is eggs and bacon for breakfast.
早餐吃蛋和咸肉。

[例 20]　There is duck and green peas for dinner.
晚餐吃鸭和青豆。

第三, 形式为复数、意义为单数的名词, 如 billiards、news、works、measles 等, 以及以-ics 结尾的表示学科名称的名词作主语时, 谓语动词也用单数形式。如:

[例 21]　There was only billiards, and the pianola to dance to.
只有台球, 还有跳舞伴奏用的自动钢琴。

[例 22]　There is an iron works in that region.
在那个地区有一个铁工厂。

第四, 两个或两个以上的并列主语, 靠近谓语动词的那一个是单数意义时, 谓语动词用单数。如:

[例 23]　Have you room for all of us? There's John, Fred, Anne and myself.

能容纳我们所有的人吗？我、约翰、弗雷德和安妮。

[例24]　　There is some paper, a dictionary and two note-books on the desk.

桌上有一些纸、一本字典和两个笔记本。

[例25]　　There was plenty of food, a good library and a battery wireless set.

有丰盛的食物、出色的图书馆和一部无线电收首机。

[例26]　　There is a book, a pen and a pencil on the desk.

书桌上有一本书、一支钢笔和一支铅笔。

有时，并列主语中的后一成分只不过是以后想起（after-thought）而加上去的。如：

[例27]　　There was biscuit left in their saddle bags, and some sausages.

例23～例25 符合概念一致原则，例26 和例27 符合邻近一致原则。此外，据 Jespersen 的意见，在口语中，当说话人还没有来得及考虑后面的主语是单数还是复数时，就说出 there is，如：

[例28]　　There's lots of people in the dining hall.

在餐厅里有许多人。

[例29]　　Sure, there's jobs. There is even Egbert's job if you want it.

当然，工作是有的，只要你肯干，甚至就可以顶埃格伯特的空缺。

[例30]　　There's some people I'd like you to meet.

我想要你见一些人。

[例31]　　Let's see, there's you and me and...

让我想想看，有你，有我，还有……

[**例32**] I'm sure there's burglars on the fire-escape.

我相信防火通道口那里有几个盗贼。

有时，甚至当同一名词的复数形式重叠使用时也可以用 there's，如：

[**例33**] There's cars and cars. (= There are all sorts of cars: some cars are good, others are bad.)

有各种各样的车（有好车也有坏车）。

[**例34**] There's cooks and cooks.

厨师有各种各样的。

这种用法是把 there is（there's）当作一种表达客观存在的一种固定形式，即不管其主语是单数还是复数，一律使用 there's 或 there is. Partridge 认为，there 存在句中的主语和动词数上的不一致情况很可能是从法语 il ya 类推而来的，美国语言学家 Evans 在他的 *A Dictionary of Contemporary American Usage* 中指出，在 there be 句型中，即使主语是复数时目前也有强烈的使用单数动词的趋势。有的人还认为，人们在讲话中，不管真正主语是单数还是复数，均使用 there's 的人占了绝大多数。这一切都说明，在口语中，there is 或 there's 代替 there are 的现象日益增加。不过，这还只局限于口语，书面语通常还是要遵循我们前面提到的三个原则。

在谈到 there 存在句作主语的名词词组是复数形式却可以跟单数形式动词时，潘欢怀教授认为，"不过用 is 时，一定要用 there's 这个缩写形式"。这个论断似乎过于绝对了一点。事实上，虽然用 there's 形式居多，但用 there is 形式也不是不可以的。如：

［**例 35**］　There is eggs and bacon for breakfast.

［**例 36**］　There is but we two.

［**例 37**］　Since I came here there has been—you.

there 存在句的动词除 be 外，还可以有其他动词。这时，自然不能用缩略形式。如：

［**例 38**］　There still remains a few wilderness areas on the continent.

第八章　There 存在句中名词词组的后续成分分析

一、后续成分为状语

大多数 there 存在句中除了主语、谓语和虚词 there 以外还带有其他成分，其中最主要的是状语。Eugene. J. Hall 在 *Grammar for Use* 一书中，以表格形式，将这种状语分为三类，如表 1 所示。

表 1　there 存在句的成分

1.	There	Be	Subject	Adverb of place
［例 1］	There	is	a lamp	on the table
［例 2］	There	are	some good books	in the library
［例 3］	There	are	four men	in the conference room
2.	There	Be	Subject	Adverb of time
［例 4］	There	is	a meeting	at 10 o'clock
［例 5］	There	was	a holiday	last month
［例 6］	There	will be	two holidays	next month

续上表

3.	There	Be	Subject	Adverb of manner
[例7]	There	was	a storm	like a hurricane

如表 1 所示，there 存在句主语的后续成分可以是地点副词、时间副词和方式副词，分别作地点状语、时间状语和方式状语。这些 there 存在句即带状语的 there 存在句。当然 there 存在句的状语不止这三类，还可以有表其他意义的状语，如方面状语（例8），比较状语（例9）：

[例8]　There is truth in what you say.

你讲的有道理。

[例9]　There are worse things than hard work.

还有比艰苦工作更糟的事情。

有些状语很难归于哪一类。如：

[例10]　There comes an end to all things.

任何事情都有个尽头。

[例11]　There was no doubt as to the crime being a political one.

毫无疑问，罪行是属于政治性质的。

很显然，例10 中的 to all things 和例11 中的 as to the crime being a political one 很难归纳为哪一类状语。我们姑且把它叫作其他状语。

二、后续成分是动词不定式或动词不定式词组

在 there 存在句中，作真正主语的名词词组可以被动词不定式所修饰。如：

[例1] There are still two more items to include in the pro-gramme.

还有两个节目要列入节目单。

[例2] There is no need to let such a trifle prey on your mind.

你无须为这区区小事而烦恼。

上述句中的动词不定式词组 to include…和 to let…都是作定语，分别修饰作主语的名词词组 two more items 和 no need。动词不定式作定语时，可以有其逻辑主语。如：

[例3] There's no reason for her to come so late.

她没有理由这么晚来。

作定语的动词不定式结构常可以代替定语从句。如：

[例4] There's plenty of work to do. （＝There's plenty of work that people must do.）

有许多工作要做。

用不定式属于口语体，而用定语从句属于生硬的正式文体（stiff formal）。

在 there 存在句中，作定语修饰主语的动词不定式常用主动语态，但表示被动意义，且可以用被动语态代替。试比较：

[例5a] There is so much work to do.

［例 5b］　There is so much to be done.

有这么多工作要做。

［例 6a］　There are many questions to settle.

［例 6b］　There are many questions to be settled.

有很多问题要解决。

什么时候用主动语态，什么时候用被动语态？并无什么固定不变的规则可循。有时仅仅是作者的个人爱好或偶然性。不过，一般说来，在口语中多用主动语态，有些习惯用法只能用主动语态。如：

［例 7］　There was never enough to eat. （i. e. We wanted to eat but did not have enough. ）

从来没有足够的东西吃。

［例 8］　There was the devil to pay with the girl's relations.

同这位女孩作亲戚会有麻烦的。

相反，有些习惯用法只能用被动语态。如：

［例 9］　There was not a sound to be heard. （i. e. No sounds were there. ）

听不到一点声音。

有时，用主动态或用被动态含义不同。试比较：

［例 10a］　There is nothing to do now. （I want to do something but cannot find anything to occupy me. = I have nothing to do. ）

现在没事干。

［例 10b］　There is nothing to be done now. （ = Nothing can be done. = We can do nothing now. = The situation is hopeless. ）

现在没有什么办法。

[例 11a]　There were no birds to see. （= Someone wanted to see some birds, but he could not.) 没鸟可看。

[例 11b]　There were no birds to be seen. （= No birds were there.) 看不见鸟。

[例 12a]　There was no general to send. （= No general could be sent.)

没将军可派。

[例 12b]　There was no general to be sent. （= It was determined that no general should be sent.)

不派将军了。

三、后续成分是形容词或形容词词组

[例 1]　There must be something wrong.

一定有什么坏事发生了。

[例 2]　There were many people sick with flu.

有很多人得了流感。

这两句中的形容词 wrong 及形容词词组 sick with flu 均作定语，可改为定语从句：

[例 1a]　There must be something that is wrong.

[例 2a]　There were many people who were sick with flu.

四、后续成分是-ing 分词或-ed 分词

[例 1]　There's a girl putting the kettle on.

有个女孩把水壶放上去了。

［例2a］　There are plenty of people getting promotion.

有许多人得到了提拔。

［例3］　There was very little work done that day.

那天做的工作很少。

［例4a］　There were twenty people hurt in the accident.

事故中有 20 人受了伤。

对 there 存在句中作主语的名词词组后面的-ing 分词和-ed 分词作什么成分的问题，不同的语法学家看法不尽相同。Jespersen、Curme 等把它们看作表语，即我们现在通常所称的主语补足语，因为它们说明主语的特征和状态。从句型转换角度来看，它们在基本句型中，本来就是作表语的。试比较：

［例5a］　There were many people sick with flu.

［例5b］　Many people were sick with flu.

［例2a］　There are plenty of people getting promotion.

［例2b］　Plenty of people are getting promotion.

［例4a］　There were twenty people hurt in the accident.

［例4b］　Twenty people were hurt in the accident.

而且，有时由于修辞的需要，可以把分词置于名词词组之前。如：

［例6］　There were stolen quite a number of very valuable jewels.

有许多珍贵的珠宝被盗。

这句如改为 "There are quite a number of very valuable jewels stolen."，则有些头重脚轻，句子失去平衡。这更加证明分词是属于谓语的一部分，即作表语。不过这种看法主要是从句型转换的角度出发。如果不从转换角度考虑，最好还是看作后置定语。国内大多数语法学家都持这种观点，因为它们实际上可看作一种省略的定语从句。如：

[例5a]　　There were many people sick with flu.

[例5c]　　There were many people who were sick with flu.

[例2a]　　There are plenty of people getting promotion.

[例2c]　　There are plenty of people who are getting promotion.

[例4a]　　There were twenty people hurt in the accident.

[例4c]　　There were twenty people who were hurt in the accident.

Hornby 把下面两句中的动词后面部分都看作主语：

[例7]　　There is no time for us to visit museum now.

现在我们没有时间去参观博物馆。

[例8]　　There was very little work done that day.

那天做的工作很少。

如果进一步分析一下，例7 的主语部分中的不定式词组 for us to visit the museum 自然只能看作定语，因此，例8 中的 -ed分词 done 看作定语也是理所当然的。

还有人认为，既然 there 存在句中的动词等于 exist，那么，不如把主语后面的-ing 分词和-ed 分词看作状语，说明谓语动词存在的状态，① 如：

[例9]　　There are lots of people talking，laughing and jostling at celebrations.

①　周定之:《关于 there be 句型》，载《外国语教学》1979 年第 5 期。

在庆祝大会上，人们谈笑风生，拥挤推搡。

这种看法不是没有道理的，因为句中的 talking，laughing and jostling 说明人们在大会上的情况，确实可看作状语。

综上所述，there 存在句中作主语的名词词组后面的-ing 分词或-ed 分词既可分析为表语，又可分析为定语或状语。不过，把它分析为定语似乎更恰当一些。

此外，-ing 分词作定语修饰 there 存在句中的主语时，有时主动形式表示被动意义。如：

［例9］　There is nothing doing.（＝There is nothing that can be done.）无事可做。

［例10］　There is a glorious dish of eggs and bacon making ready.（＝…that has been made ready.）

［例11］　I guessed there was some mischief contriving.（＝…being contrived.）

我猜想有人正在酝酿恶作剧。

五、后续成分为定语从句

［例1］　There are things that seem so far from being possible that the mind does not take them in.

有些事情看来明明不可能，所以脑子里也就不会有那种念头。

［例2］　There was no experienced person to whom she could turn for advice and few even to encourage what many thought would be a fruitless effort.

她缺少有经验的人可以请教，而且因为很多人认为那将劳而无功，因此，连鼓励她这样做的人也很少。

［例３］　There was something in his way which he could neither cut or move.

他在通道上遇到了一个障碍，既不能凿开又不能移动。

［例４］　At one time there were houses where that large factory now stands.

在现在这座大工厂所在地曾经有许多房子。

［例５］　There comes a time when patience ceases to be a virtue.

有时候忍耐不是一种美德。

［例６］　There wasn't a man in the barony but had a hundred songs in his head.　(but = that...not)

在男爵领地，没有一个人头脑里没有上百支歌。

上面各句中，that、which、who (whom)、whose、when、where 等引导的都是限制性定语从句。此外，除 that 以外，上述关联词还可引导非限制性定语从句。如：

［例７］　There is some little mistake，which will soon be put right. That's all，I am sure.

不过是一个小小的误会，马上就可以搞清楚的。没有什么大不了的，我可以肯定。

［例８］　Then there was Tommy Dukes，who had remained in the army，and was a Brigadier-General.

还有汤米·杜克斯。他一直在部队里，而且是位准将。

［例９］　There were reminiscences，as Jerry's friends reconvened.

there 存在句的主句和定语从句的时态可以相同，也可以不同。试比较：

　　［例 10 ］　　There were some paintings that were admired by everyone.

　　［例 11 ］　　There are some planets that were discovered by the accidents.

　　there 存在句中的定语从句，其关系代词 that、which、who（m）等，不但作宾语时常可省略（如例 12 和例 13），而且，在口语中，作主语时也往往省略（如例 14 ～例 16）：

　　［例 12 ］　　There is always something（that）you can do for me.

　　你总是可以为我做点事。

　　［例 13 ］　　There is a man（whom）you have met before.

　　有一个人你曾经见过。

　　［例 14 ］　　There is a man（who）wants to see you！

　　有人要见你。

　　［例 15 ］　　Julia, there's Miss Daly and Miss Power will take some refreshment.

　　朱莉亚，有一位戴莉小姐和一位包尔小姐要吃点心。

　　［例 16 ］　　There was a door（that）led into the kitchen.

　　有一条门通往厨房。

　　这种结构在都铎王朝时代，甚至更早期的英语中是屡见不鲜的，只是到 18 世纪英语"规范化"时期，才被认为不合语法。但是，由于这种结构言简意赅，富有很强的生命力，因此，不但没有被规范掉，反而在口语中广泛地使用，甚至在有插入语的情况下也可以这么用。如：

　　［例 17 ］　　There's no one, as far as I can see, has taken

their place！

据我看，没有谁能代替他们。

有时，后面带有两个定语从句，作主语的关系代词都可以省略。如：

[例18]　There was a man（that）came（who）said that he had bought many different magazines.

有个人来说他买了各种杂志。

在以 there 作为形式主语的定语从句中，作真正主语的关系代词，习惯上常常省略。如：

[例19]　The 9：15 is the fastest train（that）there is to Oxford.

九点十五分这趟车是到牛津最快的火车。

[例20]　The number of mistakes（that）there are in this homework is simply astounding.

在这份课外作业中错误简直多得惊人。

[例21]　I have seen all（that）there is left to see in the city.

市内未看完的我全看了。

[例22]　I have lost all（that）there is to love in life, death seems beautiful, a long, long rest.

我已失去了使我眷恋生命的一切；死在我看来是美好的，是一种长久的安息。

[例23]　This is the only reference there is on the subject.

这是目前这个问题的唯一资料。

例19～例23 各句中的 there is（are）作定语从句修饰前面的名词，句中作主语的关系代词都可以省略。这时，there is （are）实际上只不过起一种插入语的作用，因而也可以一并省略，而无损句子结构的完整。当然，there is（are）的有无，对句子的意义，却略有不同。there is（are）表示"存在"的意义，即在某时某地存在某物或事。试比较：

[例24a] This is the only reference on the subject.

这是这个问题的唯一资料。

[例24b] This is the only reference there is on the subject.

这是目前这个问题的唯一资料。

但是，如果是同位语从句，作连词的 that 通常不可省略。如：

[例25] The fact remains that there is no filling station here.

事实是这里仍然没有加油站。

六、后续成分是同位语从句

[例1] There is no doubt that the man is guilty.

毫无疑问，这个人是有罪的。

[例2] There is a suggestion that he be invited.

有人建议邀请他。

[例3] There is a saying that the third time is lucky.

俗话说第三次是幸运的。

[例4] There is no escaping the fact that we had made a great mistake.（＝There is no denying the fact…）

无法否认我们犯了个大错误。

以上各句中 that 引导的从句不是定语从句，而是同位语从句，表示与之同位的名词词组的实际内容。同位语从句与定语从句的区别在于：第一，引导同位语从句的 that 是连接词，不作句子成分，而引导定语从句的 that（which）、who 等是关系代词，作从句中某一成分（主语、宾语、表语等）。

第二，定语从句是修饰性的，修饰主句里作为先行词的名词词组的中心词，同位语从句是解说主句里的先行词所讲东西的实际内容，因此，带同位语从句的必须是尚需进一步解释、说明，使之意义完善的名词（词组），如 news、fact、belief、idea、answer、opinion、information、humour、truth 等。

试比较：

［例5a］　The news that had quickly spread through the town proved to be true.（定语从句）

迅速传遍全城的消息证明是真实的。

［例5b］　The news that our team had won proved to be true.（同位语从句）

我们队已经获胜这个消息证明是真实的。

第九章　There 存在句的疑问句和
祈使句形式

一、there 存在句的一般疑问句

同其他句型一样，there 存在句可以构成一般疑问句。如：

[例1]　There is a book on the desk.　→Is there a book on the desk？

[例2]　There are three tall women in the team.　→Are there three tall women in the team？

与其他句型不同的是，there 存在句构成一般疑问句时，是将动词 be 与作形式主语的虚词 there 易位，而不是与作真正主语的名词词组易位。试比较

[例3]　He is a worker.　→Is he a worker？

[例4]　There is a man in the room.　→Is there a man in the room？

回答时，通常也采用省略形式：

[例5]　—Is there a man in the room？

　　　　—Yes, there is.（No, there isn't.）

而不说：※Yes, a man is.（No, a man isn't.）

正因为如此，有的语法学家干脆把 there 看作主语，是不

无道理的。

二、there 存在句的特殊疑问句

there 存在句也可以构成各种特殊疑问句。如：

[例1]　There is a dog in the garden. 花园里有一只狗。

如对主语 a dog 提问，其问句形式为例 1a；如对状语 in the garden 提问，则为例 1b.

[例1a]　—What is there in the garden?（= What's in the garden?）

　　　　　—A dog.（There is a dog.）

—花园里有什么？

—一只狗。

[例1b]　Where is there a dog?

　　　　　—In the garden.

—什么地方有一只狗？

—花园里。

有人认为 where 和 there 并用似乎不太合理，实际上这样使用的很多。又如：

[例2]　Where is there a hotel?（= Is there a hotel? Where is one?）

哪里有旅馆？（= 有旅馆吗？在哪儿？）

试比较：

[例2a]　Where is the hotel?

旅馆在哪里？（确实知道有旅馆。）

英国作家劳伦斯在 *Lady Chatterley's Lover* 一书中就有过这

样的用例：

[例3] Mrs Bolton was almost sure she had a lover, yet how could it be? Where was there a man?

博尔顿夫人几乎确信她有一位情人，然而这究竟是怎么回事？他是什么样的人？在哪里呢？

此外，还可以借助其他疑问词来构成特殊疑问句。如：

[例4] There is a man in the room. Who is there in the room?

房里有个人。房里有谁？

[例5] There was a meeting last night. （When was there a meeting?）

昨晚开了会。什么时候开了会？

[例6a] There are three tall women in the team.

队里有三个高个女队员。

[例6b] How many tall women are there in the team?

队里有多少高个女队员？

[例7a] There is some soup in the saucepan.

锅里有些汤。

[例7b] How much soup is there in the saucepan? （There is a lot.）

锅里有多少汤？（有很多。）

[例8a] There's a holiday next week.

下星期休假。

[例8b] Why is there a holiday next week?

为什么下星期休假？

[例9a] There is some ketchup on your tie.

你领带上有番茄酱。

[例9b]　What kind of ketchup is there on my tie?

我领带上有什么样的番茄酱?

三、there 存在句的附加疑问句

[例1]　There's some ink in the bottle, isn't there?

瓶里还有些墨水, 是吗?

[例2]　There used to be an apple tree in the garden, didn't there? (or: usedn't there?)

那花园里过去有一棵苹果树, 对吗?

[例3]　There is no doubt about it, is there?

对此没有怀疑, 是吗?

there 存在句构成附加疑问句时, 疑问部分要重复 there, 而不用人称代词作主语, 这时, there 实际上起主语作用。试比较:

[例4]　There are seven of the students altogether, aren't there? (不用 aren't they?)

总共有七个学生, 是吗?

[例5]　The work is difficult, isn't it?

这工作很难做, 是吗?

there 存在句中带有定语从句时也是如此。如:

[例6]　There are many people in Africa who speak English, aren't there? (不用 aren't they?)

非洲有许多人讲英语, 是吗?

当然, 有时在询问对方的看法、征求对方的意见时, 可以

不用重复 there。如：

[例 7] There is one favour I should like you to do, will you?

我有件事想麻烦你一下。

这句中的"will you?"实际上等于另外一个句子，即"There is one favour I should like you to do. Will you do it for me?"。因此，只能用 will you。如改为"There is one favour I should like you to do, isn't there?"，在一般情况下，则是不可思议的。既然是你有某事要别人帮忙，怎么还要对方来证实呢？

四、there 存在句的祈使句形式

[例 1] Let there be light. = Let light exist. = Let light come into being.

这是 let 为引导词的第三人称祈使句，there 相当于一个作宾语的名词或代词，试比较：

[例 2] Let it be done.

但我们还是把 there be 看作一个整体，而把 light 分析为宾语。

第十章　There 存在句的非限定形式

动词 to be 的非限定形式 to be 和 being 可以与 there 连用，构成 there 存在句的非限定形式（non-finite there existential sentences），即 there to be 和 there being。there 存在句的非限定形式可以在句中充当不同的成分，可以作主语，也可以作宾语；there being 还可以构成独立主格结构，作状语。

一、there 存在句的非限定形式作主语

"there being + NP" 结构以及 "for + there to be + NP" 结构均可以作句中的主语。如：

[例1]　There being a bus stop so near the house is a great advantage.

在离房屋很近的地方有一个停车站是十分方便的。

[例2]　There not being an index（or：There being no index）to this book is a disadvantage.

书中没有索引，是一大缺憾。

[例3]　For there to be a mistake in a computer's arithmetic is impossible.

计算机计数要出差错是不可能的。

[例4]　For there to be so few people in the streets was unusual.

平时街上不止这么点人。

"there being + NP" 作主语时只能置于句首，而 "for there to be + NP" 作主语时，除可以置于句首外，还可以置于句尾，而用 it 作形式主语，置于句首。上面例3和例4都可改为：

[例3a]　It is impossible for there to be a mistake in a computer's arithmetic.

[例4a]　It was unusual for there to be so few people in the streets.

这实质上是 there 存在句限定形式的缩略。试比较：

[例3a]　It is impossible for there to be a mistake in a computer's arithmetic.

[例3b]　It is impossible that there should be a mistake in a computer arithmetic.

二、there 存在句的非限定形式作动词的宾语

"there to be + NP" 结构可以作及物动词的宾语，如：

[例1]　He doesn't want there to be any doubt about it. (There is some doubt about it.)

对此他不愿意有任何怀疑。

[例2]　They meant there to be no letters in May. （试比较：There are no letters in May.）

他们指的是五月份没有信。

[例3]　I expect there to be no argument about this.

我预期在这件事上没有争论。

[例4]　Housewives hate there to be queues everywhere.
家庭主妇们讨厌到处排队。

作宾语的 there to be 间或也可换成其他动词。如：

[例5]　You're wanted there to fetch the tinned rations.　你要自己去取定量供应的罐头食物。

[例6]　We saw there arise over the meadow a blue haze.
我们看见在草地的上空升起了一层兰色的烟雾。

后面一句中的动词不定式 arise 省略了不定式符号 to，是因为感官动词 see 的要求。

"there to be + NP" 结构的这种用法相当于 "V + 宾语 + 不定式" 结构。试比较：

[例7a]　I don't want there to be any misunderstanding me.

[例7b]　I don't want any of you to misunderstand me.
我不愿你们有任何人误解我。

能够接 "there to be + NP" 作宾语的动词是很有限的，通常只能是表示"意愿"的动词，如 want、like、mean、intend、prefer、expect、hate、consider 等，其他动词则不能接 "there to be + NP" 作宾语。如不能说：

[例8]　※John forced there to be three men in the room.
（应为：John expected there to be three men in the room. ）

三、there 存在句的非限定形式作介词的宾语

如果是介词 for，则接 there to be 作宾语，其他介词只能接 there being 作宾语。如：

［例1］　They asked <u>for there to be another meeting</u>.

他们要求再开一次会。

［例2］　They planned <u>for there to be a family reunion</u>.

他们计划全家大团圆。

［例3］　We had not a doubt <u>of there being time</u> enough.

我们丝毫未怀疑时间是充分的。

［例4］　John was relying <u>on there being another opportuni-ty</u>.

约翰指望还有一次机会。

［例5］　I'm surprised <u>at there not being an index</u>.

对没有索引我感到诧异。

作介词宾语的 there to be 和 there being 是由 there 存在句的限定形式转换而来的。试比较：

［例1a］　They asked <u>for there to be another meeting</u>.

［例1b］　They asked that there should be another meeting.

［例5a］　I'm surprised <u>at there not being an index</u>.

［例5b］　I'm surprised that there isn't an index.

四、there 存在句的非限定形式作状语

"there being + NP" 结构可构成独立主格结构，在句中作状语。如：

［例1］　<u>There being no evidence of his crime</u> the prisoner was set free.

由于没有罪证，犯人获释。

［例2］　<u>There being no farther business</u>, the meeting was adjourned.

　　没有别的事了，就休会了。

　　［例 3］　　There having been no rain for a long time, the ground was burnt black by sun.

　　好久没有下雨，地都晒焦了。

　　上述句中的"there being + NP"这种独立主格结构，作状语表原因。不过，这种用法只见于正式文体，非正式文体中常用状语从句。上面三句均可改为：

　　［例 1a］　　As there was no evidence of his crime the prisoner was set free.

　　［例 2a］　　As there was no further business, the meeting was adjourned.

　　［例 3a］　　As there had been no rain for a long time, the ground was burnt black by sun.

第十一章　There 存在句与某些同形的主谓语倒装句的比较

　　there 存在句是以虚词 there 作为引导词位于句首，而将谓语动词置于真正主语之前的一种主谓语倒装的句型。此外，还有几种句型也是以 there 开头，主谓语倒装，形式上与 there 存在句很相似。但它们并非存在句。下面我们来看看这几种句型。

　　1．引起别人注意的 there 句。如：

　　［例1］　There comes the train.

　　火车来了。

　　［例2］　There goes the bell.

　　铃响了。

　　上面这两句中的 there 不是引导词，而是表示地点或方向的副词，放在句首是为了加强语气。正因为 there 放在句首，才引起主谓语倒装，因而，形式上很像 there 存在句，但实际上却完全不同，它丝毫没有"存在"的意思。句中的 there 要重读，作谓语的动词仅限于 come、go 等少数表示运动的动词。这种句型中的谓语动词总是用一般现在时，但表示现在进行时的含义。如：There comes the train. ＝ The train is coming. 不过，又不能改为现在进行时，如不能说：※There is coming the train. 此外，如果作主语的不是名词，而是人称代词，则不引起主谓语的倒装。试比较：

[例3a]　There comes Comrade Wang!

王同志来了！

[例3b]　There she comes!

她来了！

此外，在这种句型中，作主语的常是表示确定意义的名词或代词，而在 there 存在句中作主语的通常是表示不确定意义的名词。试比较：

[例4]　There comes Charlile!　查利来了.

[例5]　There is a book on the desk.　桌上有一本书。

2. 以 there 开头，表示嘉许、赞扬的主谓倒装的句型。如：

[例1]　She looked at him for a moment, then turned to Mrs Malins and said："There's a nice husband for you, Mrs. Malins. "

她瞅了他一会，然后掉过头去向梅林思太太说："您瞧，梅林思太太，多好的丈夫。"

[例2]　"There now, Jack," said his mother, "see what you've done, you've broken a nice egg and cost me a penny. Here, Emma," she added, calling her daughter, "Take the child away, there's a dear. "

"唉，杰克，"他母亲说，"看你弄的，好好一个鸡蛋打坏了，白白浪费了我一个便士，来，爱玛，"她接着喊她的女儿来，"把孩子领走，乖乖地。"

[例3]　Tie the boat, there's a good boy!

把船系好，好孩子。

[例4]　Minnie, come to an instant, there is a dear girl.

明妮，快来，乖孩子。

[例5]　And now return to the nursery—there's a dear.

好孩子，回托儿所去。

上述句中的 there 是指示副词，要重读，表示嘉许、赞扬，常用来哄小孩。其中不能有时间或地点状语，作主语的通常是 boy、girl、child、dear 等名词，名词前往往有不定冠词。有时，作主语的名词可以是复数，但谓语动词仍用单数。如：

[例6]　There's good children. （不说：※There are good children.）

乖孩子。

3. 副词 there 作状语，置于句首，引起主谓语倒装时与 there 存在句形式上很相似。

英语中如果状语前置时，往往引起主谓语倒装。如：

[例1]　Down came the rain. （＝The rain came down.）

[例2]　Up went the flag. （＝The flag went up.）

there 作副词，位于句首，也引起主谓语的倒装，如：

[例3]　And there at last was the book I'd been looking for. （＝The book I'd been looking for was there at last.）

我要找的书终于在那儿找到了。

[例4]　There at the summit stood the castle in all its medieval splendour. （＝The castle in all its medieval splendour stood there at the summit.）

一座城堡以其中世纪的壮观耸立在山顶上。

例3和例4都不是 there 存在句。there 在句中是副词，作状语，要重读。它们构成一般疑问句的方法与 there 存在句不同。上面两句的一般疑问句形式为：

[例 3a]　　Was the book you'd been looking for there?

[例 4a]　　Did the castle in its medieval splendour stand at the summit?

there 存在句中的 there 是引导词，不重读。试比较：

[例 5]　　'There are our 'friends. （状语前置）

我们的好朋友在这里。

[例 6]　　There are 'too many 'people here. 这里有许多人。（there 存在句）

再比较下面两句：

[例 7a]　　There's a book on the floor.

[例 7b]　　There's your book, on the floor

第一句是 there 存在句，there 为引导词，意为"地板上有一本书"；第二句为状语前置而引起的主谓倒装，there 重读，on the floor 是一种追加语（afterthought），进一步说明 there，全句意为"你的书在这儿，在地板上"。

用于 there 存在句中的动词通常只是表示"存在""坐落""发生""出现"等意义的三类动词（参阅下编第三章），因此，以 there 开头的主谓语倒装的句型，如谓语动词是其他动词，而句中又再没有表示地点或时间的状语，大多不属于 there 存在句。如：

[例 8]　　There speaks my evangelical little wife. (= My evangelical little wife speaks there.)

第十二章　There 和 It 用法的比较

虚词 there 与 it 在用法上有许多相似的地方，也有不同之处。将它们之间的异同进行一番比较或许会有助于我们对 there 存在句有进一步的理解。

一、there 与 it 用法相似之处

1．there 和 it 都可以用来引导一个句子，在句中作形式主语。试比较：

［例1］　It is difficult to find a job these days.

现在要找一个工作是很困难的。

［例2］　There are two churches in the village.

村里有两座教堂。

上面两句中的 it 和 there 都是形式主语，置于句首，而真正主语 to find a job、two churches 置于谓语的后面。

2．there 存在句和 it is...句中都可以带有定语从句，引导定语从句的关系代词，不但作宾语时可以省略，在口语中，作主语时也常可省略。试比较：

［例3］　There is a man below wants to speak to you.

下面有人要同你说话。

［例4］　It isn't everybody（who）can do that.

那件事不是人人都能做的。

3．人称代词在 there 存在句中作主语，以及在 it is...句型中作表语时，都可以用宾格代替主格。如：

［例1］　It's me.

是我。

［例2］　There used to be three of us, but now there's only me.

以前我们是三个人，而现在只剩下我一个人了。

4．在黑人英语中，it 常可替代表"存在"的 there。试比较：

［例1］　Is there a man at the door?

［例2］　Is it a man at the door?

二、there 与 it 用法不同之处

1．there 和 it 虽然都可以作形式主语，但 it 作形式主语时，其真正主语是动词不定式、动名词及从句。如：

［例1］　It is difficult to learn Chinese.

汉语难学。

［例2］　It is foolish behaving like that.

这样做是愚蠢的。

［例3］　It is strange that they should refuse to cooperate.

他们拒绝合作，真是怪事。

there 作形式主语时，真正主语只能是名词（或动名词）。如：

[例4] There is a man outside.

外面有个人。

[例5] There was dancing in the streets.

街上有人跳舞。

it 作形式主语时，完全可以把真正主语前置取代 it，而全句意义不变。如例 1～例 3 均可改为：

[例1a] To learn Chinese is difficult.

[例2a] Behaving like that is foolish.

[例3a] That they should refuse to cooperate is strange.

而 there 作形式主语时，通常不能进行这种替换。如一般不说：

[例4a] ※A man is outside.

[例5a] ※Dancing was in the streets.

上面这两句虽然在语法上说得过去，不过，实际上不这么说。但是，"Somebody is outside." 却是正确的表达。

其次，两者之间的语义也不同。it 只作形式主语，并无多少具体的含义，而 there 通常含有"存在"的意义。

2．it 除作形式主语外，还可以作真正主语，表示"天气""时间""距离"等。如：

[例1] It is six o'clock.

六点钟了。

[例2] It is very cold today.

今天天气很冷。

[例3] It is a long way from Beijing to New York.

从北京到纽约很远。

［例4］　It is time to finish our work.

是结束我们工作的时候了。

上面各句中的 it 不是"先行 it"（anticipative *it*），而是"无人称 it"（impersonal *it*）。在句中作无人称主语，而不是形式主语。最后一例中的 it 似乎像形式主语，实际上不是，因为它不能改为：

［例4a］　※To finish our work is time.

there 也可以表示时间，但与 it 的用法不同。试比较：

［例5］　It is time to go home. （＝We plan to go home at six and it is six now.）

是该回家的时候了。

［例6］　There is time to go home and come back here again before the film starts. （＝We have time enough to go home… ＝ Time enough exists for us to go home…）

电影开演以前，我们有时间回趟家，然后再回来。

3. it 可以做"替代词"（substitutional *it*），代替前面所提到的东西或情况。如：

［例1］　You cannot eat your cake and have it. （it 代替 your cake）

两者不可兼得。

［例2］　—I've broken the mirror.

　　　　—It can't be helped. （it 代替 the broken mirror）

—我打破了镜子。

—那没有办法了。

there 不能作替代词。试比较下面两句：

［例 3a］　There is a man digging in the garden.

［例 3b］　（What's that noise?）It's a man digging in the garden.

上面两句尽管都可译为"有人在花园里挖洞"，但 there 和 it 的用法并不相同。there 表存在，it 是替代词，表示前面所提及的内容（嘈杂声）。例 3b 中的 it 可以改为 there，但不再表"替代"，而表"存在"。又如：

［例 4］　There is no proof that he is the culprit.

没有证据可证明他是罪犯。

这句中的 there 在下面情况下可改为 it：

［例 5］　——They say they have found his fingerprints on the window-sill.

　　　　——Even if that is true, it's no proof that he is the culprit.（= Even if that is true, there's no proof...）

——据说他们在窗台上发现了他的指纹。

——即使如此，也不能证明他是罪犯。

4. 在 it is...结构中，后续成分常是形容词，而 there is... 的后续成分是名词。试比较：

［例 1a］　It is foggy.

［例 1b］　There is a fog.

［例 2a］　It was very wet.

［例 2b］　There was a lot of rain.

［例 3a］　It won't be very sunny.

［例 3b］　There won't be much sun.

第十三章　Have 存在句与 There 存在句用法比较

　　have 可以表示"具有""拥有"（own，be in possession of）或精神上、身体上的特征或状态（own as a quality）。如：

　　[例 1]　　We have two hands.

　　我们都有两只手。

　　[例 2]　　I have an English book.

　　我有一本英语书。

　　[例 3]　　Has she blue eyes or brown eyes?

　　她的眼睛是蓝色的还是棕色的？

　　[例 4]　　She had the cheek to say such a thing.

　　她竟然厚颜无耻地说出这样的话。

　　这时 have 与 there 存在句不同义，上面几句都不能改为 there 存在句，如不能说：

　　[例 1a]　　※There are two hands in us.

　　但是，have 表示"有"时，有时确实可以表示"存在"意义，与 there 存在句同义。如：

　　[例 5]　　This room has five windows.　　（ = There are five windows in this room. ）

　　这间房有五扇窗户。

[例 6] We have much rain this year. （= There is much rain this year.）

今年雨水多。

这种用法的 have 称为 have 存在句。在 have 存在句中，除了"NP + have + NP"结构外，还可以有各种不同的后续成分。如：

[例 7] The porter has a taxi ready. （形容词）

服务员已把车准备好了。

[例 8] They have several oak trees in the garden. （介词词组）

他们在花园里栽了几棵橡树。

[例 9] I have two buttons missing. （-ing 分词）

我掉了两粒扣子。

[例 10] He has a great deal to be thankful for. （不定式词组）

他极为感激。

[例 11] I've something I've been meaning to say to you. （定语从句）

我有事同你讲。

have 存在句通常可以转换为 there 存在句。试比较：

[例 12a] The porter had a taxi ready.

[例 12b] There was a taxi ready.

[例 13a] He has several friends in China.

[例 13b] There are several friends of his in China.

[例 14a] I have two buttons missing（on my jacket）.

[例 14b] My jacket has two buttons missing.

［例 14c］　　There are two buttons missing（on my jacket）.

这两种句型的含义基本上相同，只不过 there 存在句侧重客观方面，而 have 存在句侧重主观方面；因此，表示某处"存在"什么东西时常用 there 存在句，而表示某人"有"什么东西，则用 have 存在句。there 存在句中，there 是形式主语，后面的名词词组是真正主语；而在 have 存在句中，have 前面的代词或名词词组已充当主语，因此，它后面的名词词组不再是主语，而是宾语。have 存在句中作主语的如果不是人，而是某一事物的话，那么，通常必须带有一个介词词组作状语，在这个介词词组中，作宾语的必须是指主语的代词。如：

［例 15］　　The purse had some money in it.

钱包里有些钱。

［例 16］　　The trees still had many apples on them.

树上还有很多苹果。

上面两句中的 in it 和 on them 都是不可缺少的。去掉它们，句子不成立：

［例 15］　　※The purse had some money.

［例 16］　　※The trees still had many apples.

但是，宾语如果是属于主语所代表的物体固有的一部分，则作状语的介词词组往往可以省略。如：

［例 17］　　The house has five rooms.

这栋楼有五间房。

［例 18］　　The book has illustrations.

这本书有插图。

［例 19］　　The year has twelve months.

一年有 12 个月。

例 17 ～例 19 各句中都可以加上 in it。但由于 five rooms、illustrations、twelve months 分别属于主语 the house、the book、the year 的一个组成成分，因此，通常可以省略作状语的介词词组。有时，由于使用"拟人化"修辞格，作状语的介词词组通常也可省略。如：

[例 20]　Bad news has wings.（将"坏消息"比作一只鸟）

坏事传千里。

have 存在句也可以有非限定形式。如：

[例 21]　Soon having a taxi available，Dr. Lowes was able to catch the train.

出租汽车很快就准备好了，洛斯博士能够赶上火车。

上句中 having a taxi available 的逻辑主语是句中的主语 Dr. Lowes。有时，它也可以有自己的逻辑主语。如：

[例 21a]　The porter soon having a taxi available，Dr. Lowes was able to catch the train.

服务员已将出租汽车准备好了，洛斯博士能够赶上火车。

第十四章　英汉存在句比较

一、英汉存在句的异同

英语中 there 存在句表示"某地存在某物或某人"这样的概念，如：

[**例1**]　　There is a picture on the wall.

（在）墙上有一幅画。

例 1 中英语与汉语译文对句子成分的划分是不相同的。英语中，there 作引导词，不作句子成分，表示存在的某物或某人（a picture）在句中作主语，而"某地"通常用介词词组（on the wall）表示，作状语，常位于句尾。当然，如果为了强调，也可放在句首，即"On the wall there is a picture."。汉语译文"（在）墙上有一幅画"通常看作无主句，"有"是及物动词，作谓语，"一幅画"作宾语，表示方位的词组"（在）墙上"则作状语，通常位于句首。方位词组有时也可以放在句尾，即"有一幅画在墙上"，只不过没有放在前面普遍。有些汉语语法学家认为，若表示"某地"的方位名词放在句首，而不带介词，就成为主语。① 他们把上句中的"墙上"看作主语。这种看法是不无道理的，但是，我们认为，"墙上"表示的方位意义非常强，似乎看作"在墙上"的省略结构，作状语，更为恰当一些。

此外，英语的 there 存在句和汉语的"（在）……有……"句式在词序上也是相同的，都是用 VS 这种倒装的格式。这两种句式都用来表示事物的存在、出现等。只是在英语中，谓语动词前要用引导词 there，而汉语则没有引导词。

以上讲的是带状语的 there 存在句。此外还有不带状语，但带有分词和形容词的 there 存在句。如：

　　[例2]　　There are some pictures hanging on the wall.

　　[例3]　　There is a man coming.

这两句中 some pictures、a man 都是句中的主语，同时，实际上又是 hanging、coming 所表示的动作的行为发出者，因此，与汉语中的无主递系句很类似。这两句译成汉语为：

　　[例2a]　有几张画片在墙上挂着。

　　[例2b]　有一个人来了。

上面两句中均无主语，在汉语中称为无主句。"有"为谓语，"几张画片""一个人"均为"有"的宾语，同时又分别是"在墙上挂着""来了"的逻辑主语。这种句式就是汉语中的无主递系句。汉语与英语不同的是，汉语中的"有"是及物动词，英语中的 be 是不及物动词，英语中的 having、coming 在传统语法中都分析为定语。

---

① 吴洁敏：《汉英语法手册》，知识出版社 1982 年版，第 217 页；张今、陈云清：《英汉语法比较纲要》，商务印书馆 1981 年版，第 36 页。

二、汉语递系句与英语的 have 存在句

汉语中有一种句式，其前一个动词的宾语是后一个动词的逻辑主语。如：

［例4］我有一辆汽车等我。

［例5］我有两枚纽扣掉了。

上两句中，"我"作主语，"有"作谓语，"一辆汽车""两枚纽扣"都作"有"的宾语，同时又分别作"在等我""掉了"的逻辑主语，这种句式叫递系句或兼语式，也叫主谓"有"字句。其中"有"是初系，"在等我""来了"是次系，次系所表示的动作较初系更为强烈。英语中也有类似的句式。如前面两句若译成英语则为：

［例1a］　I have a car waiting for me.（相当于：There is a car waiting for me.）

［例2a］　I have two buttons missing.（相当于：There are two buttons missing on my jacket.）

这两句中的 a car、two buttons 都作及物动词 have 的宾语，同时又分别作 waiting for me、missing 的逻辑主语。尽管 waiting、missing 是非谓语动词，但它们在句中显得比谓语动词 have 更突出。

第十五章　结论：英语 There 句型辨析

一、概述

英语中，以 there 开头的句型多为"存在句"，称为 there 存在句（there-existential sentences）。这种句型通常表示"在某处存在某人或某物"，there 为引导词，不重读，其主语大多是表示不确定意义的人或物，即作主语的名词词组通常被不定冠词、零冠词以及其他表示不确定意义的限定词所修饰，作谓语的多为动词 be 或其他表示存在意义的动词。在 there 存在句中，主谓语必须倒装。如：

[例 1]　There is a clock on the table.

[例 2]　There is ice on the lake.

[例 3]　There is someone at the door.

[例 4]　There stands a castle on the hill.

[例 5]　There lives a family of thirteen in the cottage.

以上几句都是带有状语的 there 存在句。也有的 there 存在句只带有补足语或者什么都不带。如：

[例 6]　There was someone looking for you.

[例7]　There is a thermostat that controls the temperature.

[例8]　There is nobody to type these letters.

[例9]　Undoubtedly, there is a God.

上述各种 there 存在句有一个共同的特点：都表示存在意义。但是，也有一些以 there 开头，主谓语倒装的句型，与 there 存在句形式上很相似，但并不表示存在意义。如：

[例10]　There comes the train.

火车来了。

[例11]　She looked at him for a moment, then turned to Mrs. Malins and said："There's a nice husband for you, Mrs. Malins."

她瞅了他一会，然后掉过头去向梅林思太太说："您瞧，梅林思太太，多好的丈夫。"

[例12]　There at the summit stood the castle in all its medieval splendour.

一座城堡以其中世纪的壮观耸立在山顶上。

本章对前文探讨的 there 存在句的分类以及 there 存在句与其形似的 there 句型的区别加以总结。

二、there 存在句的分类

关于 there 存在句，目前国内外已有不少的论述，对其分类情况也有所涉及，但不详尽，也不够系统。笔者从自己的教学和科研的实际出发，认为根据其结构，there 存在句可以分为以下几类。

1. 带有状语的 there 存在句。

大多数 there 存在句都带有状语。状语通常放在作主语的名词词组后面。我们可以用下列公式来表示："there + be + NP + A"。

一般语法书都认为，there 存在句必须要带地点状语（adverbial of place）。其实，除地点状语外，还可以带时间状语（adverbial of time）、方式状语（adverbial of manner）或其他状语。因为它不仅可以表示"在某处存在某人或某物"，而且还可以表示"在某个时候存在某人或某物"或"某物以某种方式或为什么而存在"，等等。如：

［例1］　There is a man in the room.

房里有个人。

［例2］　There are fifteen students in my class.

我们班有十五个学生。

［例3］　There is a meeting at ten o'clock.

十点钟开会。

［例4］　There were several parties last night.

昨晚有几个聚会。

［例5］　There was a storm like a hurricane.

刮过一场飓风般的风暴。

［例6］　There is truth in what you say.

你的话有道理。

［例7］　There is a good reason for doing all this.

他做此事是很有道理的。

有时，可以同时有两个或两个以上的状语。如：

［例8］　There weren't many students here yesterday.

昨天这里没有很多人。

不过，为了强调，有时也可以把名词词组放在状语的后面。如：

［例9］　There was in the vicinity a helpful doctor.

附近有一个好医师。

以上各例中，例 1 的 in the room、例 2 的 in my class 以及例 9 的 in the vicinity 是地点状语；例 3 的 at ten o'clock 和例 4 的 last night 是时间状语；例 5 的 like a hurricane 是方式状语；例 6 的 in what you say 是方面状语；例 7 的 for doing all this 是目的状语；例 8 有两个状语，here 表示地点，yesterday 表示时间。

这类 there 存在句中，作主语的名词词组通常必须是表示不确定意义的，作谓语的多是动词 be 的某种形式，间或也可以是其他表示存在意义的动词。

2．带有修饰语的 there 存在句。

这类 there 存在句不带状语，但带有修饰语，作修饰语的可以是-ing 分词（例 1）、-ed 分词（例 2）、形容词（例 3）、动词不定式（例 4）及定语从句（例 5）等。如：

［例1］　There are two buttons missing.

掉了两粒扣子。

［例2］　There must be no more time wasted.

再不能浪费时间了。

［例3］　There were about fifty persons present.

出席的大约五十人。

［例4］　There is nobody to type these letters.

没有人打这些信。

［例5］　There is a thermostat that controls the temperature.

有一种恒温器可以控制温度。

这类 there 存在句中，作主语的通常只能是表示不确定意义的名词词组。但是，有时，特别是当修饰语是动词不定式、定语从句时，也可以是表示确定意义的名词词组。如：

［例6］　There's the man next door to consider.

隔壁那个人需要考虑。

［例7］　There was the time when minister of the local church had seen a school boy creeping into the church late one evening.

有过那么一次，教长在一天夜里看见一个男孩爬进了教堂。

在带有定语从句的 there 存在句中，引导定语从句的关系代词，即使是作主语，也可以省略。如：

［例8］　There's a man lives in China. （但不说：※I know a man lives in China. ）

［例9］　There's no one enjoys good food more than he does.

甚至在有插入语的情况下也可以省略。如：

［例10］　There's no one, as far as I can see, has taken their place.

据我看，没有谁能代替他。

有时，there 存在句中可带两个定语从句，作主语的关系代词都可省略。如：

［例11］　There was a man （that） came （who） said that he bought many different magazines.

有个人来说他买了各种杂志。

3．无修饰的 there 存在句。

这种 there 存在句仅说明某个或某些事物的存在，它是由
there + be + 不确定的名词词组组成，不带任何状语或修饰
语。如：

[例1]　　Undoubtedly, there is a God. (God exists.)

[例2]　　Is there any other business? (as spoken by the
chairman at the end of a meeting)

[例3]　　There must be a more direct route.

这种无修饰存在句实际上是省略了名词词组的后续成分的
省略句。这或者是由于上下文已表述清楚，省略不会引起误
解；或者是由于说话人仅仅提到某物的存在，无须表示具体的
时间或地点的缘故。上面三句可理解为以下三句的省略形式：

[例1a]　　Undoubtedly, there is a God in the universe.

[例2a]　　Is there any other business for the committee at
this meeting?

[例3a]　　There must be a more direct route than the one
we're discussing.

有些 there 存在句形式上像无修饰存在句，但实际上不
是。如：

[例4]　　There have always been wars.

Quirk 等 1972 年出版的 *A Grammar of Contemporary English*
一书把这句看成无修饰存在句。然而，在 1985 年出版的 *A
Comprehensive Grammar of the English Language* 一书中作了修改，
认为它属于我们前面讲的第一类 there 存在句，只不过因为 al-
ways 是中位状语，它不在句末，而在句中而已。我们认为
Quirk 等这一修改是对的。

无修饰存在句中的谓语动词除可以是动词 be 外，还可以是其他表示存在意义的不及物动词：第一，"运动"类动词（verbs of motion），如 appear、approach、arrive、come、enter、follow、pass、rise；第二，"开始或发生"类动词（verbs of inception of happening），如 emerge、spring up、take place、happen、occur；第三，"位置或状态"类动词（verbs of stance），如 live、remain、stand、lie。如：

［例 5］　　There sprang up a wild gale.

［例 6］　　There came to his mind her beautiful and intelligent face.

4．地点状语位于句首的 there 存在句。

有一种 there 存在句可以将地点状语放在句首。用公式表示即"A + there + V + S"。如：

［例 1］　　In the garden there was a sundial. （= There was a sundial in the garden.）

［例 2］　　On the hill there stands a tall tree. （= There stands a tall tree on the hill.）

［例 3］　　In front of the village there flows a stream. （= There's a stream in front of the village.）

在状语位于句首的句子中，主谓语通常也必须倒装，因此，上述各句中的 there 可以省略如下：

［例 1a］　　In the garden was a sundial.

［例 2a］　　On the hill stands a tall tree.

［例 3a］　　In front of the village flows a stream.

有无 there，意义上差别不大。但省略 there 的现象多见于书面语中，在口语中以不省略较为自然。此外，用 there 是提供一种新信息，而省略 there，则不提供新信息，只是提出某一具体的事物，相当于 chanced to be 或 happened to be。因此，当主语被 the 等表示确定意义的限定词所修饰或主语为专有名词时，there 往往省略。这一句型中的谓语动词可以是 be，也可以是前文提到的其他三类表示存在意义的动词（"运动"类动词、"开始或发生"类动词或"位置或状态"类动词）。如：

[例4]　In the garden lay $\begin{cases} \text{Joan} \\ \text{his father} \\ \text{the old lady} \end{cases}$ (fall asleep).

5. 时间状语位于句首的 there 存在句。如：

[例1]　That night there sprang up a wild gale. (= There sprang up a wild gale that night.)

[例2]　In the afternoon there occurred an accident.

6. 以动名词为主语的 there 存在句。

与我们前面所讨论的几种 there 存在句略有不同，这种 there 存在句通常只用否定式，其结构为 "there + be + not + -ing"。如：

[例1]　There is no knowing whether we shall be able to get enough materials.

无法知道我们是否能够弄到足够的材料。

[例2]　There's no getting over it.

这是躲不了的。

[例3]　There is no denying the seriousness of the situation.

形势的严重性是无法否认的。

这种结构的含义随着各句子的上下文而变，但有一点是共同的，即表示强烈的否定意义。上面几句分别相当于：

［例1a］　It is impossible to know whether we shall be able to get enough materials.

［例2a］　It is impossible to get over it.

［例3a］　It is impossible to deny the seriousness of the situation.

这种句型中作主语的动名词不能用肯定式。如不能说：

［例1b］　※ There is knowing whether we shall be able to get enough materials.

这种句式实际上并非存在句。与此类似的还有"there is + no use + （in） + -ing"以及"there is + no sense（point） + in + -ing"结构，也表示强否定，而不表示存在意义。如：

［例4］　There is no use crying over spilt milk.（ = It is no use crying over spilt milk. ）

覆水难收。

［例5］　There is no use asking her——she doesn't know anything.（ = It is no use asking her——she doesn't know anything. ）

问她毫无用处——她什么都不知道。

［例6］　There is no sense in making him angry.

惹他生气是没有道理的。

［例7］　There is no point in talking about it again.

没有必要再谈这个。

7. 没有 there 的 there 存在句。

这主要是某些没有动词的揭示语（block language）以及广播评论中的省略句。它们虽然表示存在的意思，但句中并不出现 there 这个词。这是因为揭示语和广播评论的省略句必须短小精悍、言简意赅，凡是能省略的尽量省略的缘故。但是，这种句型表示存在意义是不言自明的。如：

［例1］　Danger！（＝There is danger.）

有危险！

［例2］　Men at work overhead.（＝There are men at work overhead.）

上面有人在操作！

［例3］　No way out.（＝There is no way out.）

毫无办法。

［例4］　No arrest without warrant.（＝There must be no arrest without warrant.）

没有证据不得逮捕。

三、存在句与倒装句

there 存在句是以虚词 there 作引导词，位于句首，而将谓语动词置于真正主语之前的一种主谓倒装的句型。有几种以 there 开头的句型，主谓语也倒装，形式上与 there 存在句很相似，但它们并非存在句，不表示存在意义。这些句型有：

1．引起别人注意的 there 句。如：

［例1］　There comes the train.

火车来了。

［例2］　There goes the last bus！

最后一班公共汽车开走了！

［例3］　There goes the bell.（There rings the bell.）

铃响了。

这种句型中的 there 不是引导词，而是表示地点或方向的副词，放在句首是为了加强语气。正因为作状语的 there 放在句首，而引起主谓语倒装，因而，形式上很像 there 存在句。但实际上它与 there 存在句完全不同，它丝毫没有"存在"的意思。句中的 there 要重读，作谓语的动词仅限于 come、go、ring 等少数表示运动的动词。这种句型中的谓语动词总是用一般现在时，但表示现在进行时的含义。如：

[例 1a] There comes the train. = The train is coming.

在这种句型中，作主语的常是表示确定意义的名词或代词，而在 there 存在句中作主语的通常是表示不确定意义的名词。试比较：

[例 4a] There comes Charlie.

查理来了。

[例 4b] There is a book on the desk.

桌上有一本书。

在这种句型中，如果作主语的不是名词，而是人称代词，则不引起主谓语的倒装。试比较：

[例 5a] There comes Comrade Wang!

王同志来了！

[例 5b] There she comes!

她来了。

2. 表示"嘉许、赞扬"的 there 句型。如：

[例 1] Tie the boat, there's a good boy.

把船系好，好孩子。

[例 2] "There now, Jack," said his mother, "see what you've done, you've broken a nice egg and cost me a penny. Here, Emma," she added, calling her daughter, "take the child away, there's a dear."

"唉，杰克，"他母亲说，"看你弄的，好好的一个鸡蛋打坏了，白白浪费了我一个便士。来，爱玛，"她接着喊她的女儿来，"把孩子领走，乖乖地。"

[例3]　Minnie, come to an instant, there's a dear girl.

明妮，快来，乖孩子。

[例4]　And now return to the nursary —there's a dear.

好孩子，回托儿所去。

上述各句中的 there 是指示副词，要重读，表示"赞扬"或"嘉许"，常用来哄小孩等，句中不能有时间或地点状语。作主语的通常是 boy、girl、child、dear 等名词。名词前往往有不定冠词。有时，作主语的名词可以是复数，但谓语动词仍用单数。如：

[例5]　There's good children.

乖孩子。

这一句式有时也可用于贬义。如：

[例6]　She is plain, spend-thrift, lazy, and what not. There is a good wife for you.

她长得不好看，又懒又挥金如土。真是个"好"妻子哩！

显而易见，这里的 good 意为 bad。

3．副词 there 作状语，置于句首，引起的主谓倒装句。

英语中如果状语位于句首时，往往引起主谓语的倒装。如：

[例1]　Down came the rain. (= The rain came down.)

[例2]　Up went the flag. (= The flag went up.)

当 there 作副词，位于句首时，也引起主谓语的倒装。这时，与 there 存在句形式上很相似。如：

［例3］　　There at the summit stood the castle in all its medieval splendour.　(= The castle in all its medieval splendour stood there at the summit.)

there 是副词作状语，at the summit 是它的同位语。

［例4］　　And there at last was the book I'd been looking for. (= The book I'd been looking for was there at last.)

我要找的书终于在那儿找到了。

以上两句都不是 there 存在句。there 在句中是副词，作状语，要重读。而 there 存在句中的 there 是引导词，不重读。在 there 存在句中，作主语的名词词组通常是表示不确定意义的，而在这种 there 句中，则不受此限制。试比较：

［例5］　　'There are our 'friends.　　(= Our friends are there.)

我们的朋友在这里。(状语前置)

［例6］　　There are 'too many 'people here.

这里有许多人。(there 存在句)

再比较下面两句：

［例7a］　　There's a book on the floor.

［例7b］　　There's your book, on the floor.

例7a 是 there 存在句，there 为引导词，意为"地板上有一本书"，on the floor 为状语，它前面不能有逗号。例7b 为状语前置而引起的主谓语倒装句，there 是副词，重读，on the floor 是一种追加语 (after thought)，进一步说明 there，意为"你的书在这儿，在地板上"。它们构成一般疑问句的方法也不相同。试比较：

［**例 7c**］　　Is there a book on the floor?

［**例 7d**］　　Is your book there, on the floor?

用于 there 存在句中的动词通常只能是 be 或其他表示"存在""开始或发生""运动'或"位置或状态"的动词，而这种状语 there 开头的主谓倒装句，则不受此限制。因此，以 there 开头的主谓倒装句，如谓语动词是其他动词，而句中又再没有表示地点或时间的状语，则大多不属于 there 存在句。如：

［**例 8**］　　There speaks my evangelical little wife. (= My evangelical little wife speaks there).

附录：作者主要作品编目

一、著作

1. 《英语语法难点例解》，陕西人民出版社 1985 年版。（该书获湖南师大 1987 年首届优秀获作奖）

2. 《英语介词特殊惯用法 150 例》，科学技术文献出版社 1992 年版。

3. 何维湘、颜钰著《大学英语惯用法集萃》，中山大学出版社 1994 年版。

4. 《研究生、留学生英语预测试题详解》，湖南科技出版社 1986 年版。

5. 《综合经济英语教程》（上、下册）科学技术文献出版社 1993 年版。（王运任主编，刘大铨、颜钰等任副主编）

二、主要文章

1. 《表示时间的 since》，《中小学外语》1980 年第 1 期。

2. 《Jokes and Humour》，《中小学外语》1980 年第 8 期。

3. 《一般过时只表过去吗?》，《中小学外语教学》1980

年第 11 期。

4. "The Yuelu Morntain：A Beauty Spot"，*China Sports Oct*，1980.

5.《表示否定的几种特殊形式》，《中小学外语》1981 年第 11 期。

6.《英语中使用不同的冠词意义上的差别》，《英语辅导》1982 年第 1 期。

7.《There be 句型的主语》，《中小学外语》1981 年第 3 期。

8.《表示肯定意义的否定形式》，《中小学外语》1982 年第 4 期。

9.《几种用否定形式表示肯定的句子》，《中小学外语（俄文版）》1982 年第 6 期。

10.《不定代词 one 的替代用法》，《中小学外语》1982 年第 9 期。

11.《可数名词用作不可数名词》，《中小学外语》1982 年第 12 期。

12.《动词不定式符号 to 的省略》，《湖南师院学报》1981 年第 1 期。

13.《英语附加疑问句的几个问题》，《现代外语》1982 年第 1 期。

14.《肯定形式和否定形式表示相同的意义》，《中小学外语教学》1982 年第 3 期。

15.《附加疑问句的主语》，《英语辅导》1983 年第 3 期。

16.《Little 用法两则》，《中小学外语》1983 年第 1 期。

17.《作状语的现在分词与谓语动词的时间关系》，《中小学外语教学》1983 年第 6 期。

18．《浅谈及物动词不带宾语》，《中小学外语教学》1984 年第 11 期。

19．《连词 when 用法上的几个特点》，《教学研究（洛阳外国语学院学报）》1984 年第 1 期。

20．《从 "much thanks" 谈起》，《中小学外语》1984 年第 2 期。

21．《引导状语从句的 As》，《福建外语》1984 年第 3 期。

22．《几组英语状语从句辩异》，《山东外语》1985 年第 1 期。

23．《动词不定式 to be 的几个特殊用法》，《外语与外语教学》1986 年第 1 期。

24．《英语 "开始" 情貌意义的表达手段》，《外国语文教学（四川外国语学院学报）》1986 年第 1 期。

25．《英语介词 in 的用法三则》，《山东外语教学》1986 年第 3 期。

26．《英语疑难解答三十题》，《湖南刊授大学》1986 年第 3 期。

27．《英语主动句表被动意义用法初探》，《湖南科技大学学报》1985 年第 2 - 3 期。

28．《试谈不及物动词用作及物动词》，《大学英语》1986 年第 2 期。

29．《语态转换问题几则》，《中小学外语》1986 年第 6 期。

30．《试论 will 用于 if 从句》，《福建外语》1986 年第 3 期。

31.《祈使句的主语——从 mind you 谈起》，《中小学外语》1987 年第 2 期。

32.《87 年高考英语试题第三大题题解》，《中小学英语辅导》1987 年第 6 期。

33.《试论英语将来时的表示法》，《湖南师大学报》1987 年外语专辑。

34.《试论 there 存在句的主语》，《现代外语》1989 年第 2 期。

35.《关于 be going to 用于条件句的主句中》，《福建外语》1989 年第 3 - 4 期。

36.《英语疑问句的一个用法——不表疑问》，《福建外语》1991 年第 3 - 4 期。

37.《引导定语从句的 As》，《福建外语》1992 年第 3 - 4 期。

38.《英语 There 句型辩》，广东商学院 1990 年学术论文报告会。

39.《there 存在句问题三则》，《苏州大学学报外国语言文学专辑》1995。